FROM THE BASEMENT TO THE DOME

FROM THE BASEMENT TO THE DOME

HOW MIT'S UNIQUE CULTURE CREATED A THRIVING ENTREPRENEURIAL COMMUNITY

JEAN-JACQUES DEGROOF

FOREWORD BY BOB METCALFE

The MIT Press
Cambridge, Massachusetts
London, England

The MIT Press would like to thank the anonymous peer reviewers who provided comments on drafts of this book. The generous work of academic experts is essential for establishing the authority and quality of our publications. We acknowledge with gratitude the contributions of these otherwise uncredited readers.

This book was set in Stone Serif and Stone Sans by Westchester Publishing Services. Printed and bound in the United States of America

Library of Congress Cataloging-in-Publication Data

Names: Degroof, Jean-Jacques, author.
Title: From the basement to the dome : how MIT's unique culture created a
    thriving entrepreneurial community / Jean-Jacques Degroof.
Description: Cambridge : The MIT Press, [2021] | Includes bibliographical
    references and index.
Identifiers: LCCN 2020050490 | ISBN 9780262046152 (Hardcover)
Subjects: LCSH: Entrepreneurship--Massachusetts. | Massachusetts Institute
    of Technology. | Corporate culture--Massachusetts. | New business
    enterprises--Massachusetts.
Classification: LCC HB615 .D436 2021 | DDC 338/.0409744--dc23
LC record available at https://lccn.loc.gov/2020050490

10   9   8   7   6   5   4   3   2   1

To my wife, Valeria. And to our niece and nephew, Valeria and Máximo.

CONTENTS

FOREWORD

When I arrived at MIT in 1964, it was not the entrepreneurial hotbed it is now. There were no dedicated classes or groups or formal initiatives. But the absence of the seething caldron of entrepreneurial activity that exists today does not mean that the ingredients for greatness were not already in place, simmering. As Jean-Jacques Degroof so astutely describes in this book, MIT's founding principles and underlying cultural values were perfectly aligned with the entrepreneurial mindset.

I did not come to MIT with the goal of becoming an internet pioneer or founding my own companies. But through what Jean-Jacques refers to as serendipitous encounters and the freedom to explore interests beyond the standard curriculum, I invented the Ethernet and founded 3Com. My introduction to entrepreneurship at MIT occurred in my junior year, through a special undergraduate systems program at Sloan taught by Professor Jay W. Forrester. Through that class, I met Edward Roberts, who would go on to become a hugely influential figure in MIT entrepreneurship. Ed and I started studying start-ups, including Teradyne and DEC. Using what we learned, I founded three start-ups in that time: MSC, DCD, PDS, all of which were consulting companies. Though the companies did not survive my admission to grad school and other circumstances, the entrepreneurship bug was with me to stay.

How I came to invent the Ethernet and found the multibillion-dollar networking company 3Com has been well documented, as has my high-profile role as an internet pioneer. Now, as the Professor of Innovation and Entrepreneurship and Murchison Fellow of Free Enterprise in the Cockrell

School of Engineering at the University of Texas at Austin, I am in the next phase of my entrepreneurial journey, working to advance the vibrant start-up ecosystem in Austin. The student is now an educator; the pioneer is now a mentor. My "To-Do List" consists of one main thing: recreate MIT.

But as Jean-Jacques points out, recreating MIT's renowned entrepreneurial ecosystem is not a simple task. There is no copying MIT's ecosystem and pasting it into another institution. The founding principles and unique cultural elements that came together to create the "secret sauce," as Jean-Jacques calls it, the ground-up nature of what has grown and thrived at MIT, are not easy to duplicate.

That does not mean that there are no concrete lessons to be learned, that there is not knowledge that can be translated and adapted for other universities and economies. Today, as a successful and seasoned entrepreneur, I still frequently look to MIT in my efforts to build a thriving entrepreneurial ecosystem at the University of Texas. I don't hesitate to reach out to my extensive network at MIT for answers to questions of theory and practice. From there, I have been able to make great strides in my goal. I may not be recreating MIT, but I am modeling what I do after the very best and adapting it to the specifics I have here in Austin.

Of course, not everyone has the level of access to the MIT brain trust that I do. But everyone can look to this book for the insights and lessons it provides as it traces the evolution of entrepreneurship at MIT, from the Institute's founding to the present-day juggernaut. For me, one of the key lessons to take from MIT (and this book) is its promotion of interdisciplinarity as critical to entrepreneurial success. I have no doubt that my successes in businesses are due to my complementary training in engineering and management. Equally important was the opportunity I had to build things, to learn by doing. Interdisciplinarity and practical experience are just two examples of things MIT has done that I know can be applied to other universities, just two examples of the many lessons detailed in this book that can be used by the individual entrepreneur, the educator, the administrator.

At this point in our history, I believe that the mission of all universities should be to become "innoversities." Universities focus on teaching and research. The innoversity places equal importance on teaching, research, and innovation. The innoversity is a three-legged stool, which we all know is far more stable than a stool with only two legs.

As I see it, MIT is leading the way in transitioning from university to innoversity. And I see this leadership as the natural evolution of its status as an entrepreneurial powerhouse. Who better to take the next step? Who better to lead the way? Who better to learn from?

—Bob Metcalfe, '68

SB Industrial Management
SB Electrical Engineering

INTRODUCTION

Entrepreneurship has long thrived at the Massachusetts Institute of Technology (MIT). The Institute's entrepreneurial ecosystem is world renowned and the source of inspiration and information for universities and economies that would like to duplicate its success. And that success is undeniable. A survey published in 2015 revealed that MIT alumni have founded at least 30,000 active companies that employed 4.6 million people. Conducted by MIT Sloan professors Edward Roberts ('57) and Fiona Murray and then-PhD candidate Daniel Kim ('19), the survey also revealed that these companies had revenues of $1.9 trillion, approximately equivalent to the gross domestic product of the world's tenth-largest economy.[1] Some of the companies founded by MIT alumni and other members of the Institute's community have achieved significant success—and even some that made history—as this book will illustrate. In 2019, MIT offered more than sixty classes in entrepreneurship.[2] In addition, it identified about eighty student clubs, entrepreneurial competitions, conferences, accelerators, and other entities providing support to entrepreneurship.[3] In the 2010s, twenty to thirty ventures per year were spun off from MIT laboratories in order to commercialize technologies whose intellectual property MIT licensed to these companies, while graduates started an estimated 100 firms per year. The percentage of MIT undergraduates choosing to work in venture capital–backed start-ups after graduation reached 15 percent in 2014[4] and seems to have grown since then.

This book explores how MIT became a world-renowned entrepreneurship powerhouse and why entrepreneurship flourished at this specific academic institution more than at others. The book also shows why it has been so difficult for other universities and policymakers to replicate this success, in spite of the numerous delegations of decision-makers visiting the Institute's campus almost weekly in search of understanding the sources of entrepreneurship's vibrancy at MIT.

In trying to answer those questions, I came to a puzzling realization: until recently, support for entrepreneurship at MIT did not result from any deliberate policy, nor from concerted actions by stakeholders within the Institute. Instead, entrepreneurship at MIT sparked and began to thrive as the result of the isolated initiatives of alumni, students, and individual faculty and staff members, primarily in the realm of extracurricular activities, especially in the early days. In fact, for a long time, MIT followed a hands-off attitude toward most entrepreneurial activities on campus, as well as firm formation resulting from technology transfer. This approach by the Institute's leadership lasted until the early 2010s. Despite the lack of formal initiatives or policy in those formative years, however, MIT's leadership supported the efforts of individuals and groups that experimented with alumni events, student clubs, business plan competitions, and classes, which allowed such entrepreneurial initiatives to thrive and multiply. But by the early 2010s, it seems that MIT's leadership realized the power and potential of the entrepreneurial initiatives—and the entities that supported them—that already existed on campus, so the Institute changed gears to explicitly adopt entrepreneurship and innovation as part of its core strategy and narrative. This emergence of interest in entrepreneurship is not atypical of the Institute, which functions very much in a bottom-up fashion.

How was it possible for interest and support for entrepreneurship to grow so strongly based on uncoordinated individual initiatives and without guidance from leadership? The thesis of this book is that MIT was such a fertile ground for entrepreneurship because entrepreneurship is so well aligned with key aspects of the Institute's culture, specifically a well-ingrained bottom-up mode of decision-making; academic excellence; a keen interest in problem-solving; a belief in experimenting and a tolerance of failure; pride at being viewed as geeky outsiders; the tradition of a multidisciplinary approach to problem-solving; and the desire to have an impact on the real world. As a result of these features, entrepreneurship not only flourished at MIT, but it became a core part of the very culture that helped to sustain it.

The congruence between MIT's culture and entrepreneurship explains that entrepreneurship largely grew there historically based not on explicit policies from its central administration, but on small local and relatively informal initiatives in which alumni, students, and individual members of faculty and staff played key roles. In this favorable environment, entrepreneurship became a logical outgrowth of the Institute's motto, *Mens et Manus* (mind and hand), and the connection between ideas emerging from labs and classrooms and the solutions to real-world problems through products that have commercial value.

The world of academia values invention and breakthroughs, but in the world outside academia, established reliable solutions to problems are generally preferred to novel alternatives for many reasons, including prior investments in certain technologies and cognitive myopia. Translating an invention into an adopted innovation requires a taste for problem-solving, experimentation, an acceptance of multidisciplinarity, examining problems and solutions from an outsider's perspective, and perseverance in the face of failure: all features common to entrepreneurship and to MIT's culture. This cultural fit might be the closest we can get to the "secret sauce" of the success of entrepreneurship at MIT.

To fully understand the fit between MIT's culture and entrepreneurship and how it formed, it is necessary to turn first to the history of MIT's relationship with entrepreneurship. The book will then move on to describing MIT's internal entrepreneurial ecosystem as it was in the late 2010s. Next, it will focus on MIT's particular approach to teaching entrepreneurship and on the impact that entrepreneurship at MIT had on the world. It will end with a reflection on lessons that can be learned by others from this particular case study, as well as useful questions and conversations that they could consider when trying to develop entrepreneurial education in their own situations.

I hope that the answers proposed in this book will help the policymakers and university administrators who regularly visit MIT's campus in search of understanding the sources of the Institute's vibrant entrepreneurial ecosystem. As is obvious from this discussion, the objective is not to present MIT as an ideal model to emulate, given the historical and cultural specificities of it achievements, but rather to use MIT's case study to trigger conversations and raise questions locally that could help decision-makers around the world find their own solutions, adapted to their local characteristics.

I HISTORY

This first part of the book is devoted to providing the context in which interest in entrepreneurship and its support grew at MIT over the years. The chapters in this part go back to the early days of the Institute's founding, the key transformations that MIT went through during and after World War II, the internet era, and the last two decades ending in 2020, which have seen a growing interest in entrepreneurship at MIT.

1 BUILDING A FERTILE GROUND: 1861–1960S

THE FOUNDATIONAL YEARS

By the mid-nineteenth century, when MIT was founded, the United States was entering a period of transformation. Factories, steam engines, and railroads began to dominate the landscape with the emergence of manufacturing and the decline of the craft tradition.[1] It was in the context of these profound changes that William Barton Rogers, a professor of geology, a field closely related to industry back then, at the University of Virginia, realized that the future of education was to prepare students for this new industrial age. He envisioned a new kind of science-based technological university that would be linked to industry and relevant to the times and the country's needs. His vision was not explicitly about entrepreneurship as we define it today, but about the university's relationship with industry.[2] However, it would put in place a culture that would lay the groundwork for entrepreneurship to flourish in the future.

Rogers was an advocate of the blending of science and the so-called practical arts and strongly believed in the role of science in supporting these arts. The practical arts (as opposed to the fine arts) focused on crafts, including tool-making, tinsmithing, and weaving, that would provide scientists, engineers, and technicians a practical but scientifically sound education. This concept of a polytechnic university, or an institute of technology, was quite innovative at a time when universities were dedicated to the humanities and sciences. Rogers saw science and technology as mutually supportive of the purpose of reorganizing craft practices in disciplines based on relevant science.

As Rogers was laying the groundwork for his ideal university, Boston industrialists wished to create a school to train engineers in the technical arts following European models of engineering schools, such as the École Polytechnique and École Centrale in France and the Technische Hochschulen in Germany, that were created at the turn of the nineteenth century. They trained a new generation of engineers with the more rigorous background in science and mathematics needed to integrate the new scientific discoveries of the times into industrial practices.

Rogers, with the support of local members of the Boston establishment, was granted a charter on April 10, 1861, by the state of Massachusetts to incorporate MIT. He created an institution "for the advancement, development, and practical applications of science in connection with the arts, agriculture, manufacture, and commerce."[3] Its motto, *Mens et Manus* ("mind and hand" in Latin), and its logo—which features the scholar and the craftsman in parallel positions—reflect the ideal of cooperation between knowledge and practice. Shortly after its founding, MIT benefited from the 1862 Morrill Land Grant Act, which awarded each state money that resulted from the sale of federally owned land. With this money, states could create colleges, but under the mandate that the colleges would provide students with the opportunity to pursue a "liberal and practical education" in the agricultural and mechanical arts. The Morrill Act also encouraged technology commercialization by requiring the participating colleges to contribute to local economic development by using knowledge generated by academic research.

Through the Morrill Act, MIT received a parcel of land in the Back Bay in Boston and $194,588 in land grant public funds. Since then, the Institute has distinguished itself among land grant colleges by its focus on newer industries, such as chemical, electrical, steel, and transportation, instead of agriculture. It was also the only private land grant university; all the others were public colleges. Ever respectful of its land grant status and mandate, MIT has always been committed to regional economic development, as we will see in this discussion and in future chapters of this book.

This new concept of the polytechnic university translated into a unique curriculum. Unlike most academic institutions of its time, MIT's classes mixed textbook studies with hands-on experience in laboratories and exposure to machine shops, engines, mills, furnaces, and chemical works. Rogers and his colleagues believed that this practical orientation would better prepare students for professional lives in industry. This initial closeness between theory and practice and the sensitivity to the needs of industry have been key influences on the evolving character of the Institute ever since.[4] The strong commitment to learning by doing and to solving real problems has endured to this day and has constituted a fertile ground for the faculty, students, and alumni to develop an interest in entrepreneurship in recent decades.

EARLY DEVELOPMENTS RELEVANT TO ENTREPRENEURSHIP

Rogers's vision of a university with strong industry linkages did not occur without tensions within the Institute over the ensuing decades. Those favoring links to industry clashed with those promoting a purer teaching and research orientation. Over the years, MIT would alternate between these two directions. The resolution of those tensions translated into compromises that laid the groundwork for the future development of entrepreneurship at MIT.[5]

By the early twentieth century, MIT was emphasizing more practical arts, with less emphasis on sciences. After World War I, faculty appointments and nominations to department chairmanships increasingly depended on consulting and development work with existing corporations. As a result of these changes, research activities came under the control of corporations, which owned the results of research and had the right to block any publication about them.[6] By the 1920s, more than half of the MIT staff regularly consulted for outside concerns. This led to a controversy concerning whether professors should be allowed to do consulting for industry. After twenty years of on-and-off debate, a compromise was reached in the early 1930s, known as the "one-fifth rule," which allowed each professor one day a week to do consulting work for a fee. Professor Edward Roberts ('57) of MIT argues that the compromise reached about consulting probably created a tolerance toward faculty and staff entrepreneurship years later. It indeed allowed them to moonlight during their one free day while being full-time employees of MIT, giving them the opportunity to test the waters of entrepreneurship before making a full commitment. In his 1991 book *Entrepreneurs in High Technology: Lessons from MIT and Beyond,* he claimed that half of all MIT spin-off enterprises, including all faculty-initiated companies and many staff-founded firms, started on such a part-time basis.[7]

During those early decades of the twentieth century, another debate arose about patenting and ownership of intellectual property. Patenting MIT's research had been controversial since the early 1900s. Should priority be given to academic publications or should these be delayed until patents were obtained (because once research results are made public, the potential rights on a patent are lost)?[8] In those years, academic researchers at MIT and at other universities generally did not involve their universities when trying to commercialize their inventions by forming companies.[9] The creation of the MIT Committee on Patent Policy in 1932 finally settled the controversy at the Institute. The compromise allowed for patenting only in cases where there was a discovery or invention of substantial promise made during the course of academic work. In other cases, priority would be given to academic publications. This patent policy was one of the earliest efforts of its type by an American university, and it was designed to structure MIT's relationship with industry.

While the policy was not intended to encourage technology transfer (the process of transferring technology from the university to the marketplace) or entrepreneurship, it serendipitously wound up stimulating the commercial activity of some faculty members, who were now able to license the results of their research and become role models for future aspiring entrepreneurs from academia. Between World War I and World War II, few MIT spin-offs were founded. The only ones that grew to a significant size were Raytheon Manufacturing Company, cofounded in 1922 (as American Appliance Company) by Professor Vannevar Bush, and Edgerton, Germeshausen, and Grier, which was founded in 1931 by Professor Harold Eugene "Doc" Edgerton ('27) and two of his students to exploit the invention of stroboscopic photography at MIT. However, the strong patent policy that MIT had created was key to facilitating academic entrepreneurship in the decades after World War II, when scientists and engineers working on defense projects would leave their laboratories at the Institute and try to transfer their expertise to the commercial realm.

In the late 1920s, the tide at MIT began to turn in favor of the concept of a research university aimed at producing new knowledge instead of only transmitting existing knowledge. Industry representatives on the MIT board of trustees expressed the need to educate engineers with a strong background in the sciences and research who could contribute to and improve upon the increasingly science-based technologies and industries of the time.[10] A critical component of this reorientation was the hiring of Karl Compton as president of MIT in 1930. Compton was a respected experimental physicist who was a member of the National Academy of Sciences and before his appointment had chaired the department of physics at Princeton University. With the help of other faculty members and administrators, including Professor Vannevar Bush, who would become the Institute's first dean of engineering in 1932, Compton steered the MIT curriculum away from providing engineers a mere technical education for positions of immediate usefulness and toward an education in the fundamental scientific principles combined with their application to solve important problems. This effort involved a reorganization of the undergraduate program and the creation of leading programs in physics, chemistry, electrical engineering, and chemical engineering, which were geared toward graduating engineers who would contribute to US industry in a creative way.[11] Compton hired star scientists as faculty members and constructed new research facilities. He thus grew the presence of science on campus and affirmed MIT's commitment to basic science as the primary goal of a research university. As a result, the MIT of the late 1930s bore little resemblance to the polytechnic school that educated practical engineers in prior decades.

Compton and Bush wanted to promote industrial collaborations, but they wanted them to support MIT's main missions of teaching and research. Their vision and efforts had one of the strongest indirect influences on shaping the future of entrepreneurship at MIT. First, in turning the Institute into a research university in the 1930s, Compton unknowingly prepared it to play a significant role in the development of new defense technologies during World War II and the subsequent Cold War. In turn, these technologies later spilled into the commercial arena, often via new business ventures. Second, Compton also played a role in trying to revitalize the local economy and was an early supporter of the then-bold idea that science gave birth to new industries.[12] He saw science- and technology-based economic development as a remedy to economic decline, drawing from the examples of firms created by MIT professors, especially Bush, who cofounded the company now known as Raytheon in 1922.[13]

In the late 1930s, Compton and other members of the New England Council, an association representing academia, industry, and government, proposed a solution to reverse New England's economic decline. The council's idea was to build on the unique assets of the region: namely, its educational and research institutions. Instead of trying to assist established companies, as is usually the case in such circles, they focused on the creation of new firms.[14] After the mixed results that occurred, Compton and his colleagues realized that it might not be enough to identify and study new technologies and then rely on local firms to finance the launch of new companies. They concluded that the launch of new ventures commercializing emerging technologies requires those companies to have access to their own source of capital. Thus, the intuition behind venture capital was born. However, in the spring of 1940, World War II started in Europe, and these projects were suspended in order to focus on the war effort that was on the horizon. During the war, however, Compton continued to work on his idea of building a new economic infrastructure based on academic research with commercial potential, and the council relaunched the project after the war ended.[15]

THE WORLD WAR II PERIOD

In 1941, Vannevar Bush was recruited by President Franklin Delano Roosevelt to head the Office of Scientific Research and Development (OSRD) to mobilize the country's best scientists and engineers in case the US went to war. OSRD did not conduct research; rather, it awarded contracts to universities as well as private and governmental laboratories. Massachusetts and MIT were major beneficiaries of the OSRD's allocation of resources, to the extent that MIT was the largest wartime research and development (R&D) contractor, sometimes referred to as the "Pentagon on the Charles."[16] The Institute's prominence in this area was likely a combination of the results of Compton's attempts to turn it into a research university and its connection to Bush at OSRD. From World War II onward, government, as opposed to the private sector, would become MIT's primary funding source.

The most memorable achievement of research conducted at MIT during the war years was probably the improvement of radar at the Radiation Lab (Rad Lab), which grew exponentially during the period and at one point had a staff of 4,000. "The atomic bomb only ended the war. Radar won it," argues Robert Buderi, who wrote a book about the history of the Rad Lab called *The Invention That Changed the World*.[17] In addition to its work on radar, the lab also developed solutions for long-range missiles and the aiming of antiaircraft guns. At the Servomechanisms Lab, the Whirlwind program, which worked to build an aircraft simulator, laid the foundation for the development and commercialization of computers. Wartime radar, inertial guidance systems, microwave technology, and the framework for modern-day personal computing all grew out of research at these labs, as did the guidance and computer systems of the Apollo rockets developed by the National Aeronautics and Space Administration (NASA). One of them carried MIT alumnus Buzz Aldrin ('63). The transistor, which revolutionized the field of electronics, is also a product of research conducted at the Rad Lab, and the digital computer owes a significant debt to radar as well. Before long, radar technology would find applications in the civilian sector, such as in ships and fishing boats, telecommunications, meteorology, sea and air traffic control, and the microwave oven.[18]

THE POST–WORLD WAR II PERIOD

The war period redesigned the physical campus of MIT, its research agenda, and the way it educated its students. Deborah Douglas, an MIT historian, wrote, "The MIT we know today—the MIT that is known around the world as a vital locus of technological creativity, scientific discovery, and education innovation—was born [as a result of its World War II activities]."[19] Another consequence of the war was that, under the pressure to achieve real results and win the war, the Institute's *Mens et Manus* culture was reinforced.[20]

After World War II, there was recognition that physicists, not engineers, had provided the critical input to developing military applications. As a result, there was a major effort to bring science into engineering disciplines in the 1950s, a trend considered to be the beginning of an era of engineering science.[21] Compton's vision of a research university was finally accomplished on campus. Many scientists and engineers who came to the Greater Boston area to work in the university labs and the new government agencies stayed on after the war and moved on to commercial firms. In the post–World War II period, spin-offs started to appear that tried to exploit wartime research in computer hardware and software, precision machinery, electronic components, machine tools, and other technologies developed at MIT's laboratories. One notable spin-off of the Rad Lab was the High Voltage Engineering Corporation, cofounded by professors Denis

Robinson, John Trump, and Robert J. van de Graaff, which supplied electro-static generators used in cancer therapy and radiography.[22]

Most of the ventures created in this postwar period conducted research that was funded primarily by government R&D contracts. As argued by Spencer Ante, the author of a biography about Georges Doriot (as discussed later in this chapter), World War II was a turning point for entrepreneurship. It proved the value of taking risks, particularly on new technologies and methods of production. In capital markets, individual and institutional investors became willing to take more risks. The GI Bill, which gave millions of Americans the opportunity to study at universities, trained the next generation of technologists and entrepreneurs.[23]

Toward the end of World War II, President Roosevelt asked Bush how to extend OSRD's wartime successes to peacetime. In a report titled "Science: The Endless Frontier," Bush recommended the creation of what is known today as the National Science Foundation (NSF). He stressed that basic research was as critical for industry as it had been for military purposes during the war. The creation of the NSF was designed to help secure the future of basic research during peacetime. It was a brilliant insight. For instance, basic research into the molecular basis of life started in the 1940s and continued in the following decades, predominantly by the NSF and the National Institutes for Health (NIH). This research led to basic techniques of genetic engineering in the mid-1970s, which in turn led in the 1980s to the emerging field of biotechnology, in which MIT would be a leading research institution.

After World War II, scientists and engineers with experience working for OSRD and the local government agencies carrying on their work started to set up new types of companies to subcontract R&D from these government entities. In doing so, they brought research skills and high-tech expertise to the marketplace. For the most part, these ventures were still only small technical consulting operations, contract R&D boutiques, and specialty hardware producers, instead of the product focused start-ups that would emerge later. The founders were primarily driven by the desire to be independent and deal with domains and technologies that they found interesting, rather than focusing on making a particular product. The firms tended to stay small and depend on the cycle of government defense spending. Although these firms were geographically and technologically close to MIT, they had limited impact on the Institute in terms of their interest in entrepreneurship.

BBN

In 1948, MIT president James Killian received a request from the United Nations to consider providing an acoustic consultation for their facilities. Killian passed the opportunity on to Professor Richard Bolt of the Acoustics Laboratory, explaining that MIT itself did not do consultations. After learning that this consultation would require a great deal of work, Bolt asked a couple of colleagues, Professors Leo Beranek and Bob Newman ('49), a graduate student of architecture, to join him in creating a consulting company in 1948: Bolt, Beranek, and Newman (BBN). From 1953 to 1969, Beranek served as president and chief executive officer (CEO), and from 1969–1971, he was the chief scientist.

BBN grew rapidly from its acoustics work and branched out into other areas that explored the relationship between human and machine. In 1961, BBN made its initial public offering (IPO) on the stock market. Over the years, BBN would produce subsidiaries and spin-offs and fund other entrepreneurs. By the late 1960s, BBN beat Raytheon, another MIT-related company, when both were vying for a contract from the government's Advanced Research Projects Agency (ARPA) to create the first network of connected computers. BBN's creation, known as ARPANET, connected the first two computers in 1969 and became referred to as the "father of the internet." Eventually, BBN evolved from an acoustical consulting firm to becoming one of the leading computer R&D firms in the US. After various mergers and sales, BBN was acquired by Raytheon in 2009, when it was valued at $350 million.

Looking back upon his successes, Beranek saw the seminal importance of his time at MIT. He lauded MIT's environment, which encouraged innovation, entrepreneurship, and the gift of guidance, plus passion. He said, "One of the reasons that MIT has been so important in the world has been that they were willing to encourage their professors to start businesses. . . . And of course MIT had the proper kind of teaching so that the students got to realize that maybe one of the best things they can do is to invent something and start a company."[24]

It was also a local anchor company that spun off many others, so it contributed to building the local entrepreneurial ecosystem, while its founders became role models for future generations of entrepreneurs.

These firms required little capital and usually obtained financing against their government contracts from local banks, such the Bank of Boston. However, new forms of financing emerged during this post–World War II period. The turning point came when President Compton and his partners at the New England Council revived their regional development project, along with an idea to create a new type of investment firm that would fund the development of technical and engineering companies. On June 6, 1946, the American Research and Development Corporation (ARD) was incorporated. It was the first institutional venture capital firm. The board of ARD included members of the Boston establishment, including Compton and two MIT professors. ARD was led for years by Georges Doriot, a Harvard Business School professor of management. This trio of MIT, Harvard Business School, and the financial community "legitimized the concept of venture capital to state governments and federal regulators."[25]

Over the years, ARD invested in 120 companies and also spun off other venture capital firms, effectively launching the venture capital industry and the venture capital-backed firm. ARD's most successful investment was the computer firm Digital Equipment Corporation. Kenneth H. Olsen ('50), an electrical engineering graduate, worked as a researcher on the Whirlwind project at Lincoln Lab, a nonprofit laboratory operated by MIT for the US Air Force to conduct research to design an air defense system. In 1955, Olsen began working on a transistor-based computer that was much more efficient, faster, and easier to build than existing computers. IBM, the partner of Lincoln Lab in the Whirlwind project, did not value his work, so Olsen concluded that the only way to continue his project was to start a new company. He and his colleague, Harlan Anderson ('53), approached General Dynamics for funding but were turned down. They finally got an investment from ARD, which offered them $70,000 in equity financing for a 70 percent stake in the company. Digital Equipment Corporation, as the firm was known, invented the minicomputer category with its PDP-8 model, which revolutionized the computer industry. By the time of Digital's IPO in 1963, the company was valued at $355 million and ARD's initial investment was valued at $38 million—a return on ARD's investment of over 500 times and a 101 percent annual return rate.[26] Digital was the venture capital industry's first home run. It proved that venture capital could generate enormous wealth by backing the right companies, and it validated the power of startups in the American economy. A model for success was born.

Prior to ARD's success with Digital, MIT's interest in venture capital had waned, due in part to the fact that Compton, a big proponent of the concept, had resigned as the Institute's president in 1948. (He died in 1954.) By the middle of 1955, MIT sold its holdings in ARD and thus missed out on the huge gain made by ARD with the IPO of Digital in 1963. MIT also adopted a more hands-off position toward emerging companies. The Institute did not become proactive with initiatives regarding technology transfer and entrepreneurship for several decades. It would even keep its local new technology companies at arm's length.[27]

The unprecedented success of Digital was transformational; it inspired a generation of technologists and executives to take the risk of leaving their corporate jobs to initiate or join a start-up. From 1955 to 1971, in the area of Route 128—the new peripheral highway surrounding Boston—the number of high-tech firms jumped from 39 to 1,200.[28] By the late 1960s, Route 128 was considered the most innovative region in the US. The genealogy of most of these high-tech firms may be traced to MIT and Digital, and the origins of the local venture capital firms were linked to ARD.[29] Companies such as Teradyne, Unitrode, Damon, Computergraphic, Bose, Analog Devices, Cullinet Software, Data General, Prime Computer, and Computervision were all founded in the 1960s. Some of the most prominent of these were founded by MIT alumni, including Analog Devices (Ray Stata, '57); Apollo Computer and Prime Computer (John William "Bill" Poduska, '59); Bose (Amar Bose, '51); Computervision and Lifeline Systems (Dennis Chapiro, '55); Proteon Associates (Howard Salwen, '58); Teradyne (Alex d'Arbeloff, '49, and Nick DeWolf, '48); and Thermo-Electron (George Hatsopoulos, '50).[30] In a 1968 article, Professor Edward Roberts found that the origin of 200 firms in the Greater Boston area could be traced to MIT.[31] As more and more sectors of the economy adopted computer technology, these entrepreneurial firms relied less on government contracting in favor of the commercial marketplace. Other sectors also blossomed, including artificial intelligence (AI), robotics, and biotechnology.

TERADYNE

In 1960, after working for a few years at Transitron, one of the first successful technology companies established on Route 128, and building a strong technical reputation, Nick DeWolf ('48) had become bored by corporate life. He intended to start a company of his own that would focus on creating test equipment for electronics. He saw an opportunity when he realized that testing performed by technicians and laboratory instruments needed to be automated in order for the semiconductor-makers to keep up with the manufacturing of electronic components. DeWolf's testing devices had the potential to significantly

---

(continued)

decrease the cost of production. For this endeavor, he reached out to a former classmate, Alex d'Arbeloff ('49). DeWolf would oversee the company's engineering component while d'Arbeloff focused on advertising and sales.

The two founders needed $150,000 to launch the company, but the doors of banks were closed to them. They had some savings and had raised another $140,000 from friends and family. ARD was the only firm in Boston willing to invest in emerging companies, so d'Arbeloff and DeWolf approached Georges Doriot, the head of ARD, for the remaining funding that they needed. Spencer Ante, the author of Doriot's biography, recalls Doriot's reaction to the pair's presentation: "Alex, you don't understand . . . If you want us to invest, we'll invest more."[32] DeWolf and d'Arbeloff walked away with $10,000 and an offer from ARD that it would invest $200,000 later if needed.

Although they bootstrapped the growth of their company with this initial investment, they were running out of money one year later because they had not been able to sell a single device. Customers did not yet see the need for automation that DeWolf had anticipated. According to d'Arbeloff, "The start-up process was like rolling a 15,000-ton boulder uphill."[33] So the two partners went back to ARD to ask for more money. It required some convincing (despite ARD's previous reassurance) because Teradyne was seen by the ARD staff as one of the problematic companies in their portfolio. But Doriot had faith in the two young founders, and he also understood that semiconductors were going to be big. In the end, they raised an additional $100,000 from ARD, which bought them time to convince customers of the value of their devices.

Teradyne's first product was the D133, a logic-controlled go/no-go diode tester. By 1962, Teradyne was profitable, and by 1970 it went international, expanding into Europe and Japan. Teradyne had launched the automated testing equipment industry, which it dominated for ten years.

Teradyne's journey was clearly made possible by the investment and support of ARD, and there is no telling if the company would have been able to get off the ground without that investment. Its example validates Compton's view of stimulating the local economy by providing funding to emerging technology companies, with direct or indirect links to MIT and the region's other universities, which would build the industries of the future.

In the 1960s, two events occurred that turned out to be pertinent to MIT's future entrepreneurial development. In 1961, NASA gave MIT a multiyear grant to study the organization and management of large-scale technology companies, especially those involved in the space program. As part of this collaboration, NASA asked MIT in 1964 to study the economic benefit of government-sponsored research. Edward Roberts, then a young faculty member, figured out that a way to achieve this goal was by studying employees who had founded companies of their own after leaving NASA and the MIT labs that were involved in publicly funded aerospace research.[34] Roberts's study was the first stream of research on entrepreneurship at MIT and the only one on the topic as it related to MIT until the late 1990s.[35] It was also a pioneering effort beyond the Institute, where researching entrepreneurship in general had not yet reached academia.

Also occurring in 1961 was the offering of the first-ever entrepreneurship course at MIT, New Enterprises. Taught at the MIT Sloan School of Management, the class was the brainchild of Richard Morse ('33), an entrepreneur and former assistant secretary of the US Army. Morse taught the class with the assistance of mostly outside lecturers (i.e., professionals such as entrepreneurs or venture capitalists who were not part of the faculty). New Enterprises would remain the only graduate course in entrepreneurship until Roberts's course, Corporate Entrepreneurship, was launched following his 1972 study on the topic. This was a sign of limited interest on the part of the students and of the low status of entrepreneurship in academic circles.[36]

ANALOG DEVICES

Ray Stata ('57) and Matt Lorber ('56) met while studying electrical engineering at MIT in the early 1960s, when they were part of the Instrumentation Lab. At the lab, which was a pioneer in inertial navigation systems, they gained experience with instrumentation and control systems. The two then took their knowledge and experience and figured out a commercially viable use for what was being created in the lab. Stata and Lorber started their first company, Solid State Instruments (SSI), with fellow alumnus Bill Linko ('66). Stata recalls that back then, there was already an infectious spirit of entrepreneurship at MIT: "It's like 'monkey see, monkey do.' If you see others start companies and become successful, you say, 'If they can do it, so can I.' Whereas if you don't see that up close and personal, there's a fear and a mystery about how to do it. The entrepreneurial spirit at MIT gives you confidence."[37]

Unfortunately, SSI was not the success that the founders hoped it would be, and they sold it after a few years. With their share of the profits from the sale, Stata and Lorber went on to found Analog Devices, Inc. (ADI) in 1965, with Lorber as CEO. In those days, venture capital was rare, but there were banks willing to fund growth. According to Stata, for every dollar that ADI

(continued)

earned, First National Bank of Boston would lend it a dollar. This one-to-one debt-to-equity ratio was a very innovative banking practice at the time. As Stata explains, "We essentially bootstrapped the company's growth with bank loans. The implication of this approach is that you have to kill to eat—every day you've got to earn those profits."[38]

ADI was a cutting-edge answer to the virgin market of operational amplifier production. It designed and manufactured the means to take outside, analog-based measurements and condition them for different types of measurements that customers needed. Over time, ADI would develop products such as data converters, amplifiers, embedded processors, power management, and interface products. ADI went public in 1969, and Stata became CEO shortly afterward. ADI was listed on the New York Stock Exchange ten years later. Because Stata had no experience as CEO, the first thing he did, in a manner that was consistent with the doer culture of MIT, was to address the issue with his employees, saying, "I don't have a clue about how to be a president, but I'm going to take the next twelve months to learn. And if at the end of that twelve months you guys collectively decide, or if the board decides, that I'm not the person who can provide leadership, I'll step down. But in the meantime, while I'm learning, you've got to help me." Fortunately, Stata's direct approach worked. "Everybody dug in, and there was then no way I could fail. Over the next twelve months I learned how to be a president, and that process has continued for four decades."[39]

Stata would continue to be CEO until 1996, when he assumed the position of chairman of the board of directors. ADI grew into an international, multibillion-dollar enterprise. Looking back at the birth and success of ADI, Stata commented, "Analog Devices is, I think, the prototypical MIT-born and bred company in every respect. I can say unequivocally that we owe our existence to this institute."[40]

While the 1960s saw the creation of a vibrant, high-tech region in the area surrounding the Institute, full of many start-ups founded by MIT graduates and former employees, it is unclear how MIT's relationship to entrepreneurship would have evolved had it not been for the growing initiative of the Institute's alumni. Starting in the 1970s, the school's alumni began to take a major interest in the development and promotion of entrepreneurial initiatives throughout the MIT community, which is the topic of chapter 2.

2 EARLY EFFORTS TO PROMOTE ENTREPRENEURSHIP: 1970S TO MID-1990S

Factors outside the MIT campus were exerting an influence on the evolution of entrepreneurship in Massachusetts. By 1970, Route 128 was considered, along with Silicon Valley, the leading center of innovation in electronics in the US. However, the combination of a recession and the reduction of military expenditures due to the end of the Vietnam War, as well as the slowing of the space race, translated into the loss of 30,000 defense-related jobs in Massachusetts between 1970 and 1972. Life was tough for entrepreneurs because the venture capital market was frozen and Route 128 was at a low ebb. These developments forced the local electronics companies to search for opportunities in the commercial sphere. The new minicomputer industry, with firms such as Digital Equipment Corporation, Data General, Prime, Wang, and Computervision, pulled the region out of the crisis. By 1975, the local high-tech sector employed 100,000 and spearheaded a decade of explosive economic growth that would become known as the "Massachusetts Miracle."[1]

EARLY INITIATIVES BY ALUMNI

The idea for the first series of entrepreneurship-focused seminars to serve young alumni emerged in the late 1960s from a small group of local alumni. The goal was to find an activity that would attract and serve young alumni.[2] Professor Edward Roberts ('57) mentions that within the alumni association, there was skepticism about dedicating any resources and effort to entrepreneurship. According to Roberts, this reflected a dominant perception that entrepreneurship was not important, nor was it a major driving force of the economy.[3] The seminar idea was accepted, however, and on October 4 and 5, 1969, a team of ten alumni organized the first weekend seminar, "Starting and Building Your Own Company."[4] It included sessions related to launching a business, such as organizing, financing, marketing, and legal issues. Instead of the 40 or 50 expected participants, around 300 alumni signed up. It was the MIT Alumni Association's most widely attended seminar series up to that point.

This unexpected success revealed great interest among Boston alumni in starting a company. "To our surprise, the greatest number of those attending were people interested in starting their own business rather than men and women who had already founded their own firms," wrote William Putt ('59).[5] It led to the replication of this seminar in eight cities across the US over the following two years, which were attended by 1,000 alumni and held by local alumni groups.[6] Putt credits Fred Lehman ('51) and Panos Spiliakos ('66) for being instrumental in making these seminars "immensely successful." Each seminar was keynoted by Roberts, who presented the results of the pioneering research on technology entrepreneurship that he had initiated a few years earlier (see chapter 1). Several MIT alumni, such as Neil Pappalardo ('64), who cofounded Meditech, Richard Spann ('61)—who cofounded Applicon, one of the first manufacturers of computer-aided design and computer-aided manufacturing (CAD-CAM) with his Lincoln Lab colleagues Fountaine Richardson, Gary Hornbuckle, and Harry Lee ('57)—and Bob Metcalfe ('68), a pioneer of the internet, the principal inventor of the Ethernet, and later the cofounder of 3Com, credited the foundation of their firms to these early seminars.[7]

Alumni involved in the seminars published the MIT Entrepreneurship Registers in 1971 and 1972, which included résumé-type information about each participant. The purpose was to facilitate networking. In 1974, the alumni founding committee wrote a book titled *How to Start Your Own Business*.[8] The book was largely based on these seminars because there were so few other sources of information on entrepreneurship at that time.[9] An interesting feature of the book is its modest tone, as illustrated by the following quote from its introduction, written by Putt: "We think this book is unique because it is not a collection of success stories. Many of the authors are still only a few years beyond the startup phase. They haven't yet had time to forget the problems of startup or to romanticize them. It is this quality of immediacy that we hope to communicate to our readers."[10] These alumni also thought that their group could contribute to improving the ties of their nascent entrepreneurial community to MIT at a time when the Institute's links to small businesses were weak. There had been an MIT Associates Program that served to connect the Institute to small businesses, but it had been merged in the mid-seventies with the MIT Industrial Liaison Program (ILP), which was geared solely toward larger firms.[11]

A follow-on initiative to the alumni entrepreneurship seminars was the New York MIT Venture Clinic, which was organized by New York–based alumni. It offered the opportunity to early-stage entrepreneurs to present their business plans and their work in progress to alumni club members and receive feedback from them. The Venture Clinic format was soon adopted by the Boston alumni group.

The Boston alumni group involved in the early entrepreneurship seminars that had started in 1969, and in the subsequent Venture Clinics, formalized their activities by founding the Cambridge MIT Enterprise Forum (MITEF) in 1978 under the umbrella of the MIT Alumni Association. The activities of the forum expanded to include an annual workshop, as well as monthly business plan presentations for existing ventures that were evaluated by a panel of experienced entrepreneurs, venture capitalists, and other experts. Following the panelists' assessment, the public was invited to ask questions and make comments. In addition, the forum had a bimonthly Startup Clinic, where entrepreneurs who were at an earlier stage of their projects and were looking for advice and funding had the opportunity to make a presentation in a friendly format. For many years, the meetings were held at MIT. The forum published a monthly newsletter, *The Forum Reporter*, and organized annual daylong workshops on topics such as business plan preparation, the selling of technology-based companies, and marketing.[12] In 1981, additional chapters of the forum were founded in Baltimore and in Washington, DC, and the organization changed its name to the MIT Enterprise Forum. The sessions of the original Cambridge MITEF grew to 200 participants in 1982 and to 300 by 1986.[13] Early organizers stressed the educational function of MITEF, which was a condition to get the endorsement of the MIT Alumni Association and avoid the conflict of interest that commercial activities could involve.[14] Founders, such as Bill Warner ('80) of Avid Technology and Eric Giler of Brooktrout Technologies, credited the

Startup Clinic of the Cambridge MIT Enterprise Forum as a key factor in the success of their ventures.[15]

During the period of the 1970s and 1980s described here, a significant regulatory change occurred that gave a boost to venture capital and technology entrepreneurship. MIT alumnus David Morgenthaler ('40) was instrumental in making this change possible through his lobbying activities to the US Congress as a president (and later chairman) of the National Venture Capital Association (NVCA). In 1978, the US government lowered the maximum effective tax rate on capital gains from 49 percent to 28 percent and allowed pension funds to invest a portion of their assets in higher-risk ventures, which was a boon for the venture capital industry. University endowments also started investing in venture capital. In 1981, the government further reduced the rate from 28 percent to 20 percent.

In 1982, the Cambridge MITEF organized the first entrepreneurship course offered during MIT's January Independent Activities Period (IAP),[16] Starting and Running a High-Technology Company, which is taught during IAP to this day. During IAP, students, and even faculty and staff, can participate in courses (mostly not for credit) on topics outside the standard MIT curriculum. Also in 1982, Stan Rich, the chair of the Cambridge MITEF, wrote with David Gumpert a book collecting the insights from the IAP class: *Business Plans That Win $$$: Lessons from the MIT Enterprise Forum.*[17] In 1991, the MITEF went global with the launch of an Israeli chapter, the first of many international chapters.

The story of the early seminars started in 1969 and of the Cambridge MITEF illustrates how critical the MIT alumni were in showing early interest in entrepreneurship and in initiating support structures from the 1970s onward—structures that would be very important to future entrepreneurs in the MIT community. MIT alumni also played a critical role in the development of the Greater Boston entrepreneurial ecosystem. For instance, Philippe Villers ('60) cofounded Computervision (1969) and Automatix (1980); John William "Bill" Poduska ('59) cofounded Prime Computer (1972), Apollo Computer (1979), and Stellar Computer (1985); the MIT Artificial Intelligence Lab spun off Symbolics (1980), which was founded by MIT scientist Russell Noftsker. In the biotech sector, Bob Swanson ('69) cofounded Genentech (1976); the MIT and Harvard professor Alexander Rich cofounded Repligen (1981).[18] The local impact of these entrepreneurs was compounded by the tendency of their firms to spin off other ventures.

Often, once a company became successful, members of management left to strike out on their own to improve upon what their parent company was producing.

In the 1980s, MIT alumni continued to promote entrepreneurship and provide associated support structures on campus. More than 700 companies presented to, and were helped by, the Cambridge MITEF.[19] This gives an idea of the impact that MITEF has had over the years on the Greater Boston entrepreneurial ecosystem, especially considering that it brought together not only entrepreneurs, but also venture capitalists, business angels, lawyers, and various types of consultants. In 1988, Michael Dukakis, the governor of Massachusetts, and Rosabeth Kanter, a Harvard Business School professor, wrote that as many as 72 percent of new firms established in the Route 128 area since 1975 could trace their origins to some affiliation with MIT.[20] The forum's sphere of influence also began to extend beyond Massachusetts.

PRIME COMPUTER AND APOLLO COMPUTER

The stories of Prime Computer and Apollo Computer are good examples of the minicomputer revolution era in New England in the 1970s and 1980s during the so-called Massachusetts Miracle. The stories also illustrate MIT's critical influence on alumni entrepreneurs of this era, in spite of the fact that the Institute did not intervene actively in facilitating company founding.

Serial entrepreneur Bill Poduska ('59) spent seven years studying at MIT, where he earned his undergraduate, master's, and doctorate degrees in electrical engineering and computer science. After graduating in 1962, he began service in the army while working as an assistant professor at MIT. He then joined the National Aeronautics and Space Administration (NASA) during the era of the Apollo missions and also worked at Honeywell in their labs located next to the MIT campus. In 1972, Poduska joined seven colleagues from Honeywell and NASA to found Prime Computer, a manufacturer of minicomputer hardware and a developer of software. Like many companies from that time, Prime was made possible in large part to the technical training that MIT gave to its founders, but, as with other companies of that era, its founding and evolution occurred outside the Institute's sphere.

It took a year for Prime's founders to secure venture capital, but the company grew rapidly from the mid-1970s onward. Poduska credited its success in part to the crucial time-sharing and computer communications experience that he had accrued during his time teaching at MIT, where he was involved with famous projects such as Project MAC and ARPANET. By 1985, Prime

---

(continued)

would become the sixth biggest minicomputer company in the US, with an estimated $564 million in revenue, and would join the S&P 500 index of the largest US public companies.

In 1979, Poduska had a fundamental difference of opinion about the future of Prime with the chief executive officer (CEO) of the firm. In 1980, he left Prime to cofound Apollo Computer, which developed and produced workstations, a revolutionary new category of computers, and developed software. Workstations were high-performance, networked, single-user machines dedicated to technical and scientific applications such as CAD-CAM. Apollo, like Prime, was quick to find success. Its initial public offering (IPO) in 1983 was recorded as one of the most successful of the technology sector. Apollo harbored great spin-off energy, as did Prime, generating at least nine different spin-offs.

In 1985, Poduska left Apollo, which Hewlett-Packard acquired in 1989, to create Stellar Computer, his third start-up. The *Boston Globe* reported that year: "Poduska, a zealous technologist, said he is responding once again to 'that siren call' of entrepreneurship."

MIT'S DISTANT RELATIONSHIP WITH THE ENTREPRENEURIAL HIGH-TECH COMMUNITY

Despite its many alumni involved with it, MIT continued to maintain a distant relationship with the Route 128 high-tech cluster. In 1986 Toshihiro Kanai ('89) interviewed a forum member (not identified for confidentiality reasons) who expressed his frustration at the lack of links between MIT and the Route 128 entrepreneurial community:

> MIT has gained much of its reputation as a leader in a high-technology area, but if you are president or operating officer of one of those [technology-based small] companies, you would have very little resources back at MIT. If you were a large company or a middle-sized company, you would have many vehicles by which you could link back and enjoy the privileges of affiliation with MIT. But as a small company, you couldn't. . . . I was outraged by that.[21]

Annalee Saxenian, the author of the book *Regional Advantage: Culture and Competition in Silicon Valley and Route 128*, reports similar testimony. Gordon Bell, vice president of research and development (R&D) at Digital, for instance, reported, "We were never able to get a good relationship with MIT. There was no cooperation or reciprocity. While I was at [Digital,] we had better relationships with Stanford and Berkeley than we had with MIT. . . . The computer science department at MIT had an arrogance that made it very difficult to work with them."[22]

MIT's attitude toward entrepreneurial companies stood in stark contrast to the approach adopted by Stanford University, which, unlike MIT, supported interaction with local high-tech firms in the form of alternative curricula to its resident programs. Stanford also established a licensing office that promoted commercialization of its intellectual property in 1969. MIT had had a Patents and Copyright Office since the 1960s, staffed with patent lawyers, but it was only upgraded and renamed the Technology Licensing Office (TLO) in 1985, when it shifted from being staffed primarily by patent lawyers to technically trained businesspeople with a greater focus on commercializing inventions.

Stanford's Industrial Affiliates program facilitated direct interaction between the university and firms both large and small by charging modest fees to enroll in it. In exchange, firms could establish relationships with the university's labs, which provided access to their research and facilitated recruiting. In contrast, MIT's ILP charged hefty fees that only large corporations could afford, according to Saxenian. The same access to labs and programs was not available at MIT. Saxenian argues that this distance between the university and the entrepreneurial community was one reason for the eventual decline of Route 128, in contrast to the success of Silicon Valley, of which one factor was the proximity of Stanford University and the entrepreneurial community.[23] One consequence of the symbiotic development of Silicon Valley and Stanford University is that the center of gravity of the venture capital industry would move to California. This would come back to haunt MIT in the 2000s and 2010s, when numerous graduates and their start-ups would move to northern California, triggering new policies at MIT to try to keep start-ups local (see chapter 4).

Why did MIT keep such an arm's-length relationship with surrounding start-ups and with the Greater Boston entrepreneurial technology community? It was probably a legacy of MIT's long-standing relationships with established corporations such as DuPont, Eastman Kodak, and Standard Oil. This focus on traditional industrial firms is reflected in the MIT Commission on Industrial Productivity, launched in 1986, which studied mostly traditional economic sectors,[24] in contrast with Production in the Innovation Economy (PIE), a follow-up, large-scale study launched in the late

2000s that devoted more attention to young firms and innovation in start-ups.[25] Finally, until recently, there has been a belief at MIT that the vibrant entrepreneurial ecosystem of the Boston area, composed of venture capitalists, specialized lawyers, and other technical consultants, would select the best ventures and provide them with adequate support. This sentiment is reflected in a comment by Lita Nelsen ('64), director of the TLO from 1986 to 2016, who said: "People say to me, 'Does MIT have an incubator?' And my classic answer has been, 'Yes, it's called the city of Cambridge.'"[26] This arm's-length relationship with the entrepreneurial sector also protected MIT and its members from potential conflicts of interest. For instance, its involvement in venture investment could have influenced its research agenda or the promotion of personnel. Investing or incubating some ventures and not others could have sent a negative message about the latter.

STUDENTS' CONTRIBUTION TO BUILDING THE ENTREPRENEURIAL ECOSYSTEM

Entrepreneurship did not get much recognition within MIT either. As Nelsen recalls, "I was a Sloan [School of Management] fellow [at MIT] back in '78–'79. And I was very disappointed because, with the exception of one or two courses, the Sloan School was primarily oriented to Fortune 500 companies and Wall Street—finance theory, that sort of thing."[27]

In the late 1980s, the Massachusetts Miracle was fading. Besides a weakening economy, a technology transition was under way that the Massachusetts companies missed out on. Personal computers and workstations were on the ascent, taking market share away from minicomputers. Local companies also continued to sell hardware and software running on proprietary systems instead of adopting a new trend embraced by their competitors in Silicon Valley, consisting of assembling off-the-shelf parts and using open architecture. By the early 1990s, most minicomputer and workstation firms in New England had disappeared or were no longer independent. Perhaps not coincidentally, given the difficult economy and layoffs in the region, a few MIT students began to show an interest in the late 1990s in starting their own businesses and to play an instrumental role in building the first initiatives to promote entrepreneurship on campus.[28]

In 1988, Peter Mui ('82), a researcher at the Strobe Lab (subsequently renamed the Edgerton Center) launched the MIT Entrepreneurs Club

(E-Club), the first student club focused on encouraging entrepreneurship.[29] Soon, Douglas Ling ('87), a graduate student, would join as one of its first members and would become instrumental in leading the club. "Entrepreneurship was not a major term in the MIT vernacular back then," says Mui.[30] He explains that the idea of the club originated from the realization that "at MIT back in the 1980s, there were lots of people with interesting ideas, but few opportunities for people to meet to discuss them or to learn how to turn the ideas into companies, and there was little interaction between the people developing technologies in the School of Engineering and those with expertise in business at the Sloan School."[31] The club was conceived as a way to meet that need and to bridge silos that existed between the management and the engineering side of the campus. Mui also wanted to provide a very informal setting and a low-pressure environment for the members, which was a contrast to the more formal approach of the MITEF. The meetings of the club followed a loose format wherein participants pitched their new venture ideas for ten minutes, followed by questions and answers for ten minutes. Presenters could come back several times to propose their ideas after refining them.[32] From the start, the E-Club was open to alumni and to non-MIT students, who included some from Harvard University and Wellesley College.

In 1988, around the same time as the founding of the E-Club on the other side of campus, a group of Sloan School students launched the Sloan New Venture Association (SNVA), with a mandate to "promote entrepreneurship in the Sloan/MIT community through a dual emphasis on academic and practical skills."[33] Its activities included facilitating the creation of new ventures using the network of faculty members, students, alumni, and business leaders. They tried to promote entrepreneurship in the Sloan curriculum via elective courses, workshops, and research projects. The SNVA, with the help of the TLO, provided its members with information and assistance about technology licensing. They also matched Sloan students with startups with the help of the Sloan Career Development Office. SNVA organized a speaker series, to which they invited successful entrepreneurs and venture capitalists. Sloan Night gave Sloan students the opportunity to share their start-up experiences. The SNVA also invited pioneers of the growing biotech industry to talk at a biotech panel.[34]

Soon, Richard Shyduroff, an early member of the E-Club, came up with the idea of launching a business plan contest to give more visibility to the club.[35] Ling, an engineering graduate student, took a few classes at the Sloan School of Management, which was unusual back then, at a time when the two sides of campus did not have much interaction. At the business school, he fortuitously came across flyers posted by the SNVA, went to one of its events, and introduced himself to Rob Aronoff ('90), then the leader of the SNVA. The two clubs decided to join forces in line with the E-Club's wish of bridging silos. The $10K Business Plan Competition (later renamed the Entrepreneurship Competition in its $50,000 and $100,000 versions) materialized in 1989 out of the clubs' joint meetings. "Dean Jack Kerrebrock of the School of Engineering was really the first supporter of the competition, putting down $1,000 and giving us the administrative staff resources we needed," says Ling. Dean Lester Thurow of the Sloan School of Management was more skeptical, wondering if entrepreneurship could be taught, adds Ling.[36] However, Thurow finally agreed to associate the name of the Sloan School with the competition once its founders lined up all their sponsors. The students reached out to MIT-related entrepreneurs who had been celebrated by MIT shortly before, at Event 128: A Salute to Founders. Of those they contacted, George Hatsopoulos ('49), founder of Thermo-Electron, agreed to sponsor the competition. Additional sponsorship was provided by the venture capital firm Burr, Egan, Deleage, & Co, IBM, the MIT School of Engineering, the MIT Sloan School of Management, the MITEF, Price Waterhouse, and Regis McKenna, according to a 1990 brochure about the first edition of the competition.[37]

Records of the first competition in 1990 vary. Some mention that fifty-four teams competed; others say sixty-four.[38] In any case, both figures represent a surprisingly high number, given the virtual nonexistence of an internal MIT entrepreneurial ecosystem back then.[39] The winner received a prize of $10,000, an amount suggested by John Preston, director of the TLO, because it corresponded to the cost of filing a patent. Preston also served as the chair of the initial judging panel. The second- and third-place teams in the competition were given $3,000 and $2,000, respectively. Teams also benefited from several thousand dollars' worth of in-kind legal and accounting services and a "trillion bucks worth of free advice," according to Joe Hadzima ('73)[40], an early advisor to the E-Club and a judge of the first $10K Business Plan Competition. Hadzima, an entrepreneur himself, would be a key contributor to entrepreneurship in general at MIT in many capacities over the years, including serving as a senior lecturer.[41]

After the first edition of the competition, Mui left MIT, and Ling continued to be the lead organizer of the $10K until 1994, when he passed the baton to Joost Bonsen ('90). During this period, Ling was able to raise $49,000 from sponsorship.[42] A brochure about the competition during the 1993–1994 academic year mentions the venture projects of students that turned into real companies. They include ACT Research Corporation, founded in 1991 by Zhen Hong Zhou ('91), the grand-prize winner of the first edition of the $10K Business Plan Competition in 1990, soon joined by Che-Chih Tsao ('95), a finalist of the 1991 edition of the competition, who commercialized a volumetric, three-dimensional (3D) display; Stylus Innovation, cofounded by the grand-prize winners of the 1991 competition, John Barrus ('87), Mike Cassidy ('87), and Krisztina Holly ('89) (Stylus was sold to Artisoft for $13 million in 1996); and QDB Solutions, founded by Mark Hansen ('91), the $5,000 prize winner in 1990, proposed a software program for database optimization and management. Another company highlighted in the brochure was Diva, cofounded by Jonathan Harber ('90) following the 1991 competition. Diva's product was a digital video editing software program that was later acquired by Avid Technology, which was founded in 1987 by another MIT alumnus, Bill Warner ('80). Novus Products, cofounded by Sam Jaffe ('93) and Nicolas DeLuca ('93), the 1993 grand prize winner, built an environmentally friendly inflatable packing system. In 1993, the $10K judge Hadzima wrote in *Mass Hi-Tech*: "This year's $10K contestants and their business plans are excellent examples of an entrepreneur's special ability to see opportunities where problems or needs exist, to forge a vision of the possible, to ask 'Why not?' and to motivate, prod, beg, persuade, and sometimes drag together the people and resources necessary to turn their vision into reality."[43]

In 1994, much-needed sponsorship came from the venture capitalist David Morgenthaler ('40), a frequent donor to MIT. In an interview given shortly before he passed away on June 17, 2016, Morgenthaler spoke of a visit to the MIT campus, during which he had the opportunity to speak to some Sloan students about the MIT $10K Business Plan Competition.[44] Hadzima further recalls in an obituary for Morgenthaler that he once asked the students about what they were trying to accomplish. They replied that they were hoping to bring together scientists, engineers, and management students to create innovative solutions to problems. They explained that their greatest challenge to achieve that goal was raising the $10,000 prize money for their business plan competition. Morgenthaler further inquired what they would do if they didn't have to raise that money. "Build tomorrow's leading companies," replied the students.[45] Edward Roberts also reports that the students approached him for funding, and in turn he solicited Morghenthaler, who agreed to donate the $10,000 prize money for the next three years and to commit money to fund Roberts's research in entrepreneurship.[46] As a result, the competition's grand prize was named in honor of David and Lindsay Morgenthaler. This funding came at a critical time; were it not for him, the $10K Business Plan Competition might have lost momentum and never turned into the world-renowned contest that it is today.

For the first ten years of the competition, the finals were held as one of the monthly programs of the Cambridge MITEF because it was the only entity on campus that had a large community linked to entrepreneurship at MIT. The business plan competition contributed to bringing the science and engineering side of campus closer to the management side. To overcome the distance between the engineering and the management sides and improve the chances of participants in the competition forming mixed teams, the student organizers of the competition initiated dinners to facilitate networking and team building.[47]

These stories about the early days of the business plan competition illustrate the practical orientation and can-do attitude of the students behind this initiative. It is also interesting to note how the interactions among students, alumni, and faculty succeeded in navigating the often-complex MIT organization to make things happen. Also, the MIT administration (or at least leaders of schools within MIT, when lobbied) provided approval and space for student initiatives to materialize. It was not always an easy ride, however, as Joost Bonsen ('90), a student leader of the $10K Business Plan Competition in 1993–1995, attests: "It was a harder sell then, because we didn't have any success stories yet, and there wasn't this visibility for entrepreneurship that exists today."[48]

The E-Club was also critical to the creation of two other notable initiatives. In 1989, a couple of members of the E-Club approached its advisor, Joe Hadzima, to teach club members how to write a business plan as a non-credit, club-sponsored IAP offering. While Hadzima was considering the request, one of the students published an announcement of the seminar in the IAP catalog, which essentially forced Hadzima to teach it! In doing so, the students followed an informal but widespread motto at MIT: "Ask for forgiveness, not permission!"[49] This was the beginning of Hadzima's IAP seminar, Nuts and Bolts of Business Plans, which he has been teaching ever since. The first session drew several hundred attendees, reflecting the growing interest in entrepreneurship among the MIT student community. By adding a writing assignment and additional course hours, the Nuts and Bolts of Business Plans seminar eventually turned into an IAP degree class in the 1994–1995 academic year, with Hadzima as the teacher. Remarkably, the E-Club organizers managed to turn their extracurricular activity into one of the first for-credit entrepreneurship classes at the Sloan School of Management,[50] which was open to both undergraduate and graduate students at the Institute. In 2009, Nuts and Bolts was ranked "one of the 10 best entrepreneurship courses in America" by *Inc.* magazine.[51]

Hadzima stressed that his seminar was one of the first classes that mixed students from science and engineering with students from Sloan School of Management. Indeed, although it was not by design, those early initiatives and later activities dedicated to entrepreneurship probably contributed to initiating bridges between both sides of campus and an appreciation of students of various disciplines for one another.

Another outcome of the E-Club was the launch in 1993 of the first undergraduate seminar outside of the Sloan School of Management, High-Tech Ventures, hosted by the Edgerton Center and initially taught by the E-Club director Shyduroff, and later Hadzima.[52] Until 2011, it was the only entrepreneurship for-credit seminar for undergraduates outside of the Sloan School.

THE INFLUENCE OF THE BAYH-DOLE ACT

The passing of the Bayh-Dole Act in 1980 fundamentally changed the nation's system of technology transfer by enabling universities to retain title to inventions and take the lead in patenting and licensing groundbreaking discoveries arising from federally funded research. This policy development had a major influence on entrepreneurship both at MIT and beyond. Recipients of federal funding—such as universities, small businesses, and nonprofits—have certain obligations to fulfill as part of the Bayh-Dole Act. These include filing patents on inventions they elect to own; working with small businesses to commercialize technology; and sharing licensing revenue with inventors. This effectively led to the creation of technology transfer as part of the mission of universities. The number of universities with technology transfer entities grew from twenty-five in 1980 to 200 in 1990. The number of US patents granted to US universities grew from roughly 300 in 1980 to about 2,000 in 1995.[53] These patents covered various scientific domains, but they became increasingly concentrated in biomedical fields. Bayh-Dole legitimized the act of spinning off ventures from universities and encouraged licensing to new, small firms. In fact, one of the act's objectives was "to encourage maximum participation of small business firms in federally supported research and development efforts."[54]

THINKING MACHINE

For his MIT PhD thesis, Danny Hillis ('78) proposed the design of a revolutionary computer architecture with the ability to recognize patterns by processing millions of pieces of data at once. Hillis envisioned a computer with parallel processing power based on 64,000 processors. Along with one of his professors, Marvin Minsky, he founded Thinking Machines Corporation in 1983 for the purpose of manufacturing parallel computers designed to advance artificial intelligence (AI).

Early on, two conflicting visions emerged regarding the focus of the company. Hillis and his supporters wanted to build the kind of computer that he conceived of in his thesis—one that would target academics conducting research on AI. Others within Thinking Machines argued for a more general-purpose computer with commercial applications. Hillis's group won the day, and within a year of its founding, Thinking Machines landed a multiyear contract from the Defense Advanced Research Projects Agency (DARPA) that was worth $4.5 million a year.

In 1985, Thinking Machines announced the production of its first computer, the CM-1, at a price of $5 million per computer. Unfortunately, the computer was unable to run FORTRAN, the standard programming language in the scientific world. Due to its limitations and cost, Thinking Machines' product was only viable for DARPA. In fact, the agency essentially kept the company afloat by brokering and subsidizing the sale of seven CM-1 computers. It also granted the company a $12 million multiyear contract in 1989 as part of a new ambitious High-Performance Computing and Communication Program.

In the meantime, Thinking Machines' competitors were able to catch up, and later surpass them in the commercial market, by utilizing cheaper and easier

(continued)

> ways to create their products, connecting off-the-shelf microprocessors used in PCs and workstations into one computer that would run on existing software. In addition to the problems of cost and accessibility, Thinking Machines failed to predict that the biggest benefit of supercomputing was not science, but data mining. After much internal debate, the leadership at Thinking Machines came to acknowledge this reality, but by then it was already late to the game.
>
> Although Thinking Machines was profitable for the first time in 1989, and there were even rumors of an IPO, decisions made in the company's early days led to its ultimate demise. While the DARPA contract appeared to validate Hillis's vision, it was a Pyrrhic victory for Thinking Machines. The early success with DARPA diverted the company from making decisions that would ensure broader, long-term success in the commercial world. By 1992, Thinking Machines reported a loss of $17 million; it filed for bankruptcy in August 1994.
>
> In spite of this commercial failure, Thinking Machines had a positive impact on the broader technology and entrepreneurial ecosystem by creating an entirely new category in the computer industry. It also served as a cautionary tale, encouraging others to think more broadly—and commercially—when creating companies based on technology developed at MIT.

To fulfill the obligations required by the Bayh-Dole Act, it became clear that MIT's patent office, which was managed by lawyers, was not equipped to meet the US government's expectations in terms of technology transfer. The Patent, Copyright and Licensing Office was restructured and renamed the TLO. Now, instead of being an office that reactively processed patent applications, the reimagined TLO was a proactive entity that helped with the commercialization of MIT-owned technology. The TLO's primary focus was now the licensing and transfer of technology. An effort was also made to hire technology specialists instead of lawyers. These tech specialists had significant backgrounds in industry, as well as in research, and could understand the commercial potential of inventions in a way that lawyers could not. The Institute sought the assistance of Neils Reimer, the director of technology licensing at Stanford University, who came to MIT on a sabbatical in 1986 to help reorganize its patenting and licensing office based on the Stanford model. Stanford University's patenting and licensing office was already emphasizing more commercialization and industry expertise over legal expertise.[55] The difficulty in meeting the obligations of the Bayh-Dole

Act was that established firms are seldom interested in licensing emerging technologies from academia for several reasons. They don't understand the potential of the technology; the time frame to develop the tech into a viable product exceeds the time horizon that most firms are comfortable with, or else they fear that they could cannibalize their existing business.[56] As a result, in 1987, the TLO's new director, John Preston, took the initiative to license technology to new ventures in exchange for equity, first as an experiment because there was a great concern at MIT about potential conflicts of interest.[57] During the first year of this policy, six companies were formed based on such licenses, including ImmuLogic and American Superconductor. Sixteen more companies were formed during the second year.[58]

Spinning off technology ventures from MIT based on the licensing of technology had a favorable effect on promoting entrepreneurship. According to Lita Nelsen, as MIT's spin-offs founded by scientists and engineers gained more visibility, master's of business administration (MBA) students started to show more interest in entrepreneurship. The TLO's licensing technology to start-ups allowed it to nurture contacts with the venture capital community. Most venture capital, however, still came from California or New York. Although American Research and Development Corporation (ARD) had launched the venture capital industry with the help of MIT in the 1940s, the center of gravity of the sector had moved to California by then.

LOCAL FACULTY AND STAFF INITIATIVES

In 1990, "in response to student requests for guidance in starting new businesses,"[59] the MIT Entrepreneurship Center (E-Center) was founded by Professor Edward Roberts of the Sloan School of Management. He recalls that students were increasingly approaching him about their desire to write their master's thesis on entrepreneurship-related topics. In Roberts, the students had found the right institutional ally, one who had conducted research on technology entrepreneurship since the early 1960s (see chapter 1) and had been involved with various start-ups. In 1990, he submitted a proposal to create the E-Center to Sloan dean Lester Thurow.[60] At the time of its founding in 1990, the E-Center was simply a tiny study room allocated by the Sloan School, where students could gather to work on their venture project, which was a reflection of the low status that entrepreneurship still had, in spite of the big step that the founding of the center represented.[61]

Bill Aulet ('94), the current director of the Martin Trust Center for MIT Entrepreneurship and a professor of practice, recalls that when he was working toward his master's degree at MIT during the 1993–1994 academic year and wanted to hold a panel discussion on campus featuring successful entrepreneurs, he got pushback from MIT administrators, who told him to "tone it down." "They would not sponsor it and did not want it on campus," explains Aulet. He says that campus leaders feared upsetting big companies like IBM because events like the one he was planning might tempt the employees studying at MIT programs for midcareer executives to become entrepreneurs instead. "At an administrative level, there wasn't a lot of love for entrepreneurship."[62]

Outside MIT, observers started to take notice of the positive impact that MIT-related companies were having on the economy. In 1989, a study by the Bank of Boston found that 636 firms founded by MIT alumni employed more than 200,000 people and had aggregate worldwide sales of nearly $40 billion. In 1990, the Chase Manhattan Bank reported in a study titled *MIT Entrepreneurship in Silicon Valley* that 176 firms founded by MIT alumni in northern California employed 90,000 people and accounted for 21 percent of the total manufacturing employment in Silicon Valley.[63]

CONCLUSION

In spite of the efforts of the pioneers who promoted entrepreneurship on campus in the late 1980s and early 1990s, there was still only an embryo of entrepreneurial ecosystem at MIT. The E-Center operated on a shoestring budget, almost like a virtual entity. There were two student clubs, one of which was launched in 1995. The Sloan School of Management offered one entrepreneurship class taught by an outside lecturer and a Corporate Venturing class taught by Roberts. The MITEF probably had the most impact in the realm of entrepreneurship, but it was operating at the periphery of the Institute by alumni, for alumni. One critical thing to note, however, is that while MIT's leadership remained hands-off, it allowed experimentation by those interested in entrepreneurship and didn't shut down or stifle their initiatives.

However, things were about to change, as the internet era would be a turning point in the second half of the 1990s, as chapter 3 illustrates.

3 THE INTERNET ERA AND THE GROWTH OF INTEREST IN ENTREPRENEURSHIP: MID-1990S TO MID-2000S

THE INTERNET ERA AND THE GROWING EMERGENCE OF ENTREPRENEURIAL ROLE MODELS

The internet era appears to have been a turning point in triggering both the public's and MIT students' interest in entrepreneurship. The middle-to-late 1990s was an era of great promise and great disruption. A gold rush mentality developed, especially among young people who did not want to miss out on the exciting technology of a new area, perceived to be similar to the emergence of the railways and electricity in the past. For the first time in the eyes of the public and of policymakers, entrepreneurship perhaps appeared as an engine of innovation and disruption, while technology entered people's living rooms.

Although the epicenter of the internet boom was in California, successful MIT spin-offs commercializing internet technologies soon gained fame and provided role models for other entrepreneurially minded members of the MIT community. Firefly Networks, founded in 1993 by Media Lab professor Pattie Maes, Max Mertal, and Yezdi Lashkari ('95), was based on Maes's research on software agents. Its product let users find and select pieces of music that they did not know just by taking cues from other people with similar tastes. According to an introduction of Maes for a TED Talk, "This brought a sea change in the way we interact with software, with culture, and with one another."[1] Microsoft bought the company in 1998 for a reported $100 million. The most emblematic MIT spin-off of the early internet era of the late 1990s to early 2000s was Akamai. That tech firm was founded in

1998 by PhD candidate Danny Lewin ('98), MBA candidate Jonathan Seelig, and Randall Kaplan, as well as their MIT professor of applied mathematics, Tom Leighton ('81), to solve the congestion of the internet with mathematical algorithms that intelligently routed and replicated content over a large network of distributed servers. The company was listed on the NASDAQ stock market on October 29, 1999, and rode the boom and bust of the internet bubble. Other examples of early successful internet-era spin-offs from MIT were Webline Communications, Direct Hit, Silicon Spice, Flash Communications, and Sohu. Several of those start-ups had participated in, and sometimes won, the $50K Entrepreneurship Competition, as the $10K Business Plan competition was renamed in 1996.[2]

Companies founded by MIT alumni in other sectors were also successful during the decade following the start of the internet era. Such companies include SensAble Technologies (founded in 1995), which commercialized a tactile computer interface, and Z Corporation, a pioneering three-dimensional (3D) printing company founded in 1994.[3] Pre–internet era companies related to MIT became significant players in their industries as well, including Software Arts, founded in 1979, which designed the first spreadsheet software; Lotus Development Corporation, founded in 1982; telecommunication software company Kenan Systems, founded in 1982; iRobot, founded in 1990; and Lexicus, a software company that specialized in speech and predictive technology systems, which was founded in 1992.[4]

Those entrepreneurs became role models for aspiring entrepreneurs. Among them, it is worth mentioning Mitch Kapor, who enrolled at the Sloan School of Management in the fall of 1979 but did not complete his degree. Kapor left the Institute in order to launch the Lotus Development Corporation in 1982 with Jonathan Sachs ('70). Its flagship product, Lotus 1-2-3, an integrated spreadsheet and graphic program, was an immediate success. It is considered the first so-called killer app of the IBM PC era because it made the personal computer ubiquitous. As a result, Lotus became the world's third-largest microcomputer software company in 1983, with $53 million in sales in its first year. It had a successful initial public offering (IPO) in 1984 and was bought by IBM in 1995 for $3.5 billion. Kapor and the success of Lotus inspired many entrepreneurs, for whom Kapor acted as a role model. This, combined with the transformational role that Lotus played in putting Kendall Square on the business map (discussed in chapter 9), left a lasting impact on the area and on the entrepreneurial community in and around MIT.[5]

Meanwhile, entrepreneurship from MIT alumni started to attract the attention of outsiders. Bank of Boston published in 1997 a report titled *MIT: The Impact of Innovation,* which stated that by 1994, graduates of MIT had founded 4,000 firms in the US that employed at least 1.1 million people and generated $232 billion in sales worldwide.[6]

HARMONIX

Harmonix is an example of how companies can spring from the fertile ground of innovation and brilliance that is so commonplace among MIT students and faculty members. However, it is also an example of a time when support for aspiring entrepreneurs remained scarce, in contrast to the seasoned advice and assistance that they enjoy today. Harmonix founders Eran Egozy ('93) and Alex Rigopulos ('92) met when they were graduate students at MIT's Media Lab, where both shared a strong interest in computer science and music. During their time at the Media Lab, they built a computer-generated music system operated with a joystick. Their example is an illustration of the multidisciplinarity so characteristic of MIT. As graduation approached, however, the two friends realized that it was unlikely that they would be able to pursue this interest while working for an established company. In an effort to remedy that situation, they decided to start their own business, Harmonix Music Systems, in 1995.

Harmonix had a tough start. It had an early product that allowed people to improvise instrumental solos by operating a joystick, but it did not catch on in the market. As a result, the founders realized that they needed to reconsider their product and their business model. In 1997, they found inspiration in the music gaming industry that was exploding in popularity in Japan. "It really struck us that videogaming was the mass-market interactive medium . . . through which we wanted to achieve our mission of bringing the music-making experience to people who are nonmusicians," says Egozy.[7] Instead of teaching gamers new skills to learn how to play music, Harmonix would build a video game that leveraged its users' existing gaming skills and repurposed them for music-making.

Egozy and Rigopulos were able to reorient Harmonix into a video game developer with the support of Sony Computer Entertainment. The company's first products won numerous awards and inspired a cult following among gamers, but they were not commercial successes. Finally, Harmonix hit the big time in 2005 with *Guitar Hero,* a game that gave users the experience of

---

(continued)

playing various types of guitar. The product fueled the growth of the music games category to more than $1 billion in sales. In 2006, Harmonix achieved additional success with *Rock Band*, which enabled players to pretend they were stars in their own rock band.

In 2006, MTV Networks (a division of Viacom) acquired Harmonix for $175 million, with the goal of building synergy between Harmonix, the game developer, and Viacom's content producer divisions. Unfortunately, that synergy failed to materialize, and the media giant sold Harmonix in 2010 back to its founders and investors, thus giving the company back its independence.

Rigopulos characterized the post-Viacom period as incredibly invigorating: "As an independent company, we can make decisions very quickly, we can change course, and we have this nimbleness that is just impossible within a big company."[8]

In 2010, the market for music games with plastic instruments dried up, so Harmonix pivoted again and created the first fully immersive, no-controller dance games, *Dance Central* and *Dance Central 2*, for Microsoft's Kinect. By 2014, the company was trying to bring music into various genres and on various platforms beyond its console business, such as PCs, smartphones, and tablets, as well as social gaming. This change in focus did have some negative ramifications, however: Harmonix had to lay off personnel in 2014 and, as a result of these struggles, Rigopulos stepped down as chief executive officer (CEO) to become creative director.

In 2015, Harmonix raised $15 million from the venture capital firms Spark Capital and Foundry Group, the latter led by MIT alumnus Brad Feld ('87), who was an early investor in Harmonix and had been on its board for some time. It is unusual for a twenty-year-old company to raise venture capital, but the new CEO, Steve Janiak, justified this move by saying that the company was being run as a start-up now that it was again independent. According to Janiak, investors were particularly attracted to the developments of the firm involving virtual reality.[9] In 2016, Egozy returned to MIT to teach courses in interactive, high-tech music while staying on the board of Harmonix. In 2018, Harmonix announced a publishing deal with the Korean video game developer NCSoft.

INSTITUTIONAL AWAKENING TO ENTREPRENEURSHIP AT SLOAN

The explosive interest of MIT students in the internet and its applications—as well as the inspiration of the aforementioned early successes—translated into a growing interest in entrepreneurship on the MIT campus.

"The internet bubble created a demand for entrepreneurship training. The demand was there before, but the internet was an amplifier. It attracted new people who were not interested in entrepreneurship before," explained Professor Edward Roberts of Sloan in a 2014 interview.[10] The internet led the Sloan School of Management to improve its offerings in terms of courses and support structure, which, as mentioned previously, was quite thin. In 1994, Sloan initiated new career tracks within its master's degree program, including a product and venture development track, which quickly became the second-largest track at the school.[11] The professional tracks, however, were abandoned some years later, following a reorganization of the program's curriculum.

The rapidly growing demand for courses in entrepreneurship and the lack of faculty members in this domain, as well as the lack of funding to hire tenure-track faculty members, forced Sloan to rely primarily on outside lecturers (i.e., professionals who teach a lecture or a class, as opposed to tenure-track scholars).[12] Most of these professionals were MIT alumni, which underscores once again the key role of alumni in the development of support for entrepreneurship within MIT. Until 1994, New Enterprises and Corporate Entrepreneurship were the only entrepreneurship courses offered at Sloan, with New Enterprises being expanded into multiple class sections to meet the demand. An analysis of the MIT course catalog *The Bulletin* indicates that in the 1995–1996 academic year, three entrepreneurship courses were being offered at MIT. By the 1999–2000 academic year, there were eleven courses, and twenty-one courses were offered in 2005–2006.

In 1995, John Preston, director of the Technology Licensing Office (TLO) and a senior lecturer, along with MIT Sloan of Management professor Eric von Hippel ('68) complemented the one-semester entrepreneurship class, New Enterprises, with a field-lab element. With support from the Kauffman Foundation, they launched MIT Entrepreneurship Lab (E-Lab), a practice-oriented class in line with the strong MIT tradition of experiential learning. The concept of the E-Lab was to give students the opportunity to work with CEOs of start-up companies on challenges relevant to their ventures, in order to work on "a problem that keeps the CEO up late at night."[13] Projects from the lab typically consisted of conducting a market survey, preparing for and taking part in a trade show, rewriting a business plan or parts of it, examining alternative distribution channels, and undertaking patent searches. Many were conducted by mixed teams of Sloan and engineering students. E-Lab would turn out to be a major teaching innovation, leading to numerous classes in line with MIT's tradition of experiential learning.

In 1996 Sloan hired Scott Shane, its first tenure-track faculty member in entrepreneurship, to teach and conduct research on the topic. More young faculty members would be hired in the late 1990s and early 2000s. A challenge to hiring appropriate faculty in this area was that thus far, entrepreneurship had not been a recognized academic subject of study, and even less so as an academic field. As a result, the pool of PhD graduates able to teach entrepreneurship classes and conduct research about the topic was small, especially at the level of excellence required by MIT. The response of the Sloan school was to hire young faculty members in academic disciplines such as sociology, economics, finance, strategy, and political science who had an interest in studying topics related to entrepreneurship from the point of view of their particular discipline. Among those young faculty members were M. Diane Burton, Simon Johnson ('89), Fiona Murray, Antoinette Schoar, and Scott Stern. Some of these recruitments were made possible thanks to significant gifts from alumni. These young faculty members, then inexperienced in entrepreneurship, were paired with outside professionals as lecturers in order to guarantee the relevance of their teaching, while also guaranteeing a degree of scholarly rigor in what would be called a "dual-track faculty."[14]

Another important step in Sloan's recognition of the demand for entrepreneurship support was the hiring in 1996 of Kenneth Morse ('68), the former managing director of Aspen Technology Europe, as the first managing director of the MIT Entrepreneurship Center (E-Center). Morse's arrival marked a relaunch of sorts of the E-Center, as it was finally operating with reasonable human and financial resources. This new chapter of the E-Center was also made possible by gifts from the Kauffman Foundation and from alumni, including David Morgenthaler ('40).[15] Morse says that Glen Strehle, then the treasurer of MIT, allocated endowment funds from the Richard S. Morse Fund that were left over from the MIT Development Foundation, which was headed by Kenneth Morse's father (see chapter 2). The income from this fund has been one of many sources of support for the E-Center ever since. Several alumni of Richard Morse's course also contributed to the fund, according to his son, Kenneth.[16] This fund allocation and the support of Glen Urban, the dean of the Sloan School of Management and a serial entrepreneur, were other early signs of institutional support for entrepreneurship at MIT.

Morse recalls fondly the way that he was recruited. He was running Aspen Technology Europe, whose mother company had just gone public. Morse called Urban, then the dean of the Sloan School of Management, with the intention of making a donation to the E-Center from some of the money that he had made through his stock options. Urban replied, "We'd love to have your money," but went on to explain that what he really needed was an entrepreneur to build the E-Center. Quitting his job, moving back to the US, and taking a serious salary cut were not on Morse's mind at the time. However, many people at MIT and at the MIT Enterprise Forum (MITEF), on whose board he had served in the early 1980s, convinced him to make that leap. And there was also the influence of Edward Roberts, who had worked with his father, Richard. Of his time at the E-Center, Kenneth Morse recalls, "The next thirteen years were inspiring and wonderful."[17]

Two of Morse's first tasks were to coteach the E-Lab practice class that had been launched one year earlier, and to convince more CEOs of MIT-related start-ups to offer internships to students. E-Lab went from a class taught once a year to being taught twice a year, and soon two sections were created each semester to meet the student demand. Under Morse, enrollment in the E-Lab class went from 20 students to 174. The E-Lab inspired professors Simon Johnson and Richard Locke to launch in 2000 the course Entrepreneurship without Borders, focusing on entrepreneurship in emerging countries. The class later added a field-lab element, the Global Entrepreneurship Lab (G-Lab), in which students advised the CEOs of ventures that were based outside the US, primarily in emerging economies.[18]

Morse also launched the Entrepreneurship Development Program (EDP) in 1999, which has since grown into a successful one-week executive education program aimed at ambitious entrepreneurs from ventures with international potential (discussed further in chapter 9).[19]

Morgenthaler said, "He [Professor Edward Roberts] and Ken made a good combination. [Ken] was a shaker and mover. Ed provided the academic cover."[20] Roberts was the center's founder and faculty director, and Morse its founding managing director. The pair presided over the growth of the

TABLE 3.1
Growth of the Entrepreneurship Center's activities 1996–1998

Attendance	1995–1996 (millions $)	1997–1998 (millions $)	2-Year Growth (%)
New Enterprises	70	270	286
Entrepreneurship Lab	20	174	770
Independent Activities Period	128	283	121
All others	70	235	236
Total	**288**	**962**	**234**
$50K Entrepreneurship Competition	# Teams	# Teams	
$50K Entries	52	83	60
Team size	2.3	3.7	61
Endowment Funds	Millions $	Millions $	
Total Pledges	N/A	10.25	N/A
Cash Received	N/A	6.74	N/A

Source: Adapted from *MIT Entrepreneurship Center Annual Report 1997–1998* (Cambridge, MA: MIT, 1998).

E-Center until 2009, when Morse stepped down. His contributions, particularly in terms of fundraising, were key to getting the center off the ground.

When Roberts was also named chair of the Entrepreneurship Center by the Sloan School of Management in 1999, he summarized his vision for the center as follows: "The mission of the center is to teach entrepreneurs how to make high-tech start-up companies successful. To do so, we will build bridges across the various schools within MIT, where expertise in areas such as engineering and marketing can be pooled to create a curriculum that teaches technology and management. Today's high-tech managers need both skills."[21] This vision sets the stage for an innovative concept of an Entrepreneurship Center that will endure over the years—one that serves the whole MIT community and combines engineering and scientific skills with management skills. Note that this vision was made possible in part thanks to sizable gifts by alumni Michael M. Koerner ('49) and Ronald A. Kurz ('54), another illustration of the key role of alumni in the support for entrepreneurship at MIT.

CONTINUED SUPPORT FROM ALUMNI, STUDENTS, AND INDIVIDUAL FACULTY AND STAFF MEMBERS

As MIT, or at least the Sloan School of Management, was awakening to the students' interest in entrepreneurship, alumni, students, and individual faculty and staff continued to drive local initiatives to support entrepreneurship during the rise of the internet era. The next piece of the entrepreneurial ecosystem was proposed in 1997 by MIT professor of engineering David Staelin ('60) and Alec Dingee ('52), each of whom were serial entrepreneurs.[22] The project became the Venture Mentoring Service (VMS), a free service offering mentorship of prospective MIT-affiliated entrepreneurs from the MIT community, including alumni, faculty, students, and staff. VMS was launched in 2000, thanks to generous donations of its founders, under the auspices of the MIT provost's office. Jerry Ackerman reported in a 2019 article that VMS was placed under the provost's office to make sure that its mentoring services would be accessible to all five schools of MIT. Dingee declared in 2001 to the *MIT Spectrum* magazine that his motivation for getting involved with the VMS was directly related to his experience as a young entrepreneur years earlier: "When I was young, I didn't have anyone to advise me and I was in over my head. With this service, entrepreneurs can bring an expert a list of questions and talk to them for a few hours to gain knowledge and contacts."[23] In 2003, Sherwin Greenblatt ('62) was named its director, a position that he still holds. Since 2000, VMS has grown to more than 170 volunteer mentors who have advised 2,800 entrepreneurs (see chapter 7).[24]

As was typical of those early initiatives to support entrepreneurship at MIT, VMS was started on a shoestring and greatly relied on the founders' energy and ability to navigate the Institute, as reflected in Ackerman's article: "At the outset, Dingee's office was sometimes his car, and he and the initial handful of other mentors frequently met with their mentees in coffee shops. Dingee spent much of his time recruiting mentees and visiting laboratories to tell students, faculty, and postdocs about the help VMS could give to commercialize their accomplishments."[25]

In 2018, Greenblatt told a publication of the MIT Alumni Association that when VMS had been founded eighteen years earlier, "entrepreneurship was kind of a quiet thing at MIT, and a lot of technical people were thinking of going to work for big companies." Greenblatt adds, "Now it's gone from being a backwater to a main driving force at the Institute."[26]

THINGMAGIC LLC

ThingMagic LLC was founded in 2000 by Bernd Schoner ('00), Rehmi Post ('04), Matt Reynolds ('99), and Yael Maguire ('04) in an effort to commercialize next-generation radio-frequency identification (RFID) sensors for the supply chain. Their venture project was based on groundbreaking research conducted at MIT's Auto-ID Center (now Auto-ID Lab) by the principal research scientist David Brock and professor of mechanical engineering Sanjay Sarma, who prompted the team to develop and commercialize more advanced RFID sensors for the supply chain.[27] It allowed companies to track products from their production site to their delivery, and one of the company's goals was to support the Internet of Things.

RFID readers gather information by reading tags that communicate information over radio waves. When ThingMagic was launched, existing RFID readers were not performing well enough to use in supply-chain management; they were too expensive and could read only one tag at a time. By using the research conducted, ThingMagic was able to build RFID readers for the supply-chain market that could read multiple tags simultaneously, across several frequencies, and from greater distances. ThingMagic also innovated by powering their RFID sensors by software instead of hardware, sparing the clients the need to rework their existing hardware. As a result, by the mid-2000s, ThingMagic became the world's first profitable vendor of RFIDs.

But their competitive technology and a growing market were no guarantee of smooth sailing for the company. At the dawn of the twenty-first century, when ThingMagic was founded, the thriving MIT entrepreneurial ecosystem—and all its various forms of support—did not yet exist to the extent that it does today. As a result, the company had no opportunity to receive the kind of expert advice and mentorship from which later MIT-related start-ups would benefit.

At first, the future of ThingMagic looked very promising. RFID technology experienced a period of hype in 2004, when retailers such as Walmart ordered their suppliers to apply RFID tags to all shipments. But the hype was both a blessing and a curse for ThingMagic. On one hand, the company had already established a name in a market that was expected to grow massively. On the other hand, the opportunity attracted a myriad of competitors. After one competitor was acquired for $200 million in 2005, the founders of ThingMagic raised $20 million in venture capital in an effort to grow the company. However, venture capital money came with its own set of challenges. ThingMagic's investors installed a more corporate style of management than the company was previously used to, hiring vice presidents in engineering, business development, sales, and manufacturing, as well as scores of middle managers. As one of those vice presidents told Schoner, who took pride in his culture of

(continued)

---

frugality, "We used to do things the cheap way. Now we are doing them the right way."[28]

Unfortunately, within two years, the boom in RFID was followed by a bust, and ThingMagic's first major deals with retailers, including Walmart, sputtered. The venture capital that had been raised was being depleted. As a result, ThingMagic had to downsize, including firing the vice presidents. The following three years were difficult, as the firm found itself in a fundraising spiral, forced to raise additional money several times, at increasingly lower valuations. In an attempt to right the ship, ThingMagic returned to its frugal way of operation and was also able to reinvent itself by designing card-level tag ultra-high-frequency-reader modules that were the size of a credit card, which companies could embed in their products to enable RFID capabilities.

The company faced new challenges when the financial crisis of 2008 hit. As is always the case in times of financial uncertainty, venture capitalists and the other risk investors that typically fund start-ups become more risk averse. Banks also started to foreclose on venture capital–funded start-ups that could not repay their loans. Fortunately, ThingMagic had drastically streamlined its business by that point, and that may have been what saved it. In the fall of 2010, ten years after the launch of the company, it was sold to Trimble Navigation, a billion-dollar public technology firm based in California. At the time of its acquisition, ThingMagic's customers included Ford, Wegmans, and New Balance, all of which used the company's technology to track inventory. In addition, hospitals have used the systems to keep track of patients and surgery tools.

In 2002, another key component of the MIT entrepreneurial ecosystem was added with the launch of the Deshpande Center for Technological Innovation, which was named after Jaishree and Gururaj "Desh" Deshpande, who established the center with a generous gift. The idea for this innovative center emerged from conversations between Deshpande, the founder and chairman of Sycamore Networks and formerly of Cascade Communications; Alex d'Arbeloff ('49), chairman of the board of MIT; and Professor Tom Magnanti, the dean of the School of Engineering. These conversations were based on Deshpande and d'Arbeloff's wish to contribute to the enhancement of entrepreneurship at MIT.[29]

Despite the fact that numerous faculty members, alumni, and students of the School of Engineering had already founded or joined MIT-related start-ups, the launch of the Deshpande Center was the first institutional initiative from the School of Engineering to support entrepreneurship.

In contrast to the Entrepreneurship Center, which focused on entrepreneurship education and building a cadre of future entrepreneurs, the Deshpande Center focused on commercialization of technologies originating from MIT laboratories by bridging the gap between government funding for basic science and the availability of private-sector funding for commercialization. The Deshpande Center does this by supporting development research and by connecting faculty and researchers to entrepreneurs, venture capitalists, and innovative businesses (see chapter 8).

The Deshpande Center's founding academic director was professor of chemical engineering Charles Cooney ('67), who took the challenge of translating the Deshpande's vision into an actionable plan. Cooney had been part of a group of MIT faculty members including Harvey Lodish, ChoKyun Rha ('62), William Roush, Anthony Sinskey ('66), Graham Walker, and George Whitesides that was involved in the founding of the pioneering biotechnology company Genzyme in 1981 (see chapter 9).[30] In addition, he had been consultant, board member, and scientific advisor for various biotechnology firms, including Genentech. The center's first executive director, Krisztina Holly ('89), was part of the grand-prize winning student team of the 1991 $10K Business Plan Competition, along with John Barrus ('87) and Mike Cassidy ('87). The three of them subsequently founded Stylus Innovation, a company sold to Artisoft for $13 million in 1996. Cooney stresses the critical role Magnanti and d'Arbeloff played in giving entrepreneurship more legitimacy in the School of Engineering. He also credits Subra Suresh ('81), Magnanti's successor as dean of the School of Engineering.[31] Although the Deshpande Center was initially a School of Engineering initiative, Cooney quickly realized the need to apply the model across MIT and started funding projects across the Institute. Over time, the Entrepreneurship Center and the Deshpande Center would have many points of intersection.

The genesis of the Deshpande Center and the VMS occurred closer to the centers of power at the university, in contrast to earlier initiatives promoting entrepreneurship that grew more at the periphery. However, both initiatives again resulted from the combination of pioneering individuals and the flexibility of the Institute to allow for the experimentation of novel ideas.

Other alumni encouraged entrepreneurship during this period by establishing prizes. In 2001, Patrick J. McGovern, Jr. ('59), an accomplished entrepreneur, established the McGovern Entrepreneurship Award, to be presented annually to a student or students for having an impact on entrepreneurship education and support across the Institute. The Adolf F. Monosson Prize for

Entrepreneurship Mentoring was established in 2005 in memory of Adolf F. Monosson ('48) by his friends, fellow alumni, and business associates and made possible by Mr. and Mrs. William S. Gringer ('56).[32]

Meanwhile, students continued to be active in the entrepreneurial realm.

In 1995, the year corresponding to the IPO of Netscape, Monica Lee ('97), a Sloan School of Management student, launched Venture MBAs, another student club for those interested in venture capital, which would later become the MIT Venture Capital and Private Equity Club (VCPE).[33]

The student-run $10K Business Plan Competition grew into the MIT $50K Entrepreneurship Competition. A memorial gift by the family of Robert Goldberg ('65) enabled the prize money to be increased to $50,000 in 1996.[34] By 1998, eighty-three teams competed (up from fifty-four or sixty-four in 1990, depending on the sources) representing 307 students.[35] It attracted increasingly prominent judges. For instance, in 1998, the judges included Jean Notis-McConarty, a partner at Coopers and Lybrand; John William "Bill" Poduska ('59), founder of Prime Computer and Apollo Computer; and Kapor, the founder of Lotus and cofounder of Electronic Frontier Foundation. The contest's impact was increasingly important. From 1990 to 1997, the contest claimed that it had contributed to over 130 companies, with a market capitalization of $180 million according to a 1998 $50K brochure.[36]

In 1997, as the MIT $50K Entrepreneurship Competition was gaining increasing attention nationally and internationally, the student organizers were receiving a growing number of inquiries from groups interested in organizing similar competitions in their regions. The student leaders of the $50K Entrepreneurship Competition reacted to these queries by hosting the first MIT Global Startup Workshop (GSW).[37] It was held for the first time in Cambridge in 1998, with Sally Shepard ('98) as lead organizer, to share best practices on how to operate similar business plan competitions across the world (see chapter 9). It was probably the first example of a student-led entrepreneurial initiative growing beyond the campus.

In 1999, Sloan students launched the MIT Sloan Entrepreneurs Club, an entrepreneurship portal for the entire MIT community.[38] The MIT Sloan Entrepreneurship and Innovation Club, as it is known today, has evolved over the years into primarily a networking entity for Sloan students, providing access to entrepreneurs and dynamic companies with the goal of facilitating access to internship and career opportunities.

MOMENTA PHARMACEUTICALS

In 1999, MIT professor Ram Sasisekharan was a member of MIT's Koch Institute for Integrative Cancer Research, where he oversaw his eponymously named lab. At that time, he and his team, including Ganesh V. Kaundinya ('89), started to sequence complex sugars (polysaccharides), just as predecessors had done with deoxyribonucleic acid (DNA) and proteins. This was a huge undertaking that was only possible using computational tools, but it was very important in providing a better understanding of the role of polysaccharides in viral infections and tissue development. Perhaps even more valuable was the processing speed, thanks to the proprietary analytics developed in the Sasisekharan Lab. It allowed researchers to understand in record time the complex molecules that make up drugs and had potential commercial applications.

The MIT ecosystem was a very important factor in Sasisekharan's decision to form a company. "We had interactions with people with business backgrounds, clinical backgrounds, which gave us very different perspectives on commercial applications for the first time," says Sasisekharan.[39] It was also important that by the dawn of the twenty-first century, the biomedical ecosystem surrounding MIT had evolved into a more sophisticated entity, with experienced stakeholders collaborating and complementing each other. As a result, Sasisekharan took the leap, and in 2001 he cofounded Momenta (then Mimeon) with Kaundinya. The company was funded by the local investor Polaris Venture Partners, hired experienced executives, and tapped into Boston's world-famous medical institutions to form a first-class scientific advisory board.

In 2006, Craig Wheeler, the former president of Chiron Biopharmaceuticals, was brought in as CEO. Momenta collaborated with medical products manufacturer Baxter International to develop generic versions of protein-based biotech drugs that were approved by the US Food and Drug Administration (FDA). That strategy allowed Momenta to gain a competitive advantage by obtaining FDA approval faster for its substitutable drugs. Collaborations with Baxter and Novartis AG allowed Momenta to share the cost and risk of introducing new generic drugs to the market. Wheeler expected that the revenue of its generic product portfolio would enable the company to eventually produce new branded-drug compounds. That year, Momenta achieved revenues of $283 million and profits of $180 million.

In addition to its widely used generic blood-thinner Lovenox, Momenta has developed several drugs, such as a generic version of Copaxone, which is used to fight multiple sclerosis. However, the road to success can be bumpy for entrepreneurial firms, especially in the medical drug development sector, where a company's fate hangs on the success or failure of clinical trials.

(continued)

In 2016, Momenta suffered a major setback when an experimental drug for pancreatic cancer, its lead novel drug candidate, did not work well enough, and had to end its clinical trial. In 2018, Momenta cut its workforce in half and reoriented its strategy to focus on the development of two late-stage bio-similar drugs, and to use its potential revenue to fund clinical trials for new drugs for immune-mediated diseases.

In 2014, Sasisekharan reflected on Momenta's journey, observing, "We're experiencing a unique window for biotech companies to go public. That's thanks, in part, to the venture capital community and MIT. It's a melting pot of people, ideas, [and] opportunities," he says. "And fundamentally it's the mindset: solving problems and focusing on things that have some inherent value to make a difference in the world."[40]

In his thesis, Joost Bonsen ('90) reports that in 2003, students from engineering and the Sloan school—inspired by the success of the practice-oriented courses MIT Entrepreneurship Lab (E-Lab) and Global Entrepreneurship Lab (G-Lab)—proposed exploring another area of entrepreneurial promise: the commercialization of scientific research conducted in MIT's labs. They first approached Professor Edward Roberts with this idea, and then Professor Charles Cooney and Krisztina Holly, faculty director and executive director of the Deshpande Center, respectively. This student initiative materialized into an experimental special studies course called Innovation Teams (I-Teams), which would become one of the earliest examples of an Institute-wide elective course. In 2004, I-Teams evolved into a formal, real-world-focused course offered by the engineering school and Sloan, through a collaboration between the Deshpande Center and the Entrepreneurship Center. It was originally taught by Cooney and Roberts and lecturer Ken Zolot ('95). It was one of the first examples of such collaboration across campus. I-Teams did not aim to prepare students to create a business plan or to launch a start-up; rather, it focused on an earlier stage, when it is not yet clear if there actually was a market opportunity for a product or service (see chapter 7 for more information).[41]

The history of I-Teams is another example of the most prevalent life cycle for entrepreneurial endeavors at MIT—an informal project at the request or initiative of students, faculty, staff, or alumni, which then grows into something institutionally recognized and supported. In addition, such projects often build on existing ones, such as in the case of E-Lab, G-Lab, or I-Teams, and regularly develop across traditional boundaries within MIT.

VentureShips, yet another student club, emerged in 2004 from a collaboration between the MIT Science and Engineering Business Club and the MIT VMS (as previously discussed). Its objective was to provide first-hand experience to students by offering a semester-long internship in an MIT-affiliated, early-stage start-up. Through the internships, students worked on real-life business issues, such as market analysis, financial forecast, regulatory approval, business development, and marketing. The start-ups selected for the VentureShips program include MIT $50K winners and finalists.[42]

THE EMERGENCE OF SOCIAL ENTREPRENEURSHIP

After the boost that it got from the internet, entrepreneurship became a powerful mode of innovation. Perhaps an unexpected consequence was that it also attracted the attention of groups with interest in social issues, groups that traditionally would have turned to philanthropy to meet their goals. The concept of social entrepreneurship was born. Social entrepreneurship tries to solve social problems with market-based solutions and pursues both financial sustainability and the fulfillment of social objectives. At MIT in the early 2000s, it materialized primarily into projects focused on solving problems encountered in developing countries (also known as *developmental entrepreneurship*).

The earliest of these was the student-founded Global Startup Lab (GSL), initially called the Africa Internet Initiative. In 2000, three MIT undergraduates from Kenya, Paul Njoroge ('00), Martin Mbaya ('00), and Solomon Assefa ('01), with the help of Saria Hassan ('01) from Sudan, launched an organization aimed at giving students in developing countries the programming skills they needed to create e-commerce applications based on the premise that information and communication technologies can aid development. Their motivation was to combat the disparity between the knowledge of information technology (IT) in the developing world and in the US. The first program was a six-week course on Java and Linux for forty-five undergraduate students in Kenya.[43] It was a great success, and the founders of GSL repeated the experience during the following years.

Another early example of social entrepreneurship was the IDEAS Competition (now called the IDEAS Social Innovation Challenge). Launched in 2001, the IDEAS Competition grew out of the efforts of Sally Susnowitz, then-director of the Public Service Center (PSC), and Amy Smith ('84), an instructor at MIT's Edgerton Center, who were investigating what public service should be at MIT.[44] The success of the $50K Entrepreneurship Competition made Smith and Susnowitz wonder if they could harness the energy of entrepreneurship to inspire innovative solutions to issues of development. The aim of the competition was to "inspire public-service-oriented innovation and entrepreneurship with awards of up to $10,000 per team for the best ideas tackling barriers to well-being."[45] Soon, winning teams of the IDEAS Competition increasingly went on to present their projects to the $50K Entrepreneurship Competition, which triggered the organizers of the contest to try to double the prize money and to create a special track for developmental ventures with social impact, which they succeeded in doing in 2006.[46]

Another relevant development involved Smith as well. In 2002, she launched a modest project called the Haiti Class out of the Edgerton Center. She took students on a field trip to Haiti to study practical solutions to local problems of development. As a result of the enthusiasm and interest of the students, the Haiti Class turned into the D-Lab.[47] The "D" in D-Lab initially stood for "Development," "Design," "Dialogue," and "Duct Tape" to stress the can-do mentality and practical orientation at the heart of the lab's philosophy.[48] The D-Lab has expanded significantly since the early days of the Haiti Class to include more than courses, but also research in collaboration with global partners, technology development, and community initiatives (see chapter 9).

Another initiative related to developmental entrepreneurship was also launched in the early 2000s. Professor Alex (Sandy) Pentland ('82) founded and led the Media Lab Asia, which connected with regions in the emerging world to use technology and design to solve acute humanitarian problems.[49] His experience with Media Lab Asia triggered his idea of creating an exploratory seminar back at MIT called Developmental Entrepreneurship Venture, which would give young people from around the world the opportunity to focus their efforts to development rather than to Wall Street. The seminar challenged its students to target the needs of 1 billion people in developing countries and to find solutions based on entrepreneurship.

Pentland indeed believed that philanthropy was not suited for such an ambitious project and that the answer required leveraging the energy of entrepreneurship. The original seminar became a course and was followed by other project-based courses, such as Development Ventures, under the leadership of Pentland and with the help of the teaching assistant (TA) and later lecturer Joost Bonsen ('90) (see chapter 6 for more information about Bonsen).[50]

THE EMERGENCE OF COLLABORATIONS AND SYNERGIES AMONG INITIATIVES SUPPORTING ENTREPRENEURSHIP

Each initiative and entity supporting entrepreneurship had its own merits, but, as an ecosystem was slowly building up on campus during those years, its strength increasingly coming from linkages and synergies that progressively developed among those entities, even if, as is inevitable, there were sometimes rivalries. As mentioned previously, some initiatives, such as the IDEAS Competition, I-Teams, or VentureShips, also built upon one another.

At this point of the nascent entrepreneurial ecosystem on campus in the mid-2000s, a dozen initiatives existed that supported entrepreneurship in the form of student clubs, alumni mentoring, contests, conferences, a technology transfer facilitator, an entrepreneurship center, and a technology licensing office, as well as twenty classes. It had mostly grown organically in a bottom-up process based on local initiatives of individual faculty and staff members, students, and alumni, with no coordination from any central authority. From the outside, it looked somewhat unstructured, even chaotic. It was difficult even for insiders to know everything that was happening on campus with regard to entrepreneurship. Keeping track of all this activity was made even more difficult because the system was in flux: initiatives came and went, merged, folded, and changed focus depending on the lessons learned and the needs of the community. The growing ecosystem was strong because there was no central authority, which allowed flexibility. Also, only the initiatives that fulfilled a need survived. The strength of the ecosystem also came from the complementarity of a number of initiatives and their collaborations. Perhaps most important, it was strong because it built on MIT's ingrained culture of problem-solving, experimenting, and making an impact. It also grew out of another part of the MIT culture: its slightly unreverential attitude reflected by the slogan, "Ask for forgiveness, not permission!" which translated into the launching of an initiative when there was a perception that the existing infrastructure did not fulfill a need. All these aspects of the entrepreneurial ecosystem made the whole greater than the sum of the individual initiatives.

Joe Hadzima ('73) elegantly characterized the state of the entrepreneurial ecosystem on campus in the mid-2000s when he wrote in a 2005 article: "MIT has developed and continues to evolve an entrepreneurial ecosystem. It starts with our founding motto: *Mens et Manus*—mind and hand. It is about solving problems and making a difference. It is a system in which experimentation occurs in the lab and in the world. There is no master plan to this entrepreneurial ecosystem; it evolves from perceived need."[51] Bob Metcalfe ('68), the inventor of the Ethernet and cofounder of 3Com, made a similar observation: "It's not just that MIT's entrepreneurial environment flourishes under its institutional commitment to technology transfer . . . What keeps MIT's entrepreneurial ecosystem accelerating is that nobody is in charge. There are at least 20 different groups at MIT competing to be THE group on entrepreneurship. All of them are winning."[52]

4 FROM INCIDENTAL TO PURPOSEFUL: MID-2000S TO LATE-2010S

GROWING STUDENT INTEREST IN ENTREPRENEURSHIP

The interest shown by MIT students in entrepreneurship, which grew during the internet era (as discussed in chapter 3), not only continued but grew significantly during the mid-2000s to late 2010s, especially after the financial crisis of 2008–2009. In a letter to the community, professor of materials science and engineering and dean of graduate education Christine Ortiz wrote in 2012:

> Student interest in entrepreneurship has exploded on the MIT campus, in particular over the last decade. The results of these activities are astounding; the $100K Entrepreneurship competition has helped launch more than a dozen companies currently valued at more than $100 million, with at least two worth more than $1 billion. Aside from the societal benefits of technology transfer, entrepreneurship activities have deep educational, professional, and personal development benefits to students and should continue to be fostered and supported by MIT. Students often seek guidance for engaging in entrepreneurial activities from faculty, department heads and internal organizations, such as the Technology Licensing Office (TLO) and the Venture Mentoring Office (VMS), and all have indicated they could benefit from a knowledge of and clarification of policies and procedures, guidelines, roles and responsibilities, and best practices.[1]

As a result, she convened a Committee on Student Entrepreneurship, composed of various interested stakeholders, to examine those topics and better meet the students' expectations with regard to entrepreneurship.

Student passion and the resulting activities were growing so fast that the Institute was initially unable to provide the necessary administrative, faculty, and/or facility support to meet student demand. In a report they wrote in 2014, professors Fiona Murray of the Sloan School of Management and Vladimir Bulović of the School of Engineering indicated that MIT offered more than fifty courses related to innovation and entrepreneurship that enrolled 3,000 students, and that extracurricular activities, such as the $100K Entrepreneurship Competition, involved thousands more. However, these programs were so popular that the Institute could not meet the demand due to a shortage of faculty and staff resources, as well as space. They reported that more than 1,000 students forming 250 teams applied to the $100K Entrepreneurship Competition. One student machine shop had a six-month, 200-student wait list. The Martin Trust Center for MIT Entrepreneurship saw a fourfold increase in student demand. Seventy-nine teams comprised of more than 225 students from across MIT participated in the 2014 summer Global Founders' Skills Accelerator Program (renamed delta v). In 2015, the IDEAS Global Challenge (later renamed IDEAS Social Innovation Challenge) received fifty-nine submissions from 200 team members. Around 300 students engaged with D-Lab in over twenty countries in the developing world.[2]

This growing interest of students also showed in the extracurricular activities that they launched. They created more initiatives on their own supporting entrepreneurship than in any other previous period, confirming their key historical role in the growth of the entrepreneurial ecosystem on campus. Increasingly, such initiatives catered to specialized entrepreneurship interests in either social entrepreneurship, specific industries, geographical zones, or social groups (see appendix 4.1, "Student-Led Initiatives Supporting Entrepreneurship 2006–2019," at the end of this chapter).

Why this explosion in interest in entrepreneurship on the part of MIT students? One factor seems to be changes in the labor market for MIT graduates caused by the consequences of the financial crisis of 2008–2009.[3] Indeed, following the crisis, the traditional employers of MIT graduates in manufacturing, finance, and consulting hired much less. As a result, the risk and opportunity cost for graduates of joining or launching a start-up decreased significantly.[4] According to Professor Murray, what was first a cyclical phenomenon in the labor market due to the financial crisis turned into a trend.[5] Students increasingly considered entrepreneurship as a credible career path, whereas before this point, most of them confined it to the realm of extracurricular activity.[6] Applications to MIT from undergraduate and master's of business administration (MBA) students indicated strong interest for entrepreneurial careers.[7] In 2014, 20 percent of incoming undergraduate students expected to launch a start-up or a nonprofit during their studies.[8] In 2015, professors Edward Roberts and Murray, along with Daniel Kim, wrote that "the proportion of MIT undergraduates selecting employment in venture capital–backed start-ups upon graduation increased from less than 2 percent in 2006 to 15 percent in 2014."[9] They also referred to a 2014 MIT Graduating Student Survey suggesting that approximately 20 percent of graduating seniors joined early-stage companies.[10] While the median age of first-time MIT alumni company founders was thirty-five years old in 1980, it was only twenty-seven in the 2010s.[11]

The second factor explaining students' attraction to entrepreneurship was the innovations in the technology sectors that had multiplied since the mid-2000s. More opportunities appeared among younger disrupting firms that were commercializing applications based on new technologies. This included such innovations as mobile phones (Apple launched the iPhone in 2007); the Internet of Things; cloud computing; autonomous vehicles; the genome revolution in biotech; the convergence of biotech and information technology (IT); engineering at the nanoscale; clean energy; and the explosion of data and information in general. Innovations in technology sectors also spilled into established industries using technology, which increasingly began to look and feel like IT businesses.[12] Meanwhile, new competitors increasingly used digital technologies to displace incumbents in one industry after another. Facebook was opened to anyone in 2006 after operating exclusively on college campuses, and Twitter was spun off from its parent company in that same year. Google bought YouTube in 2007, creating enormous competition in the media and advertising industries. Airbnb (with roots in Professor Steven Eppinger's ('83) Product Design and Development class) was launched in 2007 in an apartment, and by the mid-2010s, it was the largest hotel operator in the world, all without owning any rooms or buildings. Uber was founded in 2009 to revolutionize the taxi industry and other forms of delivery. Amazon began its ascension to dominate the retail sector and to become a major actor in cloud computing.[13] As a result, the center of gravity of the economy increasingly moved from the traditional employers to new corporate leaders, such as Amazon, Apple, Google, and Biogen, as well as to a growing number of challengers to these new giants.

Another incentive was that the cost of launching a venture decreased significantly. As argued by the *Economist,* by the 2010s the basic building blocks for digital products had become cheap, ubiquitous, and so sophisticated that they could be easily combined, whether they were open-source code, services that offered developers on demand, or application programming interfaces (APIs) that served as digital plugs that allowed one service to use another, such as PayPal. Platforms such as Amazon Web Services could host the services of start-ups, the Apple Store could distribute their products, and marketing would happen on Twitter or Facebook. The know-how to grow a start-up was being widely disseminated, as illustrated by the popularity of the Lean Startup movement, a methodology to shorten product development cycles. The standardization of term sheets, the basic agreements between entrepreneurs and investors, also helped simplify and accelerate the formation of new firms.[14]

THE INSTITUTIONAL RESPONSE TO MIT STUDENTS' GROWING INTEREST IN ENTREPRENEURSHIP

As it is often the case, support at the level of MIT's departments, centers, and labs, as well as the Sloan School of Management, was among the most responsive to students' growing interest in entrepreneurship, and they were the earliest to experiment with activities supporting it, generally at the initiative of individual faculty or staff members. In 2006, the Media Lab launched a new program in developmental entrepreneurship, the first entrepreneurship program outside the Sloan school but in close collaboration with it, which built on exploratory seminars and courses initiated by Professor Sandy Pentland ('84). The same year, the Media Lab hired Frank Moss ('72), a serial entrepreneur, as its new director. He would be succeeded by Joi Ito, another serial entrepreneur, in 2011. In 2012, the Developmental Entrepreneurship program evolved into the Media Lab Entrepreneurship program, with a wider scope.[15] Another notable example of building on the growing interest of students in social entrepreneurship is the D-Lab Scale-up Program, which was launched in 2011 to increase the impact of its projects in the developing world.[16] The Entrepreneurship Center considerably expanded its portfolio of activities under the leadership of its managing director, Bill Aulet ('94), who succeeded Ken Morse ('68) in that position in 2009.

SANERGY

Lindsay Stradley ('11) Ani Vallabhaneni ('11), and David Auerbach ('11) chose
to tackle a huge problem with Sanergy,[17] their social entrepreneurship venture. The United Nations and the World Health Organization report that poor
sanitation creates a global loss of $260 billion annually and more than 2 mil-
lion preventable deaths each year, the majority of which are children.[18]

While they were still students, Sanergy's founders imagined a solution to
this huge problem: constructing toilets, franchising their management, collecting the waste, and turning it into fertilizer. They went on to create a business model that they tested in Kenya. The Sanergy team refined their idea
during their time at MIT thanks to grants from D-Lab and the Legatum Center
for Development and Entrepreneurship. In 2011, it became the first social
entrepreneurship project to win the grand prize at the MIT $100K Entrepre-
neurship Competition.

After graduating, Stradley, Vallabhaneni, and Auerbach settled in Nairobi's
slums in Kenya. Sanergy structured its operations into two independent entities, a for-profit one and a not-for-profit one, so the firm could receive both
investments and donations. The for-profit side collected waste and sold fertilizer and insect-based animal feed to farmers, while the nonprofit side raised
money from philanthropies while building the sanitation infrastructure and
providing support to franchise operators of toilets. The Sanergy founders had
to adjust their business model several times to reach scale. In 2013–2014, it
started a new line of business that offered synergies and turned out to be very
profitable: cultivating black soldier fly larvae to make insect-animal feed. Sanergy could use its solid waste to raise the larvae, which it then sold as animal
feed to farmers. In 2016, after five years of operations, they realized that they
were limiting their growth by charging their franchisees upfront for the toilets instead of over time. Thus, they decided to move toward a sort of pay-per-
service model, offering the toilets at no charge and increasing the price of waste
removal instead. As a result of this change, the rate of toilet installation tripled.

By 2020, Sanergy planned to have 4,900 toilets (compared to 750 in late
2016) operating in the slum of Mukuru in Nairobi, serving 200,000 people,
which represents 36 percent of the population.[19]

The Sloan School of Management was the first school that responded to
students' growing interest in entrepreneurship. It did this by strengthening
its class offerings in entrepreneurship, which reached twenty-five courses
in 2005–2006.[20] In 2006, Sloan announced the launch of the Entrepreneurship and Innovation Track (E&I) within its MBA program. With the
E&I track, Sloan started to incorporate entrepreneurship in its curriculum

beyond isolated classes and support for extracurricular activities. The track focused on teaching students how to launch and develop emerging technology ventures and led to a certificate in Entrepreneurship and Innovation in addition to the MBA degree. The strong interest of students was confirmed when one-third of the MBA cohort applied to the new track the first year it was offered.[21]

In contrast, the School of Engineering's involvement with entrepreneurship education was much slower, although its members and alumni probably formed the largest group of entrepreneurs at MIT. Companies such as 3Com, RSA, Akamai, iRobot, Meraki, ITA Software, and Rethink Robotics originated in the school. The school had also been a pioneer in promoting entrepreneurship by bringing science from the lab to the marketplace with the founding of the Deshpande Center for Technological Innovation. However, it started its offering of entrepreneurship courses slowly, first in 2004 with I-Teams (jointly with the Sloan School of Management), and then in 2009 with an introductory class titled The Founder's Journey, taught by senior lecturer Ken Zolot ('95), and a companion course, Entrepreneurship Projects.[22]

MIT's administration's previously established hands-off approach to entrepreneurship started to change in the early 2010s. First, in 2011, MIT president Susan Hockfield initiated seminar sessions titled From Ideas to Impact: Lessons for Commercialization, which were open to all faculty members, and created a Faculty Committee on Innovation and Entrepreneurship to better coordinate existing educational opportunities in innovation and entrepreneurship.[23]

Then, in 2013, President L. Rafael Reif announced the launch of the Institute's Innovation Initiative, which arguably marked the official embrace of entrepreneurship by MIT's leadership, especially in terms of entrepreneurship education. As one insider pointed out, the Innovation Initiative formalized what had been brewing for some time at the Institute in relation to entrepreneurship and innovation. The initiative extended MIT's mission beyond its primary roles of education and research to entrepreneurship and innovation as well.[24] In practice, the Innovation Initiative mostly gave an institutionalized recognition to what was already in place, in the form of dozens of local formal programs and extracurricular activities dealing with entrepreneurship. However, elevating it organizationally to the Office of the President and making it a central part of MIT's narrative gave a new legitimacy to entrepreneurship on campus, which was a key turning point. The appointment of two associate deans for innovation, one from the School of Engineering and one from the Sloan School of Management, contributed to this legitimization. At the curriculum level, the Innovation Initiative helped to realize the recommendation of the Faculty Committee on Innovation and Entrepreneurship, which had created an undergraduate minor in entrepreneurship and innovation, jointly offered by the School of Engineering and the Sloan School of Management. With this minor, entrepreneurship confirmed its acceptance into MIT's official curriculum at the Institute level, in great contrast with the previous periods.[25]

In coordination with the Innovation Initiative, the School of Engineering launched several efforts related to entrepreneurship education, particularly as extracurricular activities. In 2014, the Department of Electrical Engineering and Computer Science launched Start6, a two-and-a-half-week extracurricular crash course introducing students of the School of Engineering to entrepreneurship, which was held during the Independent Activities Period (IAP). Start6, under the leadership of Professor (and department head) Anantha Chandrakasan, offered practical sessions on relevant topics ranging from bootstrapping to venture capital. Fifty students were selected to participate in the first year of the course. In 2015, a trip to Silicon Valley was added to Start6 during spring break to expose the students to the Valley's entrepreneurial culture. In 2016, Start6 was renamed StartMIT, and it became open to students from all five schools of MIT. At that point, it was run by the Trust Center and organized under the coleadership of Chandrakasan (who had become dean of the engineering school) and Dean David Schmittlein of the Sloan School, reflecting a symbolic effort by the two sides of the Institute to promote entrepreneurship. Entrepreneurship was no longer a local initiative promoted by an individual faculty or staff, but an activity sanctioned jointly by the deans of the business school and the largest engineering department.

In early 2016, Dean Ian Waitz of the School of Engineering announced a more ambitious project: the launch of the Sandbox Innovation Fund program led by the School of Engineering in close partnership with the MIT Innovation Initiative.[26] The explicit goal of the Sandbox was to help students to develop the knowledge, skills, and attitudes needed to be more effective when they graduate and enter the business world.[27] As such, it met the students' demand for better preparation for a job market in which entrepreneurship and an entrepreneurial mindset had become increasingly important. The Sandbox was controversial in that it broke with the MIT tradition of not directly funding the entrepreneurial projects of members of the community, especially students.[28]

With the adoption of support for entrepreneurship at higher levels, other institutional initiatives appeared. The Center for the Arts at MIT hopped onto the entrepreneurship bandwagon in 2013 with the launch of the $15K Creative Arts Competition, a business plan competition modeled after the famous $100K Entrepreneurship Competition but reserved for projects dealing with the arts and creative industries.[29] The same year, the Media Lab launched a seed fund called the E14 Fund, to support the entrepreneurial projects of its students. Like the Sandbox, it also broke the Institute's long-standing policy of not funding the start-up projects of MIT community members.[30] And like the Sandbox, the break from tradition was all the more notable because E14's funding was provided by venture capitalists and other outside investors. In 2014, STEX was created in order to connect established companies that are members of the Industrial Liaison Program (ILP) with MIT-related start-ups. In 2016, the School of Architecture and Planning started MITdesignX, an entrepreneurship program specific to the school, aiming at educating its students about how to create entrepreneurial solutions to the challenges faced by cities and the built environment.[31] (For more information, see appendix 4.2, "Estimate of the Institutional Response to Growing Interest in Entrepreneurship.") In 2019, MET Fund, an independent legal entity unaffiliated with MIT, but with the support of the School of Architecture and Planning, was launched to provide support to ventures that complete the MITdesignX program.[32]

MIT leadership's embrace of entrepreneurship was further confirmed in 2016 with the launch of The Engine as a reaction to the perceived broken process of bringing scientific inventions to the marketplace.[33] Corporations had closed their research and development (R&D) labs for the most part, and venture capital had too short a time horizon for science-based ventures to develop. Faced with this perceived market failure, MIT's leadership pointed to the need for patient capital to bring ventures that are trying to commercialize tough science and need more time than do digital businesses to reach a stage where they are ready for venture capital. In October 2016, President Reif announced the creation of The Engine, a for-profit but public benefit corporation, separate from MIT, that would act as an accelerator for start-ups trying to commercialize "tough techs" by providing advice and physical facilities, as well as an investment fund of patient capital.[34] In addition to going against MIT's policy of not funding entrepreneurial projects, The Engine also broke with Institute tradition by incubating the entrepreneurial projects of its members, which certainly raised substantial objections within the MIT community. MIT's policy up until then was motivated by avoiding conflicts of interest and the belief that MIT's regional entrepreneurial ecosystem was well equipped to select and support its best spin-off ventures at arms' length.[35] What distinguishes The Engine from entities like the Sandbox and the E14 Fund, however, is that it is a separate legal entity with its own staff and is located outside of campus. The Engine has been diligent in putting in place a process for governance to avoid conflicts of interest and introduce an arm's-length relationship with MIT.[36]

SMARTCELLS

During the 2000s, while pursuing his PhD in chemical engineering as a member of the MIT's Nanostructured Materials Research Laboratory, Todd Zion ('04) chemically modified insulin for diabetics and noticed that the modified insulin automatically adjusted to changing levels of blood glucose, requiring only one injection per day. The technology used a biodegradable polymer to produce stimuli-responsive nanoparticles for controlled drug delivery. After three years of painstaking trials, Zion had invented the first glucose-regulated insulin for treating diabetes. It was a major improvement to help diabetics keep their blood sugar level constant. He called his invention SmartInsulin. It solved the most complex challenge of diabetes therapy: achieving tight blood glucose control without hypoglycemia to reduce the serious complications of the illness.

The MIT entrepreneurial support system, although still modest in the early 2000s, played a key role in the formation of a company called Smart-Cells. In 2003, Zion and four other students[37] participated in the $50K Entrepreneurship Competition and won the Robert P. Goldberg Grand Prize. "It really clicked that building a business could be the right way to bridge the gap between interesting technology and commercially viable products," Zion says.[38] He licensed the technology from MIT and, with the $30,000 prize money from the competition, founded SmartCells to commercialize the SmartInsulin drug. From there, Zion recruited his SmartCells cofounders: his fellow PhD student Tom Lancaster ('04), Professor Jackie Ying, his former advisor, and experienced entrepreneur James Herriman, whom he met through the

(continued)

MIT Venture Mentoring Service (VMS). The creation of SmartCells was followed by seven years of development that proved that its product was nontoxic, nonimmunogenic, and nonantigenic.

Boston's local entrepreneurial ecosystem also played a supportive role. From the outset, the founders opted to build their firm in the most cost-effective way possible. SmartCells only had a small in-house lab, but it leveraged a network of collaborators at Boston's Massachusetts General Hospital (MGH), the National Institutes of Health (NIH), and other medical institutions. SmartCells was also efficient with capital. It relied mostly on 150 local angel investors across a number of groups that invested $9.8 million in the company between 2004 and 2010. Besides the modest angel investment, the firm funded itself more with nondilutive money via grants. At its peak in 2010, the company had only seventeen employees. Once the company was about to reach the stage of human clinical studies, Zion believed that it was the right time to transition to an established pharmaceutical company with the resources to conduct the trials and bring the drug to market. This goal materialized in 2010 when Merck bought the company and conducted further development to bring the drug to market. The success of SmartCells relaunched the interest of business angels for biomedical ventures and, in so doing stimulated the local ecosystem. SmartInsulin illustrates the long development time and patient capital required to commercialize science-based technologies ("tough tech," as President Reif would label them).[39]

Zion said in 2014 that he was looking forward to seeing SmartInsulin available to the public, "not only because the hope it offers diabetics, but also because it proves the basic research model works."[40]

Why did MIT's administration change from a hands-off approach to a new interest in entrepreneurship and a proactive policy toward firm formation? The answer can be traced to a number of forces converging in the same direction in the decade prior to 2016.

It seems that the growing interest and activities of the students in the area of entrepreneurship sent signals to MIT's schools, and then to its hierarchy, which felt compelled to replace their traditional hands-off approach to entrepreneurship with a more proactive policy. Evidence of the pressure resulting from the students' interest can be seen in numerous statements from leaders of the Institute. Referring to the Start6 introductory course of entrepreneurship, Professor Chandrakasan declared to the *Boston Globe*, "You will see more of these types of programs because students want it."[41] In 2014, Professor Vladimir Bulović also commented on the pressure from the students to the *MIT Spectrum* magazine: "The Innovation Initiative is driven by our students' demanding from us a change—change in the way we educate them to be more effective."[42] And to the *Boston Herald*, he declared, "We're bursting at the seams. There is a tremendous drive by students for more and more entrepreneurial activity."[43] In the 2016 report that laid out the plan for the Innovation Initiative, Fiona Murray and Bulović stated that one factor shaping it was a new generation of students: "They come here [to MIT] to learn the basic principles of science and engineering and build capabilities in innovation so they can go on to provide solutions that scale rapidly and achieve broad impact, whether through making and commercializing new discoveries, developing innovative businesses within global corporations, or launching new ventures."[44] Similarly, Dean Waitz recognized that MIT was institutionalizing what students had already initiated through their extracurricular activities when he stated that "the ability to identify a need, create and communicate an innovative solution, and build a team that produces a positive impact are things we ought to better prepare our students to do, especially as the data indicate they are doing it already."[45]

Meeting the aspirations of students was also motivated by a more prosaic consideration: the need to attract students and retain graduates locally who were increasingly seduced by the mystique of Silicon Valley and the appeal of Stanford University, the alma mater to founders of giants like Google, Yahoo!, and Cisco.[46] In early 2010, the School of Engineering was increasingly losing promising applicants to Stanford.[47] In addition, start-ups founded by MIT students and researchers had been moving to California in growing numbers, including some high-profile ones.[48] Dropbox, cofounded by Drew Houston ('06), was probably the most visible instance. In his commencement speech in 2013, Houston declared that Silicon Valley was "where the real action was happening" at the time when he and his partners launched the company in 2007.[49] When he was a student in the mid-2000s, Houston noted that there were fewer opportunities for aspiring entrepreneurs to turn their ideas into reality. Even in 2014, when he was interviewed by the *Boston Globe*, Houston said that MIT graduates have the reputation of being outstanding engineers, but not as savvy in business as their peers at Stanford.[50] Meraki, a start-up founded in 2006 by three CSAIL PhD students that was sold to Cisco in 2012 for $1.2 billion, is another example.[51] According to Sanjit Biswas, Meraki's cofounder and chief executive officer (CEO), his team was forced to relocate to San Francisco because the Boston entrepreneurial ecosystem was not supportive enough in the mid- to late 2000s.[52]

Curt Woodward of *Xconomy* reported that "[Professor of Electrical Engineering Dave] Gifford joked that he wanted to have Stanford University send over 'a 55-gallon drum of whatever they put in the water in Palo Alto. People here are just as smart as people out there. But I think that we need to be more proactive about starting companies,' Gifford said. "It would be good for our students, and it would be good for the New England economy if we could get [these companies] to stay here."[53]

"Is it possible MIT is feeling inadequate—insecure even?" This was the question asked by reporter Michael Farrell in the *Boston Globe* in early 2014.[54] He stressed that MIT was facing increasing competition from Stanford University, which had "emerged as the center of gravity for this exciting new era, in which seemingly every other bright young student is starting a new company, and more than a few of them are becoming overnight millionaires." The *Globe* added, "The mere idea of MIT being left behind in the zeitgeist sweeping the technology world seems farfetched. But the aggressive approach that its president is pushing also speaks to the speed at which change is happening in its core subjects." The *Globe* article quotes Dane Stangler, vice president of research and policy at the Kauffman Foundation, who said, "[These efforts on the part of MIT] might not be enough to woo the most promising students and even donors who increasingly look to universities to be a catalyst for industry . . . Even a place like MIT feels like they've got to do more to keep up."[55]

Some donors voiced the same concerns. In the *Globe* article, Ray Stata ('57), the cofounder of the computer chip manufacturer Analog Devices, Inc., was quite straightforward when he said: "The facts are that until quite recently MIT didn't do anything explicit to promote innovation other than the research and education part. The graduates who have been in the entrepreneurial world think MIT can do an even better job by being deliberate about entrepreneurship and not being derivative." The *Globe* added that "based on input from Stata and other prominent alumni and faculty, MIT's new president Rafael Reif has launched a campuswide effort to make the school the unquestioned leader of technological innovation and entrepreneurship in the 21st century."[56] Donors have a powerful voice at MIT, which needs to raise $150 million every year in order to operate.[57]

The launch of the Innovation Initiative and the central administration's embrace of entrepreneurship so close in time to the start of MIT's "Better Worlds" capital campaign is probably no coincidence. For the most part, the largest donors in the prior decade have been entrepreneurs, including Stata; Alex d'Arbeloff ('49) cofounder of Teradyne; Amar Bose ('51), founder of the Bose Corporation; Martin Trust ('56), cofounder of MAST Industries, a significant player in the apparel sector; Neil Pappalardo ('64), cofounder of Meditech; Kenan Shahin ('63), founder of Kenan Systems and TIAXX LLC; Patrick McGovern ('59), founder of IDG, and his wife, Lore McGovern, cofounder of Vector Graphics; Ely Broad, founder of KB Home; Edwin C. "Jack" Whitehead, founder of Technicon; Ashar Aziz ('81), founder of Fire-Eye; and Charles ('57) and David Koch ('62) of Koch Industries.[58] As these examples and the cases of Silicon Valley and Stanford University illustrate, wealthy graduates are a major source of funding. Keeping them engaged with the university (and preferably geographically close to it) in order to build a vibrant entrepreneurial ecosystem is a significant advantage.[59]

Donors were indeed showing increasing interest in entrepreneurship. The Legatum Center for Development and Entrepreneurship was founded in 2007 thanks to a major gift from a donor.[60] Legatum was built on the notion that scalable business models provide long-term solutions to poverty. In 2011, Trust—a serial entrepreneur best known as the founder of MAST Industries—made a significant gift to the Entrepreneurship Center, which was renamed the Martin Trust Center for MIT Entrepreneurship in his honor. Samuel Tak Lee ('62) made one of the largest donations in MIT's history in 2015 to establish the MIT Real Estate Entrepreneurship Laboratory. In 2018, senior lecturer Robert Pozen endowed a summer entrepreneurship internship program for an undergraduate student.

It seems that the change of policy toward entrepreneurship education and firm formation can also be traced to broader concerns about the US losing its capacity to innovate due to the decline of manufacturing. Not coincidentally, President Reif announced the launch of the Innovation Initiative at a 2013 MIT conference titled "Production in the Innovation Economy (PIE)," which presented the result of a large-scale study initiated in 2010 by former MIT president Susan Hockfield. The study concluded that the loss of manufacturing in the US could impede its innovation capacity because a lot of learning occurs at each stage of manufacturing, and those lessons feed back into each stage of the process, including R&D. University labs often are at the origin of novel ideas and inventions that end up in the manufacturing value chain. The loss of the manufacturing process could adversely affect the labs and their capacity to innovate and invent.[61]

PIE also examined the implications of the loss of manufacturing capabilities on start-ups, specifically production-oriented start-ups that need advanced manufacturing capabilities, which require more time and capital to scale up than nonproduction firms.[62] The study found that the US ecosystem was supportive in the early stages of the development of these firms. But when these firms were ready to move into larger-scale production, the need for more capital and manufacturing capabilities incentivized them to move production overseas or to sell out to competitors, often from Asia (more specifically from China), which threatens the future capacity of the US to innovate.

The PIE study helped spread the realization that innovation and manufacturing were so intertwined and that the loss of the US manufacturing base affected its innovation capacity, a critical part of its prosperity.

MULTIPLE PATHWAYS TOWARD ENTREPRENEURSHIP

By the late-2010s, entrepreneurial projects could rely on myriad supporting structures, whether in the form of classes and programs, student clubs, contests, mentoring services, accelerators, and networking opportunities (see figure 4.1). Students, researchers, and faculty members increasingly used multiples resources of this type sequentially, or even in parallel. The fact that aspiring entrepreneurs used multiple resources indicates that the strength of the ecosystem was the sum of its multiple parts rather than any one individual form of support. The stories of ReviveMed and Biobot Analytics illustrate this point in an exemplary way.

TRENDS EMERGING BY THE END OF THE 2010S

GROWTH OF INTEREST IN ENTREPRENEURSHIP
As figures 4.2 and 4.3 illustrate, the decades leading to 2020 saw growth of interest in entrepreneurship on campus in terms of both extracurricular activities and course offerings, with an acceleration in the last decade. Start-up formation by MIT graduates followed a similar growth pattern. In a 2015 report, Edward Roberts, Fiona Murray, and Daniel Kim estimate that approximately 3.5 active companies were founded per 100 alumni during

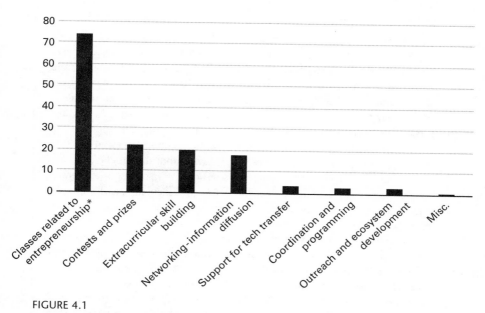

FIGURE 4.1

Estimate of resources supporting entrepreneurship in 2019 (N = 145).

2019 Annual Report—Martin Trust Center for MIT Entrepreneurship (Cambridge, MA: MIT, 2019), https://entrepreneurship.mit.edu/annual-report/ (accessed November 15, 2019).

REVIVEMED

After graduating with a PhD in biological engineering, Leila Pirhaji ('16) cofounded ReviveMed[63] with her PhD advisor, Professor Ernest Fraenkel ('98). ReviveMed was based on Pirhaji's doctoral research and uses artificial intelligence (AI) technology that she developed at MIT to leverage data from metabolites (small molecules in the human body) to accelerate drug discovery. ReviveMed has been working with pharmaceutical companies while also pursuing internal programs focused on discovering therapeutics for metabolic diseases.

Pirhaji and her cofounders' path from idea to venture founding involved taking advantage of many resources offered on campus. First, Pirhaji got a minor at the Sloan School of Management during her doctoral program. While at Sloan, she took part in the I-Teams course, in which students work on a commercialization, "go-to-market strategy," with principal investigators of research conducted at MIT. Pirhaji also participated in Start6, a two-and-a-half-week crash course held during the January Independent Activities Period (IAP) that

(continued)

introduced students to entrepreneurship. Pirhaji's session of Start6 included a trip to Silicon Valley, during which she presented her project to local venture capitalists. She also benefited from StartIAP (renamed MIT Fuse), a mini four-week accelerator also held during IAP that had the objective of getting participants to work at "entrepreneur speed" and of taking them from concept all the way to company. These experiences, along with valuable mentoring, landed the ReviveMed team in the semifinal of the $100K Entrepreneurship Competition, where they won a $10,000 prize from Booz Allen Hamilton. The venture project got nonequity funding and advice from the Sandbox Innovation Fund Program. ReviveMed's team also participated in delta v, the summer-long accelerator of the Trust Center for MIT Entrepreneurship, and they took advantage of the advisors of the MIT Mentoring Service that same year. In total, ReviveMed won over $50,000 in entrepreneurship prizes.

Pirhaji stated that the start-up was made possible by the abundant support that she received at MIT. Her very first presentation was "super not-clear and super scientific," but she eventually learned, on many levels, how to focus her ideas. Her progress was such that her first pitch session is now held up against the final one as a class example—an illustration of the trajectory from unshaped to finely honed."[64] The example of ReviveMed and other MIT start-ups suggests that their participation in contests and other forms of support at MIT prepares them to be strong competitors in contests outside MIT. Indeed, ReviveMed, like many other MIT-related start-up projects, went on to win several prestigious entrepreneurial contests outside MIT. Describing MIT's entrepreneurial ecosystem, Pirhaji said, "The culture of innovation is so common . . . The support is really instrumental. I would never [have been] able to do any of this without it."[65]

BIOBOT ANALYTICS

Biobot Analytics is an example of a company that benefited from the help of many elements of the MIT entrepreneurial ecosystem.[66] It resulted from a large collaboration within MIT across six labs, from the School of Architecture and Planning to Biological Engineering, as well as Civil and Environmental Engineering and Computer Science and Artificial Intelligence. Its technology combines several disciplines, including urban studies, computational biology, chemistry, virology, engineering, and data analytics. Biobot is based on research led by the laboratories of Carlo Ratti, professor of the practice in the MIT Department of Urban Studies and Planning and director of the MIT Senseable City Lab, and Eric Alm, associate professor in the MIT Department of Biological Engineering, director of the Alm Lab, and director of the MIT

(continued)

Center for Microbiome Informatics and Therapeutics. Biobot's cofounders, Newsha Ghaeli, an architect and urban innovation researcher, and Mariana Matus ('18) who has a PhD in computational biology, together with scientific cofounder Eric Alm, aim to foster community health at all scales by detecting infectious disease and other health outbreaks early on to prevent pandemics. They achieve this by building predictive health analytics from molecular data present in human waste and collected from sewers. Biobot's first product tracked the use of opioids based on the analysis of wastewater to help city administrators react more proactively to epidemics (see the epilogue for Biobot's work regarding the detection of COVID-19 in wastewater).

Ghaeli and Matus started their entrepreneurial journey by conducting proof-of-concept studies with the financial backing of the Kuwait-MIT Center for Natural Resources and the Environment. Matus kickstarted this foundational scientific research and made it the topic of her PhD dissertation. They transitioned from research to pursuing a business project by taking part in the preparatory stages leading to the $100K Entrepreneurship Competition. During the IAP period of January 2017, they took part in the mini four-week accelerator program called MIT Fuse, which helps participants go from concept to a company project.

In 2017, Ghaeli and Matus were part of the first cohort of venture projects selected by MITdesignX, the entrepreneurship program launched by the School of Architecture and Urban Planning the year earlier. They took advantage of the funding and mentoring provided by the Sandbox Innovation Fund Program and participated in the IDEAS Global Challenge (renamed IDEAS Social Innovation Challenge), the contest for social entrepreneurship projects, due to the potential social benefits of their product. It was among one of the eight winners and was awarded $10,000. The team continued over the summer of 2017 by participating in delta v, the accelerator program of the Trust Center for MIT Entrepreneurship. It was Matus's second time participating in delta v; the previous time, she had a somewhat similar idea and a different team, but it was not the right opportunity, and she decided not to move forward. Illustrating the argument that the MIT entrepreneurial ecosystem prepares its participants for outside contests and other support structures, Biobot were selected by the prestigious Californian accelerator Y Combinator for the Winter 2018 cohort.

the 1960s; by the 1980s, this figure had jumped to 10.7 and rose again in the 2000s to 13.4 (see figure 4.4). The figure that they projected for the 2010s was 18 companies per 100 active alumni based on an extrapolation of this growth rate. In annual terms, this suggests that in the 2000s, around 1,300 firms were founded each year by MIT alumni entrepreneurs."[67]

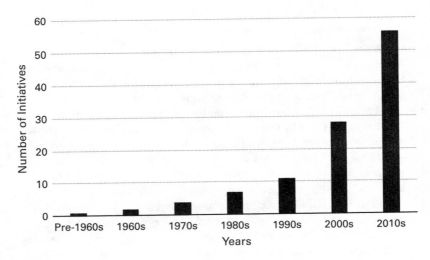

FIGURE 4.2
Estimate of initiatives supporting entrepreneurship over ten-year periods (excluding classes) (N = 109). Includes known sources of support that have been discontinued.

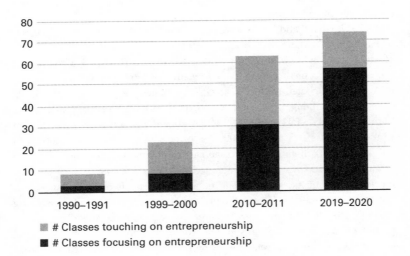

FIGURE 4.3
Estimate of growth in the entrepreneurship course offerings (1990–2019). The data starts in 1990 because earlier data is less relevant (only one course was offered between 1961 and 1993).
Source: MIT Course Catalog (MIT Bulletin) 1990–2010–2011. Annual Report of the Trust Center for MIT Entrepreneurship 2015–2016 and 2019–2020.

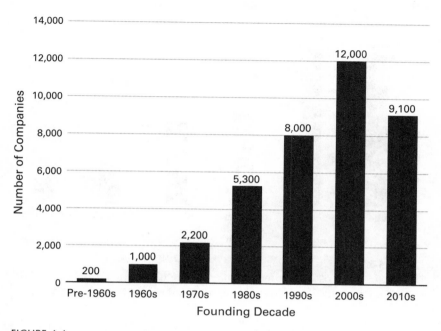

FIGURE 4.4

Estimated number of companies founded by MIT alumni, by founding decade, pre-1960s through April 2014.

Source: Edward B. Roberts, Fiona Murray, and J. Daniel Kim, "Entrepreneurship and Innovation at MIT: Continuing Global Growth and Impact," MIT Sloan School of Management, 2015, http://web.mit.edu/innovate/entrepreneurship2015.pdf (accessed February 2, 2020), 14. The authors specified that they normalized the figures in order to address differences in the size of the alumni base over time. They divided the number of companies founded by MIT alumni in each decade by the number of existing alumni in that decade.

Unfortunately the survey reported in the 2015 report has not been replicated more recently.

Support for entrepreneurship has come from various sources over time: alumni, students, individual faculty and staff members, departments, labs, schools, the MIT central administration, and sometimes nonalumni donors. Figure 4.5 shows an estimate of the number of times that certain stakeholders were primarily at the origin of initiatives supporting entrepreneurship. Of course, reality is more complex, and in many cases, several stakeholders were involved in launching an initiative supporting entrepreneurship. It appears that alumni and students were responsible for 43 percent of the

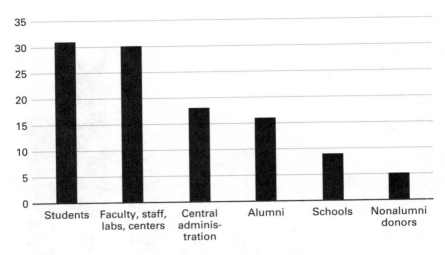

FIGURE 4.5
Estimated sources of support for entrepreneurship (excluding classes) (1946–2019)
(N = 109). This includes known sources of support that have been discontinued.

initiatives. This number grows to 50 percent if we add the support initiatives for which faculty and staff were responsible, because faculty and staff generally followed a similar process, acting on their own impulses, from a local position in the Institute and navigated the organization to turn their or their students' project into reality, as earlier chapters have discussed. If we further include initiatives started by departments, centers, and labs, often also acting under the impulse of an individual faculty or staff member, the number grows to 70 percent. These statistics support the argument that the story of support for entrepreneurship at MIT is largely a bottom-up dynamic supported by the Institute's strong *Mens et Manus* (mind and hand) culture, at least until the early 2010s, and Institute leadership that stood back and allowed experimentation at the department, lab, and center levels. Importantly, it is clear that eventually, most stakeholders were involved with entrepreneurship. A total of 77 percent of initiatives taken by the central administration occurred in or after 2010.

SPECIALIZATION OF INTEREST IN ENTREPRENEURSHIP
For a long time, support for entrepreneurship did not distinguish between industry or geographical scope, nor did it differentiate between traditional for-profit entrepreneurship and social entrepreneurship. Starting in 2000,

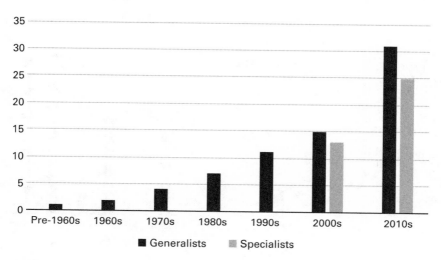

FIGURE 4.6

Estimated generalist modes of support of entrepreneurship, as opposed to specialist modes (1946–2019) (N = 109). This includes known sources of support that have been discontinued.

however, an increasing number of specialized forms of entrepreneurship support began to emerge, as shown in figure 4.6. This can be interpreted as a sign of growing sophistication in the internal ecosystem supporting entrepreneurship on campus.

One line of specialization was across industry. New initiatives emerged that catered to specialized sectoral interests, such as the Clean Energy Prize (CEP) in 2006, the Hacking Medicine initiative in 2011, the Healthcare Innovation Prize and Hacking Arts in 2012, and the $15K Creative Arts Competition in 2013. (To learn more, see appendix 4.3, "List of Industry or Professional Specific Support for Entrepreneurship.")

Another line of specialization has been the emergence and growth of interest and support for social entrepreneurship since 2000 (see figure 4.7). The growth of interest in social entrepreneurship probably reflects in part the millennial generation's wish to lead lives driven by social conscience as well as personal gain.[68] Increasingly, in the 2010s, the social dimension of entrepreneurship was incorporated in mainstream entrepreneurship (see appendix 4.4, "Support for Social Entrepreneurship").

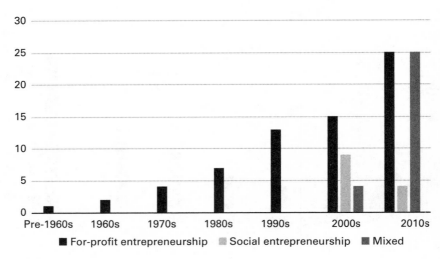

FIGURE 4.7
Estimate of the growth of social entrepreneurship (1946–2019) (N = 109). This includes known sources of support that have been discontinued.

GEOGRAPHICAL EXPANSION OF INTENDED IMPACT OF ENTREPRENEURSHIP

At first, support for entrepreneurship focused on the local impact, with students and other members of the community as the beneficiaries. Over time, however, support for entrepreneurship with an intended impact beyond campus was added, especially after the year 2000. This intended impact beyond campus largely targeted international settings. This trend derives in part (but not solely) from the growing interest in social entrepreneurship in the developing world, as described earlier. Roughly 23 percent of initiatives supporting entrepreneurship created over time until 2019 were started with an intention to have an impact internationally. From 2000 onward, the proportion increases to 29 percent. In addition, a growing number of initiatives with an initial focus on campus or the local ecosystem internationalized over time.

GROWING RATES OF FEMALE ENTREPRENEURSHIP

The rate of female MIT students who become entrepreneurs within five years of graduation is still much lower than compared to their male counterparts. However, female student participation in entrepreneurship has grown, especially after 2010, as illustrated by the 41 percent of female participants in delta v in 2020. This increased female representation resulted in a number of initiatives taken by students, alumni, and the Institute's leadership to meet and support that interest. In 2014, a student-run group called Sloan Women in Management (SWIM) added a Female Entrepreneurship Pitch Contest to its annual conference. The contest featured ten start-ups that had been selected from thirty candidates. In 2016, SWIM created a vice president of entrepreneurship to liaise with women interested in entrepreneurship at Sloan and across campus.[69] In 2018, twelve female students organized MIT FoundHers, a weekend retreat for emerging female founders. Erika Ebbel Angle, founder and chairman of Science for Scientists, and Marina Hatsopoulos ('93), founder and former chief executive of Z Corporation, organized the first Women in Innovation and Entrepreneurship networking reception in 2015.

The Institute has also stepped up in supporting women in entrepreneurship, which translated into the deliberate choice of bringing in a number of talented female entrepreneurs and investors to campus as senior lecturers in the early 2010s. These lecturers included Katie Rae, the managing director of Techstar; Jean Hammond ('86), a Boston-based angel investor and former entrepreneur; and Elaine Chen, an entrepreneur and vice president of product development for Rethink Robotics, who later became an entrepreneur-in-residence at the Trust Center. In 2016, StartMIT organized a panel highlighting women entrepreneurs. The trend of promoting women in leadership position in the area of entrepreneurship continued, including Georgina Campbell ('11) as head of the Legatum Center for Development and Entrepreneurship in 2016; Jinane Abounadi ('90) as executive director of the Sandbox Innovation Fund in 2016; Trish Cotter as executive director of the Trust Center for MIT Entrepreneurship in 2017 (after she had been an entrepreneur-in-residence and lecturer there); and Lesley Millar Nicholson, who succeeded Lita Nelsen ('64) as the director of the TLO in 2019. In 2017, Rae became the CEO and managing director of The Engine. Murray, who has conducted research on female entrepreneurs and scientists, also underlined the key role that female entrepreneurs who are on the MIT faculty play as role models, such as professors Angela Belcher, Karen Gleason ('82), Sangeeta Bhatia ('93), and Dina Katabi ('99).[70] As testament to the importance of female entrepreneurs, The Engine organized a Celebration of Female Entrepreneurs in 2018.[71]

The outside world started to notice the impact of women entrepreneurs among MIT graduates. For instance, *Forbes* named Clara Brenner ('12), the cofounder of Tumml, an urban impact accelerator, to its 2014 "30 under 30" list. Similarly, *Inc.* included ten MIT alumni on its "Female Founders" 100 in 2018. Among them were Natalya Bailey ('15) of Accion Systems, which is building a new microelectric propulsion system for spaceships; Ayah Bdeir ('06) of littleBits, an education start-up that uses electronic and magnetic building blocks to introduce children to tech innovation; Rana el Kaliouby ('06) of Affectiva, a company providing software that measures human emotions; and Limor Fried ('05) of Adafruit, an open-source hardware company that builds electronic learning tools for all ages.[72]

CONCLUSION

As a result of the convergence of student demand and a need to improve the entrepreneurial ecosystem at MIT and at the local and national levels, the Institute put entrepreneurship and innovation at the center of its offerings starting in the early 2010s, building on the existing cluster of initiatives and entities that had been built primarily from the bottom up by members of the community—and later by its departments, centers, labs, and schools. The major difference in the dynamic compared to earlier periods was well summarized by Lita Nelsen in 2016 when she said that that support for entrepreneurship "has gone from incidental to purposeful,"[73] or as the *Smithsonian Magazine* wrote: "The school's commitment to innovation and entrepreneurship has gone from being a talking point to an institutional prerogative."[74]

APPENDIX 4.1. ESTIMATE OF STUDENT-LED INITIATIVES SUPPORTING ENTREPRENEURSHIP (2006–2020)

Initiatives	Year Started
Music Hack Day @MIT*	2009
Education Ideastorm	2009
MIT Sloan Africa Business Plan Competition	2010
Entrepreneurship Review (MITER)*	2010

(continued)

Initiatives	Year Started
Hacking Medicine	2011
MIT China Entrepreneurship and Innovation Forum (CHIEF)	2011
StartLabs	2011
Hacking Arts	2012
Launch*	2012
Female Entrepreneurs Pitch Contest*	2014
FinTech Club and Business Plan Competition	2015
Sloan Healthcare Innovation Prize	2016
InnovateEDU	2016
MIT Water Innovation Prize	2019
RaboBank—MIT Food and Agribusiness Innovation Prize	2019

* Discontinued

APPENDIX 4.2. ESTIMATE OF THE INSTITUTIONAL RESPONSE TO GROWING INTEREST IN ENTREPRENEURSHIP (2006–2020)

Initiatives	Year Started
Sloan MBA Entrepreneurship and Innovation Track	2006
Building Global Innovators	2010
Entrepreneurship seminar for faculty, "From Ideas to Impact: Lessons for Commercialization"	2011
Faculty Committee on Innovation and Entrepreneurship	2011
StartIAP (renamed MIT Fuse in 2018)	2011
Committee on Student Entrepreneurship	2012
Innovation Initiative	2013

(continued)

Initiatives	Year Started
E14 Fund	2013
Entrepreneurship Online classes	2014
StartMIT	2014
Inclusive Innovation Challenge (IIC)*	2016
The Engine	2016
Undergraduate minor in entrepreneurship	2016
MIT Entrepreneurship and Maker Skills Acclerator (Memsi)	2016
Innovation@ONE	2016
MITdesignX	2016
Sandbox Innovation Fund Program	2016
MIT Entrepreneurship and Fintech Integrator (MEFTI)	2018
Innovation venture mentors	2018
Proto Venture Program	2019
Mission Innovation Program	2019

* Discontinued

APPENDIX 4.3. LIST OF INDUSTRY- OR PROFESSIONAL-SPECIFIC SUPPORT FOR ENTREPRENEURSHIP (2006–2020)

Initiatives	Industry	Year Started
ClimateTech & Energy Prize (CEP)	Energy	2006
Music Hack Day @MIT*	Music	2009
Hacking Medicine	Health care	2011
Hacking Arts	Creative industries	2012
15K Creative Arts Competition	Creative industries	2013
Samuel Tak Lee MIT Real Estate Entrepreneurship Laboratory	Construction—real estate	2015
Fintech Club and Conference	Financial services	2015

(continued)

Initiatives	Industry	Year Started
MITdesignX	Architecture–real estate–urbanism	2016
Sloan Healthcare Innovation Prize Competition	Health care	2016
MIT Entrepreneurship and Maker Skills Integrator (MEMSI)	Manufacturing	2016
Innovation@ONE	Civil and environmental engineering	2016
MIT Entrepreneurship and Fintech Integrator	Financial services	2018
MIT Water Innovation Prize	Civil and environmental engineering	2019
RaboBank—MIT Food and Agri-business Innovation Prize	Food and agriculture	2019

* Discontinued

APPENDIX 4.4. SUPPORT FOR SOCIAL ENTREPRENEURSHIP

Initiatives	Year Started
Primary focus on social entrepreneurship	
Global Startup Lab (GSL)	2000
D-Lab	2001
IDEAS Social Innovation Challenge	2001
Sloan Entrepreneurs for International Development	2001
Media Lab Developmental Entrepreneurship Program	2006
Legatum Center for Development and Entrepreneurship	2007
MIT Sloan Africa Business Plan Competition	2010
Inclusive Innovation Challenge (IIC)*	2016

(continued)

Initiatives	Year Started
Mixed for-profit and social entrepreneurship	
delta v	2012
Media Lab Entrepreneurship Program	2012
15K Creative Arts Competition	2013
Female Entrepreneurs Pitch Contest*	2014
Undergraduate minor in entrepreneurship	2016
Sandbox Innovation Fund Program	2016
Sloan Healthcare Innovation Prize	2016
MITdesignX	2016

* Discontinued

II ENTREPRENEURSHIP AND MIT'S CULTURE

This part of the book will explore the cultural elements of MIT, how they influenced the powerful emergence of entrepreneurship at the Institute, and the uniquely ad hoc and informal nature of that emergence.

5 CULTURAL FIT AND THE GROWTH OF ENTREPRENEURSHIP

Why did the strong interest in entrepreneurship develop so early and so spontaneously among members of the MIT community, particularly at a time when there was scant interest in entrepreneurship in most US universities and in the wider society? To answer that question, we must turn to the Institute's distinctive culture. As Lawrence S. Bacow ('72), former MIT professor and current president of Harvard University, suggests: "MIT is more than just a collection of buildings on the Charles River populated by brilliant students, faculty, and staff. MIT represents a particularly unique and often poorly understood culture. Anyone who seeks to replicate or simply understand MIT must first try to understand and appreciate a culture that celebrates quirkiness, choice, independence, entrepreneurship, focus, creativity, and intensity."[1] This chapter will explore how entrepreneurship, in its essence, has grown out of—and been supported by—a number of features of the unique culture of MIT. By this, I mean more specifically its organizational culture, as defined by Professor Emeritus Edgar Schein[2] of the MIT Sloan School of Management, which can be seen as an internal conventional wisdom that unconsciously guides the responses of members of an organization and informs how they solve everyday challenges. It signals implicitly what works and what does not, what is acceptable and unacceptable, what things mean, and what to pay attention to.[3]

In the case of MIT, for instance, the values represented in its motto, *Mens et Manus* (mind and hand) are still strong after more than 150 years of history and continue to inspire the MIT community at all levels. The argument that MIT's culture is important to entrepreneurship is not new and is part of a common narrative at the Institute. For instance, MIT president Susan Hockfield said in 2011: "I wish I had the recipe for what makes MIT such a fountain of innovation and entrepreneurship. But I think the simple answer is it is in our DNA.[4] The 2013–2014 annual report of the Trust Center for MIT Entrepreneurship mentions that "MIT's motto . . . is an integral part of MIT's entrepreneurial culture."[5]

But what is it about this culture that has been supportive of entrepreneurship? The argument of this book is that entrepreneurship is particularly congruent with at least six elements of MIT's culture: a well-ingrained, bottom-up organizational dynamic; excellence in all things that one studies or attempts to do, as well as a belief in hard work and fortitude; an interest in problem-solving and having a positive impact on the world; a belief in experimenting and a tolerance of failure; the pride of being viewed as rebels, sometimes eccentric and even a bit geeky, pursuing unconventional solutions; and the tradition of a multidisciplinary approach to problem-solving. This fit made MIT fertile ground for entrepreneurship to flourish largely spontaneously, from local initiatives and outside of centralized policy guidance, in a bottom-up dynamic involving various stakeholders of the community, as detailed in the previous chapters. This cultural fit also explains how entrepreneurial projects could emerge so frequently from informal initiatives and serendipitous encounters outside of structures devoted to promoting entrepreneurship, as will be documented in chapter 6.

BOTTOM-UP ORGANIZATIONAL DYNAMIC

As one long-term participant and observer of life on the campus pointed out, "There are very few top-down initiatives at MIT. Most examples of a top-down approach are relatively recent, such as The Energy Initiative, the Innovation Initiative, and Solve. Everything else [has been] bottom-up."[6] Similarly, Vice President for Research Maria Zuber said, "MIT is a very bottom-up organization. Faculty self-organize to do things that are interesting to them. They look at senior administration to facilitate what they want to do, as opposed to tell them what they ought to do."[7] This statement indicates that the bottom-up emergence of interest and experimentation in entrepreneurship fits into MIT's broader cultural dynamic of ideas and projects starting with experimentation at local levels. Thus, there was room for pioneering individuals interested in entrepreneurship to test new ideas and projects with the tacit acknowledgment of the hierarchy because this was the way that the broader organization operated. This bottom-up organizational dynamics is particularly strong at the level of centers and laboratories, whose numbers have multiplied in the decades after World War II. They are set up by individual faculty members—who need to find funding to sustain these structures—to pursue their interests and conduct their research. As such, they are academic entrepreneurs in a way. As a professor and founder of the Media Lab, Nicholas Negroponte ('66) says, "MIT as an institution is divided into church and state, where the church side are the academic departments, and the state are the labs. The labs have, if you will, the money, and the departments have the power."[8] The money thus gives the labs and centers some latitude to experiment locally. Indeed, they often were the places where initiatives supporting entrepreneurship found a home. This tolerance of a bottom-up organizational dynamic allowed space for individuals who wanted to experiment over the years with various forms of support for entrepreneurship, which would have been much more difficult in a more top-down organization. In an interview about the founding process of the Venture Mentoring Service (VMS), which was proposed in the late 1990s by MIT professor of engineering David Staelin ('60) and alumnus and serial entrepreneur Alec Dingee ('52) (see chapter 3), Lita Nelsen ('64) said: "Typical MIT, things start experimentally. They don't get planned from above."[9] Following the sharing of their initial idea with Provost Bob Brown, a number of consultations occurred with interested parties, which led to the founding of VMS in 2000.

EXCELLENCE IN ACADEMIA AND BEYOND

MIT ranks among the best universities in the world. As of now, MIT has had 154 members of the National Academy of Engineering, 59 National Medal of Science winners, 29 National Medal of Technology and Innovation winners, 95 Nobel laureates, 77 MacArthur fellows, and 15 A.M. Turing Award winners.[10] Those professors, who are world experts in their field, set the bar very high for their students. Students admitted to MIT come from the top 5 percent of their high school class. Typically, 50 percent of MIT undergraduates go on to graduate school, and of those, half get a PhD. "Being an undergraduate at MIT is like auditioning for a major symphony orchestra. You either cut it or you don't," writes Professor Emeritus Jay Keyser.[11] As former president of MIT Jerome Wiesner famously said, "Getting an education from MIT is like taking a drink from a fire hose." Meritocracy is also reflected in the fact that MIT does not deliver honorific degrees.

Exceeding one's expectations and improving on them are thus embedded within the MIT cultural mindset. It is a concept that also seems to exist with the MIT student psyche, and it serves to create a climate of peer pressure that pushes everyone to continue to reach for new heights. Keyser quotes Benson Snyder, the author of the 1973 book, *The Hidden Curriculum*, who describes how MIT departments compete for students by emphasizing how hard their courses are: the harder the courses, the higher the department's reputation.[12] Snyder further reports that in the 1970s, students were allowed to take as many courses as they wanted in their freshman year. Students competed to see who could take on the most subjects—and pain—which they saw as a badge of honor. Ann Friedlander, a former dean of the School of Humanities and Social Sciences, told Keyser that MIT students saw themselves as having enlisted in the "mental Marines,"[13] an outlook that echoes the philosophy of the Trust Center for Entrepreneurship, which states that entrepreneurs need the spirit of a pirate and the discipline of a Navy SEAL. In the extracurricular arena, MIT students also tend to overload. This tradition of challenging oneself continues today. A longtime MIT insider commented recently about how impressed he was by MIT students who, in addition to their demanding course load, were involved in numerous extracurricular endeavors, such as volunteering for a good cause, working on a start-up project, or playing in the symphony orchestra.

What does all this have to do with entrepreneurship? Launching and growing a company may be somewhat romanticized nowadays, but it also feels like hell at times. It is actually extremely difficult (most start-ups fail) and thus requires excellence and dedication in all aspects of the entrepreneurial process, including technology, marketing, distribution, managing people, etc. Founding a company also requires immense persistence and hard work, all of which can be found in abundance at MIT. The MIT experience absolutely prepares its people for uphill battles and humbling escapades. "In the early days of a company there are a bunch of different 'fire hoses' you're drinking from, and you have to wear a ton of hats. MIT forces you to learn how to handle that . . . That's exactly what a startup is like. You have to be really deliberate about only working on the most important things," says Jamie Karraker ('12), cofounder of Alto Pharmacy.[14]

PROBLEM-SOLVING

One of the first steps of an entrepreneurial project is to identify a problem—an "opportunity," in entrepreneurial lingo—that can be solved through
a commercial solution. Entrepreneurship is only a variation on the strong
problem-solving tradition embedded in MIT's culture. Bill Aulet says "It's in
the DNA. . . . From the time of its founding, MIT's *Mens et Manus* philosophy
of hands-on education has always fostered the kind of roll-up-your-sleeves
attitude essential for an entrepreneur."[15] References to this cultural feature
are omnipresent in the narrative of members of the community, from the
top of the hierarchy to the undergraduate students, all of whom live by it. As
current MIT president Rafael Reif wrote:

> We believe in learning by doing—and by making, exploring, designing, invent-
> ing, and performing too. Much of the daily work of our faculty and students
> happens in extraordinarily advanced laboratories, in fields from cancer, brain sci-
> ence, robotics, and nanomaterials to alternative energy and astrophysics. But we
> also have our own machine shop, a wind tunnel, an aerospace research hangar, a
> research nuclear reactor, and a glassblowing lab. We like to make things—and we
> like to make an impact. Taken as a whole, our campus is a workshop for invent-
> ing the future.[16]

Sangeeta Bhatia ('97) is a professor at MIT's Institute for Medical Engineering and Science and in the Department of Electrical Engineering and
Computer Science, as well as director of the Marble Center for Cancer
Nanomedicine. Reflecting on the same worldview, she says, "I'm mostly
driven by how to fix things. I'm always thinking about how to solve problems by repurposing tools. As an engineer, I have a hammer, and look for
the next nail. But as a physician, I also want to pick problems with the most
clinical impact."[17]

There is perhaps no other person on campus better placed to comment
on this characteristic of MIT than Professor Martin Culpepper, who is leading Project Manus, an effort to upgrade makerspaces on campus and foster
student maker communities. Maker spaces offer space and tools for three-
dimensional (3D) printing, wood and metal working, robotics, circuitry,
and other types of projects. "Building a solution to a problem isn't the same
as committing something to memory. It's something you live, and when
you are done, you own it," says Culpepper.[18] Ray Stata ('57), the legendary
entrepreneur and benefactor, concurred with this view when he said, "It's a

'hands-on' place; if there's a problem, students are encouraged to go down to the basement, build the appropriate equipment, and develop a solution."[19]

Students apply to MIT for these *Mens et Manus* characteristics. In 2012, *Boston Magazine* profiled second-year MIT Sloan student Ash Martin ('10), who said that he felt right at home at MIT: "It's full of my people, . . . the roll-up-your-sleeves-and-get-it-done people. This is where it's at and where I want to be."[20] Ben Vigoda ('99), cofounder of Lyric Semiconductor, explains that a core principle of his life at MIT was conveyed to him by Professor Neil Gershenfeld, the director of MIT's Center for Bits and Atoms: " 'Always think with your hands' . . . essentially, start building a prototype right away and learn as you go." He points out that it is how architects operate. They mess with material, learning as they go to eventually build a viable model. "That 'just start building' mentality at MIT is awesome and is how we developed our technology and company early on," says Vigoda.[21]

The importance placed on solving problems and learning by doing is not just a narrative; it translates into reality. MIT had always had hobby shops, but by 2015, growing interest from students had put so much strain on the 120,000 square feet of available space (divided into forty workshops) that MIT launched Project Manus to upgrade makerspaces. Similarly, since Professor Neil Gershenfeld started teaching his rapid prototyping class, How to Make (Almost) Anything, the class has been oversubscribed each year by hundreds. The practice-oriented class Entrepreneurship Lab, which challenges Sloan School of Management students to solve real-world problems in start-ups, was so successful that its model was soon replicated for other areas of interest.[22] In 2020, there were thirteen such labs.

One should also mention the huge success of the class Design and Manufacturing, which Professor of Mechanical Engineering Woodie Flowers transformed in 1974 from a largely pencil-and-paper class into one to prepare students not only to design an object, but also to build it in a format of a get-your-hands-dirty, build-competition experience. The final presentation of students' projects has become the most popular event, Innovation Day, staged by the Mechanical Engineering Department.[23] Reflecting his belief in experiential learning and problem-solving, Professor Flowers said that "nobody is getting hired to solve the multiple-choice problems at the end of the chapter."[24] This philosophy is reflected in the opportunity that undergraduate students have to conduct research alongside graduate students and faculty members through the hugely successful Undergraduate Research Opportunities Program (UROP). Through their work in the lab, they can apply firsthand what they learn in class to solving real-world problems.[25]

Finally, the congruence of MIT's culture and problem-solving in particular perhaps appears most clearly when Professor Charlie Cooney ('67) says, "We like to solve problems. Entrepreneurship is that link between identifying innovating ways of doing things and translating, applying, implementing them in the solution to problems."[26]

EXPERIMENTATION AND TOLERANCE TO FAILURE

Related to problem-solving is the value that MIT places on experimentation. It involves an element of fortitude, a tolerance of failure, a stick-to-it ethos, and patience toward the process, as well as a sense of belief in oneself, or at least in one's ideas. Of course, experimentation lies at the core of all scientific endeavors, but it is also central to how the Institute operates. In addition, it is central to its pedagogy. At the outset, William Barton Rogers's new type of polytechnic university was an experiment. It was embodied in the central role that laboratories have played in MIT's pedagogy, which was originally a radical departure from traditional teaching methods. This approach has been carried out to this day. For instance, Eugene "Doc" Edgerton ('26), a legendary professor and pioneering engineer, inventor, mentor, and entrepreneur best known for his work on high-speed imaging, sonar, and deep-sea photography (see chapter 1), told his students that you have to try your ideas for yourself and expect that you will never get it right the first time. MIT experimented and innovated in many ways, as discussed in previous chapters, such as with its relationship to industry, its early patent policy, its invention of engineering science, and the launch of American Research and Development (ARD), to name just a few. The sanitary engineering department evolved into MIT's Department of Biology, which conducted basic research on the cellular and molecular mechanisms underlying cancer. Professors Tyler Jacks and Phillip Sharp built a major cancer research lab at MIT, where they were able to bring together engineers and biologists without the benefit of an associated medical school or a hospital. Professors Nicolas Negroponte ('66) and Jerome Wiesner ('37) built the Media Lab within the School of Architecture and Planning.

MIT also experimented with entrepreneurship by allowing extracurricular activities or experimental classes related to entrepreneurship to develop
into formal classes and sometimes full-fledged programs. This highlights
a key institutional capability that has helped interest in entrepreneurship
grow at MIT: a tolerance of local, informal experiments and initiatives,
some of which, when they succeeded, were incorporated as intrinsic parts
of the Institute. This was the case, for instance, when Amy Smith ('84) started
the Haiti Project, the precursor of D-Lab, and when a few students launched
the Entrepreneurship Club (E-Club) and later the $10K Business Plan Compe-
tition. It was also the case when Professor David Staelin ('60) and Alec Dingee
('52) convinced Provost Bob Brown of the need for a mentoring service for
aspiring entrepreneurs belonging to the MIT community, which led to the
foundation of the VMS (see chapter 3). When some needs are unmet by the
Institute, students and other stakeholders tend to take the initiative to fulfill
them.

Romi Kadri ('14) is a perfect example of this uniquely MIT trait. Kadri
noticed that students come to MIT with a desire to make a positive impact on
the world and recognized that entrepreneurship is a key factor to make their
ideas real. However, he noticed that undergraduate students in the School of
Engineering were not aware of most of the entrepreneurship-related resources
available on campus and did not have access to entrepreneurship courses
that gave them credits. Kadri managed to navigate the system and to have
the undergraduate program in mechanical engineering introduce a concentration in entrepreneurship. He did this with the help of entrepreneurship
champions like Trust Center founder Edward Roberts and managing director
Bill Aulet, as well as professors Sanjay Sarma and Peko Hosoi.[27]

Not all experiments are successful, of course, but valuing experimentation implies a tolerance of failure. Entrepreneurship perfectly fits into such
a worldview because it relies on iterative experimentations and risk-taking.
One of the first principles taught in entrepreneurship classes at MIT is the
early incorporation of customer feedback to improve the venture's product
iteratively. As Lita Nelsen of the Technology Licensing Office (TLO) wrote,
"Our culture at MIT stresses that risk taking is necessary for achievement.
We assume that our students are good enough to take risks and succeed.
They have sufficient talent, energy, and self-confidence to recover rapidly
from failure and to learn from failure to become more effective in their next
endeavor."[28] Vinnie Ramesh ('12), who cofounded the health data science

start-up Wellframe when he was a senior at MIT, exemplifies this view. "If I fail, I'm probably going to try again and start another company," he laughs. "And if it doesn't work, you've still learned a lot, and you'll come out a stronger person."[29]

Several testimonials collected in this book about initiatives supporting entrepreneurship refer to the value of the safe space that MIT provides for everyone to experiment and (sometimes) to fail. The student-led E-Club is such a space, according to Josh Siegel ('11), who was one of its organizers in 2011. "The emphasis is on hearing from people in the midst of grappling with the financial, organizational, interpersonal, and legal issues involved in getting a company up and running," he says. "We give you the nitty-gritty. It's a club for people who are very hands-on, who want to do it themselves, make mistakes, and keep struggling until they succeed. We turn away people who are looking for a get-rich-quick scheme."[30] A willingness to take risks and the ability to learn from failure are critical for entrepreneurship. As seen in previous chapters, early initiatives by members of the community to pursue entrepreneurship were made possible by MIT's tolerance of failure in experimentation. It appears in many examples in this book, such as in 1969, when a group of alumni organized a weekend seminar titled, "Starting and Building Your Own Company," which eventually led to the founding of the Cambridge MIT Enterprise Forum (MITEF). It was also the case when Amy Smith ('84) started D-Lab in 2000 out of an experimental seminar. Professor Sandy Pentland followed the same process when an experimental seminar held in 2001 led a few years later to the launch of the Media Lab Developmental Entrepreneurship Program.

A more radical form of experimentation that has a strong tradition at MIT is called "hacking." It is generally assumed that the term "hack" originates from the Tech Model Railroad Club (TMRC), which builds railroads and train models. Founded during the 1946–1947 school year, the TMRC is one of MIT's oldest student clubs. In the 1950s, members of the club began to understand the potential of computers to model their increasingly complex railroad models. The railroaders used the computer in the Department of Electrical Engineering during off-hours to explore the possibilities. While pursuing their hobby, they also programmed system tools, music programs, games, and even a time-sharing program. "The modelers sometimes called themselves 'hackers,' which they meant in the traditional sense of pranksters or jesters, people who didn't take life or work too seriously. Soon, the rest of the computing world was using the term as well,"[31] according to Fred Hagwood, the author of *Up the Infinite Corridor*. In his book *Hackers. Heroes of the Computer Revolution*, Stephen Levy credited the TMRC students with developing the "hackerism" movement that influenced the development of the personal computer.[32] The hacking culture, according to Levy, is based on access to computers and any other resource useful in helping people understand how the world works; freedom of information; mistrust of authority; decentralization; and personal recognition based on individuals' hacking.

Ever since then, the hacking culture has been strong at MIT, permeating the circles of people interested in entrepreneurship. It involves similar values: possessing the ingenuity to access resources that one does not control, stretching the rules, and pushing limits. Appreciation for the hacker spirit can be found in the logo of the Trust Center, showing a pirate ship. The Trust Center's website stresses that it is important to "embrace the hacking mentality of MIT . . . the pride in being different and embracing what we call 'the spirit of a pirate.'"[33] Aulet adds that what is needed to be an entrepreneur is the spirit of a pirate combined with the discipline of a SEAL: "It is this dichotomy that makes for great entrepreneurs. . . . It is not just this craziness. It is actually that they execute like hell when they get down to it."[34] The hacker spirit is also illustrated by the enthusiastic adoption of hackathons in the late 2000s and early 2010s by students interested in entrepreneurship. "Hackathon" is a portmanteau of the words "hack" and "marathon." It is thus a race to solve challenges against time. Students participating in Hacking Medicine, for instance, try to disrupt the silos in the health care sector to create innovations.[35] Steven Leckart of *Wired* magazine suggests that hackathons fit MIT so well because they are a variation of the "marathon bursts" that took place in the 1960s there, when students programmed in twenty-four-hour stretches to demonstrate stamina, as well as their skill in building software.[36] Aulet noted, "There's no other place where the president of the university will urge students at graduation to go out and 'hack the world,' to rewire society's circuits."[37]

EMBRACING THE OUTSIDER

MIT is called an institute, not a university. Although the distinction is no longer relevant, it was at the school's origin and for a long time afterward.

William Barton Rogers, its founder, was inspired by the European models of engineering schools of the turn of the nineteenth century. These schools were designed to train high-level engineers, who were expected to lead new industries that emerged with the Industrial Revolution, such as the École Polytechnique and École Centrale in France and the Technische Hochschulen in Germany. However, they were set up as separate institutions of higher education; they were denied the title of "university" because they did not teach classical subjects such as philosophy, medicine, law, and theology. They were not allowed to deliver doctorates until the twentieth century.

Similarly, for a long time, MIT was seen as an outsider by its peers in academia and looked upon as a mere vocational school. The Morrill Land Grant Act, which provided the original funding to launch MIT in 1861, specifies that the money was to be used "to teach such branches of learning as are related to agriculture and the mechanic arts . . . in order to promote the liberal and practical education of the industrial classes in the several pursuits and professions in life."[38] MIT was established in spite of great opposition from its senior neighbor and beacon of the establishment, Harvard University. MIT continues to show features that set it apart from other universities and underscore its meritocratic ethic, such as not delivering honorary degrees and not accepting legacy admissions.

This identity of being an outsider is another cultural feature specific to MIT and its community members, but it is accompanied by a sense of pride in being disruptors, upstarts, and even a bit geeky. With this background, MIT did not draw its students from the establishment, as reflected by a comment from a student in 1899: "A college education does not mean quite the same to a tech man that it does to the average college man. . . . Men go to tech not to have their alma mater seal them gentlemen, but to make them workers."[39] This identity is also embodied in appearances.

This trait was espoused by Professor Noam Chomsky in his response to visitors from Japan who were surprised by the dilapidated facilities of his department: "Our motto is: Physically shabby. Intellectually first class."[40] The facilities may not be pretty, but the excellence of the research conducted within the walls is unparalleled. Perhaps no other building illustrates the "Don't judge a book by its cover" side of MIT than the legendary Building 20, which hosted the famous Rad Lab during World War II, which led to the improvement of radar, a decisive achievement in winning the war (see chapter 1). It had been constructed at the beginning of World War II as a temporary plywood structure, but it survived until 1998.[41] In the postwar years, it hosted various laboratories, offices, and meeting rooms for student groups. The temporary nature of the building made it possible for its occupants to knock holes in the walls to adapt them to their needs. There was not much space, so people pulled the doors open. As a result, people wandering down the creaky corridors saw what was going on in the rooms, and in the process, learned many things in addition to their own work, according to Professor Walter Morrow ('49).[42] This characteristic may have contributed to the decisive breakthroughs that happened in Building 20. Building 20 was also the site of the TMRC, from which many first-generation hackers emerged—hence its nickname, "the Magic Incubator."[43] Building 20 is even related to entrepreneurship. It was indeed where Bose Corporation, founded by Professor Amar Bose ('51) got its start, as well as Bolt, Beranek, and Newman (BBN; see chapter 1), which became a pioneer of the early days of the internet.

Sofia Roosth, who conducted an ethnography of a group of MIT researchers, illustrates the laid-back sartorial culture of MIT in her description of Professor Drew Endy: "Despite the intervening decade between earning his PhD and arriving at MIT, Endy continued to dress like a graduate student, a quirk that was tolerated, if not embraced. . . . On any given day, Endy would wear a T-shirt advertising some aspect of his work in synthetic biology: shirts emblazoned with logos of the Biobricks Foundation, MIT, or Creative Commons."[44] In *Up the Infinite Corridor*, Hapgood suggests that at MIT, an Armani suit is not a sign of success, but of a lack of self-esteem: "At MIT you dress up by dressing down."[45] Substance definitively takes precedence over appearance. The mythical figure of the nerd and the hacking culture express the continuity of this feature.

Having an identity outside the establishment fits entrepreneurs well. Many choose not to join corporate settings or, if they do, they eventually leave their employer out of frustration that their innovative ideas are dismissed, such as Ken Olsen ('50) and Harlan Anderson ('53), who cofounded Digital Equipment Corporation (see chapter 1), and Bob Metcalfe ('69), the cofounder of 3Com. Noubar Afeyan ('87), born in Beirut to American parents, argues that entrepreneurship is a form of intellectual immigration, consisting of leaving one's comfort zone and going somewhere where you cannot take anything for granted: "This [MIT] is the place where you can do that."[46] According to Aulet, "Entrepreneurs create an organization that didn't exist before. They have a scarce amount of resources with which to do that. They are the underdog."[47]

Entrepreneurs by definition try to challenge incumbents. As student Peter Reinhardt said when trying to rally his colleagues in the mini-incubator that he set up in his dorm room, "Try to imagine working at a large corporation for the rest of your life. If this irks you, keep thinking about it until you are ready to quit and start your own company."[48] As argued by professors David Mindell ('96) of MIT and Fred Turner of Stanford University and MIT, there are remnants of the counterculture movement of the 1960s that mutated into a cyberculture, which saw in information technology (IT) and computer networks tools to empower individuals for building egalitarian societies.[49] Originally, this cyberculture's intellectual backbone was systems theory—specifically cybernetics, developed by MIT professor Norbert Weiner. It later found a home in Professor Negroponte's Architecture Machine Group and its successor, the Media Lab.[50] The resurgence of some of these ideas can be seen in the students turning their backs on traditional employers in favor of young entrepreneurial ventures, and in the increasing appeal of social entrepreneurship to the millennial generation.

ROBERT S. LANGER: THE EMBODIMENT OF MIT'S CULTURE AT ITS BEST

Since the founding of MIT, there have been countless men and women—faculty, students, administrators, and others—who exemplify the best elements of MIT's culture. Dr. Robert Samuel Langer is definitely one of those people, as evidenced through his persistence in the face of failure and rejection, his commitment to bettering the world through his work, and his ability to think outside the box and create a new road map to entrepreneurial success.

Today, Dr. Langer is widely known as the "Edison of Medicine" for his biomedical engineering genius. Over the course of his prolific career, Langer has won more than 220 prestigious awards and is one of only four individuals alive today to have been awarded both the National Medal of Science and the National Medal of Technology and Innovation. At age forty-three, he became the youngest person to be elected to the three American science academies—the National Academy of Science, the National Academy of Engineering, and the Institute of Medicine—and is one of thirteen MIT Institute Professors, the highest title bestowed upon MIT faculty. The Langer Lab is the largest biomedical engineering lab worldwide, researching topics including drug delivery, polymer

(continued)

structures, tissue engineering, removal of specified drugs or other substances, and targeted inhibition, just to name a few. Many of the students and fellows who have passed through his lab have gone on to become high-profile and successful scientists and entrepreneurs.

Langer's road to renown was not easy, but as a true product of MIT, he never gave up and was never deterred by delayed gratification or failure. When he graduated from MIT in 1974, his first steps as a chemical engineer were riddled with rejection. He contacted medical schools and hospitals with the intent of working on engineering solutions for important medical issues. However, at the time, the medical field generally felt that engineers had no place in biology. Finally, after numerous rejections, Langer was added to a team at Boston Children's Hospital. There, he made a great deal of progress, including the discovery of a new way to deliver drugs. But the nation's health care establishment was still slow to recognize his contributions or his potential, rejecting nine of his grant proposals.

Being rejected so often for grants ended up helping Langer in the long run, however, by pushing him to look for unusual means of funding. At a time when no one else was doing it, he wrote patent applications and reached out to pharmaceutical companies to fund the additional development of his research. His hope was that these companies could take his products to market and thereby do what he ultimately wanted—make a real impact on patients. Eventually, the tide began to turn in Langer's favor as scientists and companies saw results from his work, allowing him to finally gain funding from the National Institutes for Health (NIH).

In 1987, Langer cofounded his first company, Enzytech, which produced a microsphere drug delivery system. The following year, he founded a second company, Neomorphics, which was focused on generating materials that were optimal for growing tissue.

During this time, Langer gained wider acceptance for his commercial successes, and MIT offered him a position as full professor. By the 1990s, he began to lay the foundations of a methodology for spinning off companies that successfully took academic research from the bench to the market.

Langer and his teams pushed to publish findings in prestigious journals and then work with the TLO to apply for various broad blocking patents. The careful timing between publishing and applying for patents was a critical step in ensuring successful spin-offs from Langer's lab. The publications attracted the attentions of possible investors, while the broad blocking patents protected the promise of the platform technology for various spin-offs, even potentially from subplatforms. If more patents are filed after founding, these can attract even more possible investors. As evidence of the success of Langer's

(continued)

> approach, spin-offs resulted from eighteen of the twenty-one ventures that his lab produced between from 1987 to 2013.
>
> As of today, Langer's forty companies altogether have an approximate market value of over $23 billion and are estimated to have affected the lives of over 2 billion people around the world. How fortunate for him—and the world—that his MIT-ingrained tenacity, commitment to excellence, and willingness to work outside traditional avenues helped to keep him from giving up when the going got tough.

EMBRACING A MULTIDISCIPLINARY APPROACH TO PROBLEM-SOLVING

Innovating through entrepreneurship generally requires imagining solutions that are outside the box, which often involves several disciplines and going beyond the silos that separate them. One of the few reliable rules drawn from research in entrepreneurship is that diverse teams of start-up founders perform better on a range of outcomes.[51] Bridging silos and promoting a multidisciplinary approach lie at the core of entrepreneurship at MIT. A general prerequisite of most MIT entrepreneurial contests or accelerators, for instance, is that participants form mixed teams of scientists and engineers with management students. Besides discipline, diversity of gender and culture is encouraged.

This is consistent with MIT's tradition of multidisciplinarity, related to the fact that solving real-world problems often requires solutions combining multiple approaches. Former MIT president Karl Compton (see chapter 1) recognized in the early 1930s the potential of the convergence of physics and engineering, and helped encourage interdisciplinary collaborations that lead to technologies such as radar, jet propulsion, nuclear power, and digital computing, as well as products including radios, telephones, planes, televisions, lasers, magnetic resonance imaging (MRI) and computer tomography (CT) scanners, rockets, satellites, global positioning system (GPS) devices, and smartphones.[52]

This convergence of physics and engineering started a new technological age. The impetus of multidisciplinarity can also be traced to World War II and postwar large academic labs, such as the Rad Lab and its successor, the Research Laboratory of Electronics (RLE), which conducted research for the military. Those labs developed key technologies for winning the war, including radar, the atomic bomb, submarines, aircraft, and the digital computer. In those labs, scientists, engineers, mathematicians, designers, and planners belonging to various disciplines crossed boundaries of traditional disciplines for the first time. They developed nonhierarchical, interdisciplinary collaborations, and independence of the mind was encouraged.[53] "In order to achieve this goal [of winning the war], they had to become entrepreneurs, assembling networks of technologists, funders, and administrators," says Professor Turner of Stanford University.[54]

The Rad Lab, for instance, had a collaborative, flexible, and nonhierarchical management style, where scientists and engineers demonstrated the immediate applications of new technologies and their ability to transform existing social systems. These networks of administrators, engineers, and scientists in various disciplines developed new ways of thinking and speaking. Peter Galison, a historian of science, argues that they developed "contact languages" with which to trade ideas and techniques toward the common goal of inventing weapons.[55] In his history of the Rad Lab, Bob Buderi wrote that "the wartime labs deeply influenced the style of research—interdisciplinary, cooperative, hard-driven—that would be conducted at academic, industrial, and government facilities."[56] He quotes a veteran of the Rad Lab as saying that after the war, he and his colleagues tried to abandon this way of operating, but it had become ingrained in their outlook and would be fundamental in the emergence of large-scale scientific and engineering projects known as big science. It notably materialized at MIT in the launch of the RLE in 1946, which mixed aspects of the electrical engineering and physics departments.[57]

Multidisciplinarity continues to this day and is even growing. In the early days of her tenure as MIT president, Susan Hockfield met as many young faculty members as possible. She reports that, based on the description of their research, it would have been difficult to guess which department they belonged to. "Their research crossed boundaries between disciplines without any celebration or permission, and I realized that flexibility was critical to the rapid translation of new ideas from the lab to the marketplace," writes Hockfield.[58] She mentions Professor Angela Belcher as a poster child of mixing disciplines. In 2019, Belcher directed the Biomolecular Materials Group, was an active member of the Energy Initiative, and had appointments in the Department of Material Science and Engineering, the Department of Biological

Engineering, and MIT's Koch Institute for Integrative Cancer Research. She was trying to combine biology and engineering to create a new generation of electronics, including batteries. Her lab included researchers with training in applied physics, chemical engineering, biology, and material science. Hockfield argues that Belcher and her colleagues illustrate a revolutionary convergence between biology and engineering that has as much potential as the convergence between physics and engineering experienced in the decades since the 1930s. She provides examples of boundary-crossing technologies, such as viruses, that can self-assemble into batteries; nanoparticles that can defeat cancer; prosthetic limbs that can read minds; and computer systems that can increase crop yields.[59] Many professors have understood this trend, as illustrated by the fact that one-third of almost 400 engineering faculty members use the tools of biology today.

Multidisciplinarity can also be observed in the Koch Center for Integrative Cancer Research, which mixes biologists with electrical, chemical, mechanical, materials science, and biological engineers. The same applies to the McGovern and Picower institutes, wherein psychologists, psychiatrists, electrical engineers, neurologists, and radiologists study the brain's multiple dimensions. "Bringing people together around a shared ambition amplifies their impact," writes Hockfield.[60] More generally, MIT's matrix organization mixes the discipline-centric schools and departments with the project-centric labs, which facilitates opportunities for interaction across organizational borders, from which ideas emerge. Increasingly, labs mix researchers with different backgrounds.[61]

Multidisciplinarity also shapes the curricular and extracurricular experiences of MIT students. Professor of Mechanical Engineering Ian Hunter stresses that multidisciplinarity is an intrinsic part of how MIT operates: "Our students are people who march across any discipline to find solutions to problems. And that's very much the MIT way. It's not only important for research, it's also important for successful startups."[62] Describing his rapid prototyping class How to Make (Almost) Anything, Professor Gershenfeld says, "What I enjoy the most is how this crosses classroom boundaries, with students ranging from new undergrads to new faculty members, and with artists teaching engineers about engineering, and engineers teaching artists about art."[63] Probably a reflection of the growing complexity of problems in today's world, the demand of students to have interdisciplinary flexibility and to combine opportunities across schools and departments has increased.[64] Increasingly, students describe their aspirations not in terms of majoring in biology, electrical engineering, or economy, but rather increasingly in terms of problem-solving, such as curing cancer or building sustainable energy solutions. MIT's response was to organize the undergraduate experience around disciplinary study and problem-based activities, such as undergraduate minors in energy and entrepreneurship.[65]

Multidisciplinarity is also reflected in the early architectural decisions that MIT made with regard to its campus. Instead of opting for a Harvard-style campus of independent buildings, writes Philip Alexander, author of *A Widening Sphere: Evolving Cultures at MIT*, MIT opted for "one megabuilding that was flexible on the inside and could be expanded on the outside. The architecture reflected the porosity of the organization, its flexibility, and facilitated collaboration across departments and schools."[66] Although this early architecture was followed by an ad hoc approach to building, more recent architecture is more reminiscent of the original tradition. The Stata Center, which was designed by Frank Gehry, houses a wide range of departments and disciplines. The *Boston Globe* reports, "Within the lobby café you might run into the creator of the world wide web, the founder of the free-software movement, and some of those who let loose the first computer worms."[67] The Kendall Square Initiative, MIT's ambitious redevelopment of Kendall Square (discussed further in chapter 9), aims to create a connection between the campus and Main Street, the central artery of the square. Interdisciplinarity is facilitated nowadays by the ease of cross-registration in various schools, such as when engineering students take business classes, which facilitates the collaboration that often leads to strong founding teams in start-ups.

This openness to multidisciplinarity was taken advantage of by early entrepreneurs within the MIT community. For instance, among examples mentioned earlier in the book, Biobot[68] (discussed in chapter 4) resulted from a large collaboration within MIT across six labs in the School of Architecture and Planning, Biological Engineering, Computer Science, and Artificial Intelligence. Davide Marini ('03), a PhD in mechanical engineering and cofounder of Firefly Bioworks in 2009, said that he enjoyed the interaction with the Biology Department, and that it was through this that he became interested in the complexity of living systems (see the box in chapter 8).[69] Eran Egozy ('95) cofounded Harmonix Music System (see the box in chapter 3) thanks to his ability to mix his interest in electrical engineering and his passion for music while studying at MIT. "MIT has no boundaries. No one says no to crazy ideas or non-traditional combinations," says Egozy, and "I feel that the fundamental principles of learning how to learn, embracing exploration, and breaking down boundaries, are helping me every day."[70]

Early entrepreneurship thrived at MIT because it presented a natural fit with some key aspects of the culture, to the point of becoming an ingrained part of it. This congruence and fusion have not constituted a static phenomenon, but rather one that has been reinforced over time through the learning process at the core of culture building, as the members of the organization learn what works and what does not. Such lessons were provided, for instance, by early entrepreneurs associated with MIT, who served as role models for future generations of entrepreneurs.

As an illustration, Peter Mui ('82), the cofounder of the student-run Entrepreneurship Club, says that Ken Olsen was an inspiration for him. Similarly, Noubar Afeyan ('87) recalls that he was inspired to start his first biomedical company by a conversation he had during his graduate studies with David Packard ('36), the cofounder of Hewlett-Packard.[71] Role models provide validation, leading younger members of the community to think, "if they could make it, I can as well"; and they also offer legitimacy. Leon Sandler, the executive director of the Deshpande Center for Technological Innovation, confirms this: "With such a long history of spinoffs . . . 'you start to build a mythology, a narrative around things that have happened. You have this sort of spirit here about doing things, an environment that encourages and supports people in doing entrepreneurial activities.'"[72]

CONCLUSION

The natural fit between entrepreneurship and MIT's culture provides an understanding of the vibrancy of the entrepreneurial ecosystem on campus, particularly the numerous initiatives and entities supporting entrepreneurship. It particularly explains how so many initiatives could grow from informal, local, bottom-up ideas into formal policies of MIT's central administration. This congruence also helps to explain the many entrepreneurial projects that emerged from traditional classes and research activities that were not designed to teach or support entrepreneurship, and also how many success stories grew out of serendipitous encounters between community members, as chapter 6 will explore.

6 THE ROLE OF SERENDIPITY

This chapter will illustrate the symbiotic relationship between MIT's culture and its thriving entrepreneurial ecosystem by examining how entrepreneurial projects emerged outside formal structures devoted to supporting entrepreneurship. The focus here is on projects born unexpectedly from the Institute's social and extracurricular activities, living spaces, fraternities, and eating and drinking establishments. We will also look at entrepreneurial enterprises that arose from academic activities that were completely not related to or focused on entrepreneurship. These projects often result from fortuitous encounters and informal relationships built across these porous spaces. This phenomenon was accurately described by Joost Bonsen ('90), a longtime participant and observer of entrepreneurial life on the MIT campus, when he writes:

> There are certainly institutional boundaries which delineate time in lab from activity in a class or drinks at the campus pub, but each of these elements form an MIT triad of activity. The borders are porous, and the back-and-forth between elements of the triad are incessant. Students bring their hobbies into the lab; they wonder about the commercial implications of their research—and they talk about challenges with their friends in social settings.[1]

Entrepreneurial projects that originated in such contexts could have been brought to fruition only because of an implicit message ingrained in MIT's culture: it is acceptable and legitimate for people to turn an idea or a research project into an entrepreneurial one in order to solve a meaningful problem. This is what sets MIT apart from most other universities, who have similar organizational and social settings but lack this distinctive culture conducive to entrepreneurship. Those entrepreneurial projects that emerged in unplanned and informal ways can be documented only anecdotally, but they nevertheless represent important evidence.

ENTREPRENEURIAL PROJECTS PERCOLATING IN INFORMAL SETTINGS

SOCIAL SETTINGS

Entrepreneurial projects often bubble up in places where students and other members of the community socialize. Such places played an important role in the development of entrepreneurship at MIT, especially before the Trust Center for MIT Entrepreneurship became the magnet for entrepreneurially minded members of the community.

The Muddy Charles Pub is a vibrant venue for brainstorming and networking on campus.[2] Many student clubs and initiatives have been conceived at the "Muddy," initially out of informal discussions, including TechLink, a networking student club; the TinyTech Club, which focuses on microtechnologies to nanotechnologies; and the MIT Energy Club. The Muddy Charles Pub was also the site of entrepreneurial networking nights. In her book *The Venture Café*, Teresa Esser ('95) says, "The Muddy Charles Pub isn't a pretentious place . . . and the people who come to the pub like it that way. . . . On most evenings, the pub is the kind of place where janitors and engineering professors can sit elbow to elbow and shoot the breeze." Adds Joe Contrada, manager of the bar,[3] "It's always been a great place for people to hang out and talk about baseball, their love lives, or how they are going to make their next million. And it's all very parallel. You always do your best stuff when you're comfortable and not under pressure to do something that has a very tiny vested interest."

The MIT Energy Club is one of the many ventures to emerge from the casual atmosphere of the Muddy Charles. In early 2004, Dave Danielson ('08), a material science doctoral candidate, took the Sustainable Energy class, which was taught by Professor Jefferson Tester, who was finalizing a textbook on the topic. Tester and his coauthors challenged his students with a reward of $1 for every mistake they could find in the draft of the book. Danielson earned $300 in this way. He suggested to his fellow students to continue the conversations about sustainable energy via regular meetings at the Muddy and to pool the money that they had gained from Tester's challenge to cover the cost of beers. The Energy Club was born out of those informal conversations.[4] Soon the members of the Energy Club realized that they needed to consider the commercial dimensions of energy, so they collaborated with the MIT Enterprise Forum to organize the Ignite Clean Energy (ICE) competition in 2005, in which numerous clean-tech start-ups have competed.[5] After Bill Aulet ('94) created the MIT Clean Energy Prize (CEP) in 2006 with Tod Hynes ('02), members of the Energy Club have run it.[6] It grew over the next few years into the oldest and largest student-run, clean-energy business plan competition in the US. The CEP has spawned numerous start-ups, including Ubiquitous Energy, which permits solar cells to be printed on flexible surfaces such as paper, fabric, glass windows, and mobile devices; Ayar Labs (formerly Optibit), which developed chips that move data around with light but compute electronically, and whose application in large data centers promises to cut total energy consumption by 30 to 50 percent; and PolarPanel, which has developed a solar refrigeration system to power refrigerated railway cars to replace diesel generators, resulting in savings of $20,000 to $25,000 in diesel fuel per railway car annually.[7]

Similarly, in the early 2000s, Pehr Anderson ('96) and Chris Gadda ('98) were wondering what to do with their idea for a new kind of telephone when three people at the Muddy told Anderson to look up Alex Laats at MIT's Technology Licensing Office (TLO). Like many of the engineers hanging out at the Muddy, Anderson was too shy at first to introduce himself to Laats, but at the third recommendation, he found the courage to do it. Laats had a trusting relationship with venture capitalist Charles Harris, who in turn knew executive headhunter Chuck Ramsey, whose career was built on pairing bright young technologists with experienced chief executive officers (CEOs). This chain of informal connections allowed Anderson and Gadda to launch NBX Corporation, which grew into a ninety-person, successful business and was acquired in 1999 by 3Com.[8]

Many other places at MIT have fulfilled the same function over the years as the Muddy Charles in terms of facilitating impromptu encounters that led to entrepreneurial projects. There was also the Thirsty Ear Pub in the basement of the Ashdown student residence. In his remarks about the Tech Model Railroad Club (TMRC; see chapter 4), Fred Hapgood, author of the book *Up the Infinite Corridor*, paints a wonderful picture of the value of these informal spaces: "TMCR was a combination of fraternal organization, neighborhood bar, wilderness hut, and safe house, an oasis of communitas [sense of belonging]."[9] John Harthorne ('07) remembers going to a mixer at

Walker Memorial on campus and meeting an engineering student who was bringing solar energy to sub-Saharan Africa and a scientist who was removing arsenic from drinking water in Bangladesh. "I told them I wanted to be a consultant," says Harthorne.[10] This experience lead to some soul searching on the part of Harthorne and to his cofounding of the MassChallenge in 2010, which became the largest accelerator in the world and one of the few nonprofit ones.[11]

Hubspot, the company founded by Brian Halligan ('05) and Dharmesh Shah ('06), is renowned for having invented inbound marketing, a new approach to marketing. It got its start thanks to a fortuitous encounter when the founders met in 2004 at a cocktail party for new students. Shah, a self-proclaimed introvert, sat in a corner while his wife searched for interesting people he should talk to, and one of the people he ended up speaking with was Halligan.[12]

Thomas Leighton ('81), an MIT professor of applied mathematics and the cofounder of Akamai, commented at a conference in 2016 that a serendipitous encounter triggered the idea of submitting a business plan to the students' entrepreneurship competition. The research that would lead to the founding of Akamai generated a series of academic papers on how to optimally deliver content on the internet; and it would have stayed that way, says Leighton, were it not for an encounter that one of his PhD students, Danny Lewin ('98), had in 1997 with an apartment house neighbor, a Sloan student named Preetish Nijhawan ('98). Lewin was concerned about his financial situation, as he was struggling to support his family with his doctoral student stipend. Leighton relates Nijhawan encouraging Lewin to enter the $50K Entrepreneurship Competition, suggesting that, if Lewin won, he could pay back his debts. (Actually, he could not have used the prize money that way, as the winnings must be used to start a company.) Soon, Lewin and his friends were poring over books in the library on how to write a business plan and consulting local experts.[13]

LIVING SPACES

Group living spaces are other vibrant places where entrepreneurial projects can percolate. Bill Aulet, director of the Trust Center for MIT Entrepreneurship, has noted that some of the best teams in his delta v entrepreneurial summer accelerator program have come from fraternities, dormitories, and varsity sports teams. He cites the origins of Perch as an example. When

Jacob Rothman ('16), an undergraduate in mechanical engineering, hurt himself while playing on MIT's varsity baseball team, he used his recovery time to brainstorm with fellow athletes about a device that could help athletes find the right form while strength training. Rothman eventually participated in delta v and cofounded Perch in 2016 with his fellow teammates Bowen Baker ('16), Nate Rodman ('16), Jordan Lucier ('17), and Zach Churukian ('17). Perch's product uses three-dimensional (3D) cameras fixed to a weight rack and a computer that analyzes the athlete's movements using machine learning to predict injuries and determine what exercises would push athletes to their best performance when working out while avoiding injury.[14]

The idea of a robotic kitchen came to Luke Schlueter ('16), a graduate student in mechanical engineering, when he ran out of time to cook for himself every night and found other options too expensive. To turn his idea into reality, he pitched it to Michael Farid ('14), Braden Knight ('16) and Kale Rogers, ('16), his fellow members of Delta Upsilon fraternity, and they built a prototype in the frat house's basement. Today, Spyce Kitchen is the world's first restaurant featuring a robotic kitchen.[15]

In 2011, the undergraduate Peter Reinhardt[16] and his friends launched the Incubomber, a mini-incubator, in their dorm room, "where Bomb Ideas Come to Life,"[17] according to Reinhardt. His description of Incubomber's inception illustrates reflects the irreverent style of undergraduate dorm life at MIT: "I lofted my bed, we shoved in two long tables that seat five people total, brought in eight [liquid crystal display] screens for four people, and [one of us worked] in the closet. We threw up some posters, got a ton of canned food, and invited a bunch of awesome people to stop by and hang out."[18] Reinhardt described the motivation behind his group's initiative as follows: "Entrepreneurship exists around MIT, but it doesn't run out and bite your kneecaps off unless you go mucking around. Every MIT student has a couple ideas, why don't they start companies to develop them? Right now?" The Incubomber was founded to help answer those questions. Among the projects developed in the Incubomber's "Bat Cave," as Reinhardt called his dorm room, was a heart-rate-sensing bracelet that connects via Bluetooth to a smartphone.

Che-Chih Tsao ('95) recalls that one day he called up several fellow Taiwanese students living in the Westgate dormitory to organize a weekend dinner party that he hoped would also serve as a "brainstorming kind of informal invention club."[19] Among the attendees was Zhen-Hong Zhou ('91), from China, with whom he had taken a course in electrical engineering. He said:

> I didn't even know about the $10K competition at the time until Zhen won the grand prize [in 1990, the first edition of the competition]. During that time, I had the original "volumetric 3D display" idea, and Zhen suggested that we could form a team around that technology to compete in the second $10K competition. A volumetric display forms a visual representation of an object in three physical dimensions using a number of visual effects. We entered the contest and made it to the finals, but did not win.

The team continued with the idea and in 1991 it became the commercial focus of ACT Research Corporation, which Zhou had created a year earlier after winning the inaugural $10K.

SIDE PROJECTS AND EXTRACURRICULAR ACTIVITIES

When he worked at Dropbox, Dan Wheeler ('06) once told *The Tech* that the best preparation for entrepreneurial projects comes from personal experiences and side projects. Wheeler stressed that he was impressed by the projects that his classmates developed during their free time. In his view, working on side projects is a good way to find cofounders. "When you build stuff for fun, it gives you the highest likelihood of meeting similarly minded people. And when you've already worked with people before on past projects, there's much less risk and a higher chance of success later on," says Wheeler. Indeed, he believes that the group project environment is extremely similar to working at a start-up. "It's like working on a big group project with people that you like and respect."[20] Andrew Sutherland ('12), who founded Quizlet in 2005, supports Wheeler's view. During his time at the Institute, he found inspiration in his living group, as well as from the general atmosphere of MIT. He says, "Everyone here is really interesting and creative and curious. Almost everything I've learned is from other students—everyone is a genius at something, and everyone is always working on a project."[21]

Undergraduate students have been particularly instrumental in starting and cultivating informal gatherings. They have, for instance, organized a weekly event known as SLACK (which stands, nonliterally, for "Stay Late and Hack"). Delian Asparouhov ('15), now chief of staff at Khosla Ventures in San Francisco, recalled that at one SLACK event a student expressed the opinion that students spent too much money on taxis to the airport and it would be great if they could split the fare. Not only would they save money, but they would also make friends from school. Out of his pitch to fellow students, SplitMyTaxi was born at the end of 2012. One of the students, Adam Eagle ('16), developed the first version of the app during winter break, and fellow students rushed to use it on their way back to campus. "A lot of students, like Adam, had these side projects, dorm-room startups as I like to call them," writes Asparouhov.[22]

As Professor Eric Grimson ('80) said in a 2011 interview in *The Tech*, "Half of what happens here is not in a lab."[23] Hobbies and extracurricular activities play an important role in the student experience, and they are regularly a source of inspiration for start-up ideas. The story of Z Corporation is a great example of this. Z Corporation's story started with Tim Anderson and Jim Bredt ('82), who worked in mechanical engineering for Professor Ely Sachs's Three-Dimensional Printing (3DP) group as a technician and a doctoral student, respectively. Anderson's first assignment was to build a machine that would sculpt new parts by spraying wet cement through a tiny nozzle, which was a technically challenging task. In their free time, Anderson and Bredt fiddled on their own with discarded equipment at the MIT Electronics Research Society (MITERS) space in MIT Building 20. One day, they decided to build a "hack" 3D printer, a project that they believed would not pose the same technical problems that they faced in their day jobs.

Observing how an old Hewlett-Packard inkjet printer was shooting ink out of a tiny head, they wondered how they could use the printer to sculpt objects in three dimensions. One evening, while hanging out at MIT's twenty-four-hour coffeehouse, Anderson performed some experiments on sugar crystals. After putting them inside a microwave, he observed how the tiny solid particles would transform from solid to liquid, and then back to solid again. Encouraged by the ability to build sugary solids, he borrowed an old inkjet printer, put some sugar on an index card, and put the card inside the printer. The card came out exhibiting 3D letters. As he had expected, applying ink to sugar crystals transformed them into sculpted solids.

Encouraged by these results, Anderson and Bredt built their next machine with parts from an old inkjet printer and an abandoned wafer-transfer machine rescued from a dumpster outside an MIT lab. The partners took their invention to the TLO and tried to convince it to give them a simple license so that they could build 3D printing machines in their garages. However, the licensing officer sensed that the duo had created a huge breakthrough and encouraged them to launch a company. He introduced them to Marina Hatsopoulos ('93) and her husband, Walter Bornhorst ('64), who were searching for a promising technology around which to launch a new venture. The four of them started Z Corporation in 1994, which became a pioneering business in 3D printing, with clients including Sony, the National Aeronautics and Space Administration (NASA), Lockheed Martin, Adidas, Ford, United Technologies, and many others.[24]

Another example of a venture growing out of an extracurricular activity is the story of Adam Goldstein ('10). As an undergraduate, he was a member of the MIT debate team and served as the de facto travel agent of the student club, which travelled a lot internationally. One day, he realized that he had spent three hours searching for flights for his teammates and came to the conclusion that the process was broken. He figured that the problem was worth tackling, although it meant facing established brands in the arena, such as Expedia, Orbitz, and Kayak. His efforts resulted in the 2010 the founding of Hipmunk,[25] a venture proposing a better user interface for online travel planning. After graduating from MIT, Goldstein and his cofounder, Steve Huffman (also a cofounder of Reddit), were admitted to the Y Combinator incubator. One year later, they raised a round of venture funding and had ten employees based in San Francisco. Hipmunk would raise additional venture capital over the years and be acquired by Concur Technologies in 2016.[26]

ENTREPRENEURIAL PROJECTS EMERGING FROM ACADEMIA: RESEARCH ACTIVITIES AND CLASSES

Research projects, classes, and extracurricular activities are more formal settings, with no mandate or mission to encourage or support entrepreneurship. Yet these settings are regularly the catalyst for spontaneous entrepreneurial projects.

Sometimes entrepreneurial endeavors flourish out of research projects that were not initially destined to be commercialized. The case of Akamai is a perfect example of this. The research project at the origin of this company, itself the result of a serendipitous encounter, was not meant to be a start-up. In 1995, Tim Berners-Lee, the father of the World Wide Web, an MIT faculty member, and head of the World Wide Web Consortium at the Lab for Computer Science at MIT,[27] foresaw the problems caused by the congestion of the internet. He had an office in the same corridor as Tom Leighton, a professor of applied mathematics. Their shared location led to informal conversations during which Berners-Lee challenged his MIT colleague to solve this internet congestion bottleneck. To mathematician Tom Leighton, it was an interesting optimization challenge. Leighton assembled a team of researchers, including his PhD student Daniel Lewin ('98), whose thesis would become the basis of the technology of what would later become Akamai. The group worked on the coding of consistent hashing, an innovative algorithm for optimizing internet traffic.

Because the team was convinced that their algorithm could have a positive impact in the real world, it offered to give it to corporations such as AOL and UUNET, but these large companies refused. That led the team to reconsider forming a company. Lewin contacted his long-time friend and Sloan MBA student Jonathan Seelig to help with the business plan. In 1998, after licensing the technology from MIT, Lewin, Leighton, Seelig, and Randall Kaplan incorporated Akamai. The company was listed on the NASDAQ stock market on October 29, 1999, and rode the boom and bust of the internet bubble. However, Akamai survived, and in 2020 the company had revenues of $2.89 billion.

Research conducted in the early 2000s by the Media Lab group led by Professor Sandy Pentland ('84) provides another example of an unforeseen entrepreneurial project growing out of academic activity and resulting from a serendipitous encounter. Pentland's group created a wearable device, the Sociometer, that captured the conversations of participants in social groups, as well as the characteristics of these networks in controlled scientific experiments. This stream of research opened new possibilities of analyzing social interactions in real time and at a large scale, without imposing any restrictions on the participants' interactions, in contrast to unreliable prior methods based on surveys and diaries. But at that point, their technology was a solution in search of a problem. The problem they needed appeared in 2007, when the researchers in Pentland's group fortuitously met Peter Gloor, a scientist at the MIT Center for Collective Intelligence. Gloor was taking surveys of employees of a German bank to understand how its physical layout affected productivity and job satisfaction. The Media Lab researchers developed and prototyped sociometric badges that they deployed at the bank to measure when employees were talking to each other and for how long. They drew conclusions from the data that improved the workers' productivity and satisfaction. This success led researchers Ben Waber ('11), Daniel Olguin Olguin ('07) and Taemie Kim ('11) to found Sociometric (since renamed Humanize) in 2011, with Pentland serving as scientific advisor. By 2015, Humanize had twenty companies in the banking, technology, and pharmaceutical industries as clients.[28]

Sometimes classes can also lead to venture projects, as the case of Thomas Massie ('93) and SensAble Devices illustrates. In 1992, Massie took a mechanical engineering course called Design and Manufacturing, taught by Professor Woodie Flowers ('68), and entered its robot competition, one of the most popular contests on campus. His project was a robotic arm, which he called the Phantom, that would operate contrary to traditional arms: instead of reaching out, the arm would react to a person touching it and give him or her the feeling of touching an object or a surface. The Phantom had numerous applications: It could allow engineers to test the physical qualities of their designs while they were still on the drawing board. It could also train doctors for surgery by helping them become familiar with various types of tissues before a procedure. Massie began manufacturing the Phantom in his dorm room and went on to win the robotics competition. He was further rewarded for his invention in 1995 with the inaugural Lemelson-MIT Student Prize and won the MIT $10K Business Plan Competition that same year. He founded SensAble Devices and marketed the Phantom from his dorm room. The Phantom haptic interface was sold in more than seventeen countries to firms such as Hewlett-Packard, General Electric, Toyota, and Brigham and Women's Hospital, as well as to other multinational companies and medical schools.[29] In the $10K Competition, as he was looking for help, he met Aulet, with whom he would later reincorporate the company as SensAble Technologies.

Another example of a class leading to a venture project is the case of Robopsy, which originated in Professor Alex Slocum's Precision Machine Design class,[30] in which students were challenged to create an innovative medical device to the specifications of a client with a current problem. For the class, clinicians at Massachusetts General Hospital presented their problems to MIT engineering students, who chose the most challenging one and built a working prototype that would solve it. In 2004, MIT students Conor Walsh

('06) and Nevan Hanumara ('06), along with Cambridge University's Steven Barrett (who was part of the Cambridge–MIT exchange program) chose to address Dr. Amar Gupta's problem with lung cancer biopsy. Doctors used a computed tomography (CT) scan to find a suspected tumor in a patient, but they could not stay in the room during the scan due to the radiation emitted by the equipment. They had to watch the scan on a computer monitor in another room and then return to the original room to manually find the right spot to perform the biopsy. This process was complex and sometimes required more than one puncture as doctors tried to perform the biopsy. This could be painful for the patient and cause complications, as well as requiring a hospital stay. The student team's answer to these problems was Robopsy, a lightweight, plastic, dome-shaped device that holds a biopsy needle and can sit on a patient's chest during a CT scan. Robopsy allowed doctors to look at the CT scan on a computer while remotely controlling the movement of the biopsy needle. The students' invention earned the $5,000 Boeing Prize at the 2005 MIT IDEAS Competition and won the 2007 $100K Entrepreneurship Competition.[31] It also earned third place and a cash prize in the Biomedical Engineering Innovation, Design, and Entrepreneurship Award competition sponsored by the National Collegiate Inventors and Innovators Alliance.[32]

There are also cases where the process of teaching leads to the formation of a start-up, as with Yonald Chery ('88). Chery served for several years as the head teaching assistant (TA) for Introductory Digital System Laboratory, a core MIT electrical engineering course, while he was a PhD student in the early 1990s. As a TA, Chery used whiteboards, but he noticed that he often had to rewrite the same explanations or that the students copied his notes erroneously. His frustration led him to the idea of the Automatic Whiteboard Mimeographic System, a portable, retrofitted pen-tracking system that records handwritten notes from a conventional whiteboard to a personal computer. Chery submitted a venture proposal to commercialize his product idea, which he called Mimio, to the $50K Entrepreneurship competition, and he won a $10,000 prize on his second attempt in 1997. Chery founded Virtual Ink in 1997 with graduate school colleagues, turning his TA assignment into a product idea and eventually into a venture. The business was launched while Chery was still at MIT, and he served as chief technology officer (CTO) and director until early 2001. Virtual Ink was eventually acquired by Newell Rubbermaid in 2006.[33]

David Young ('13), an MBA student and a captain in the US Army Reserves, did not expect that coteaching an Independent Activities Period (IAP) class on military leadership would lead to an entrepreneurial project. For the class, Leadership Lessons Learned from the Military, Francisco Aguilar ('12) interviewed Young on the topic of the class for his master's thesis at Harvard's Kennedy School of Government, where he was pursuing a joint degree with MIT's Sloan School. Rapidly, the conversation between the two men turned to a project that Aguilar was working on following the 2010 Haiti earthquake. Aguilar knew that the cumbersome fiberoptic cameras used by rescuers did not allow them to easily find people under the rubble, so he imagined a low-cost, throwable, ball-shaped camera. Young and Aguilar decided to join forces to create this ball-shaped camera, and Aguilar founded Bounce Imaging to sell it commercially to first responders and police departments, and Young became the company's first employee (see the box in chapter 7 for more on Bounce Imaging and the support that the founders received from the MIT entrepreneurial ecosystem).[34]

These examples of entrepreneurial ventures arising out of informal settings where students and members of the community socialize or have random encounters—from living spaces, extracurricular activities, classes, and research activities—illustrate Sloan professor Fiona Murray's statement: "We know innovation happens when you have these serendipitous collisions, when people who understand problems and people who understand solutions come together."[35]

INFORMAL NETWORKERS AND POLLINATORS

The spontaneous emergence of entrepreneurial projects is often facilitated by MIT students, alumni, mentors, staff members, and faculty who play key roles as connectors and pollinators that facilitate the flow of information. For instance, Joost Bonsen ('90) has been involved in various capacities with numerous initiatives supporting entrepreneurship since he was a student in the late 1980s. Perhaps more important, Bonsen has been a self-proclaimed catalyzer, connecting the dots of the entrepreneurial ecosystem on campus for many people. He describes his role as orchestrating serendipity. People like him bridge gaps, serve as sounding boards for new projects, and help people overcome stumbling blocks. He described facilitators like himself as information routers who lower psychological and social barriers. He argues that they are particularly important when people try to do things beyond their usual sphere, such as when scientists try to devise an entrepreneurial project requiring additional knowledge and social contacts than their usual academic expertise and social capital.[36]

Another facilitator of connections was Thad Starner ('91), whose passion for wearable computers during his tenure as a student turned him into a pioneer in a new area of investigation. By acting as an evangelist and network facilitator, Starner played a critical role in building a community of people interested in the nascent field. This community inspired numerous people in academia to research the area of wearable computers and others to found ventures based on the technology.[37] As mentioned in chapter 2, Joe Hadzima ('73) is an example of an alumnus who has been instrumental in helping early student interest in entrepreneurship since the 1980s. Since then, he has continued to be an advisor, a lecturer, and an officer of the Cambridge MIT Enterprise Forum (MITEF), helping connect multiple dots over the years.

Some faculty and staff members have also served as important facilitators and pollinators within and beyond their official positions. For example, Professor Edward Roberts has for many years been *the* go-to person for those interested in entrepreneurship, and his research on entrepreneurship since 1963, as well as his founding of the Entrepreneurship Center in 1991, have put him at the heart of the entrepreneurial ecosystem on campus. More recently, Kenneth Morse, the former managing director of the Trust Center for MIT Entrepreneurship, and his successor, Aulet, have been essential contributors to various networks of stakeholders interested in entrepreneurship education. This observation does not apply only to faculty and staff members involved in entrepreneurship. Professor Charles Cooney ('67), a bridge-builder between the School of Engineering and the Sloan School of Management, was instrumental in facilitating the launch of the Deshpande Center for Technological Innovation, the CEP, and the I-Teams class. Bonsen also praised Media Lab professors Alex Pentland, Rosalind Picard, Pattie Maes, and others for what he calls their "incubation ethos."[38]

CONCLUSION

The culture at MIT created an environment in which serendipitous connections yielded opportunities for entrepreneurship, even outside of formal structures designed to support budding entrepreneurs. In most cases, nobody told MIT's aspiring entrepreneurs to work on start-up projects, but they embarked on their entrepreneurial journeys because implicit norms in MIT's culture conveyed the sense that it was acceptable (even desirable) to bridge silos, experiment, and hack in order to solve a relevant problem and make a positive impact on the world.

III THE ENTREPRENEURIAL ECOSYSTEM AT MIT IN THE LATE 2010S

Parts I and II of this book detailed the history of the emergence of interest in entrepreneurship at MIT and the genesis of initiatives supporting entrepreneurship over the years, as well as the critical role of MIT's culture. Part III provides a snapshot of MIT's complex entrepreneurial ecosystem today. Chapter 7 specifically addresses entrepreneurship education targeting students, while chapter 8 covers entities supporting entrepreneurship for technology transfer, which involves more faculty members and researchers.

7   CREATING ENTREPRENEURS: SUPPORT FOR STUDENT ENTREPRENEURSHIP

MIT's entrepreneurial ecosystem is not stagnant. As has been examined in earlier chapters, it has expanded and evolved to meet the needs and demands of students, alumni, and faculty, particularly as they seek to create and navigate entrepreneurial solutions for a rapidly changing world. There are now myriad offerings that support student entrepreneurship at MIT, ranging from over sixty classes at the school to initiatives and resources outside the classroom. The genesis of many of these resources has been covered in the book's earlier chapters, but this chapter will focus on the identification and categorization of those resources today and the description of some representative examples.

The discussion begins with the Martin Trust Center for MIT Entrepreneurship (Trust Center), which provides students with a portfolio of services promoting and coordinating specialized support structures for entrepreneurship that exist across the campus. Next, it describes specialized support structures, which can be broadly grouped into four categories and are designed to build specific entrepreneurial skills, mainly through training and mentoring following an experiential learning approach. Another category is entrepreneurship contests, such as business plan competitions, hackathons, and pitch challenges, as already covered in other chapters. Yet another kind of support is related to networking and community- and career-building events and entities. This category consists primarily of student clubs. Finally, there is the group of entities focused largely on outreach activities.

Because of the sheer breadth and depth of entrepreneurial support opportunities for students at MIT, it would be too cumbersome to examine them all in depth here. As a result, it will highlight some representative cases of each type of support and showcase start-ups that benefited from those support modes. (The appendixes at the end of the chapter provide a more exhaustive list of programs and other initiatives supporting student entrepreneurship.)

MARTIN TRUST CENTER FOR MIT ENTREPRENEURSHIP

The Trust Center, previously called the Entrepreneurship Center (E-Center), is the hub for student entrepreneurship at MIT. The Trust Center serves all MIT students across schools and disciplines.[1] It sees its mission first and foremost as educational. In addition to teaching students how to launch businesses, its objective is to teach students how to develop an entrepreneurial mindset.[2] This translates into the promotion and coordination of myriad activities and the provision of infrastructures, as well as linkages with other initiatives on campus supporting entrepreneurship.

The Trust Center's educational mission thus focuses on instilling an entrepreneurial skillset and mindset within students, as opposed to churning out start-ups. In striving to do that, it also tries to meet various levels of interest students might have in entrepreneurship. Some students apply to MIT with the clear idea of launching a company after graduating. Others are content with just an introduction to entrepreneurship, while still others realize that the best fit for them is to join an existing start-up. A number of students become "intrapreneurs" (i.e, entrepreneurs within large corporations), while others learn that they are more attracted to being changemakers in social entrepreneurship or the philanthropic world. As a sign of its dynamism and vibrant community, more than 1,000 people pass through the Trust Center on weekdays, and 300 to 400 on weekends.[3]

The Trust Center also is committed to being an honest broker, and as such, providing a safe learning space to students. This means it is a place absent of conflicts of interest, particularly when it comes to ensuring that mentors provide their services with no expectation of financial gain or involvement with promising student ventures.

FACILITIES

A new 7,200 square-foot facility to house the Trust Center and support its many activities was finalized in 2016. It includes various "neighborhoods," allowing students to pursue different activities, ranging from socializing and brainstorming and researching to crunching numbers and making prototypes. There is a "beehive" space that facilitates student engagement and activity and a "quiet car" area for students who need to study. There are classrooms to host courses and the ProtoWorks makerspace that allows students to do rapid prototyping.[4] All this is complemented by ten conference rooms. The facility was carefully built for different uses and to facilitate serendipitous encounters.

DIVERSITY

Because successful entrepreneurship requires a variety of perspectives and opinions, the Trust Center stresses the importance of a diverse community of people. In its activities, mixed teams of master's of business administration (MBA) students and science or engineering students are usually required. The Trust Center puts a special effort into increasing the number of female students in entrepreneurship. For instance, in the 2017 delta v accelerator program, 45 percent of the participants were women and 75 percent of the teams had at least one female coleader.[5] The participation of foreign-born and first-generation Americans is also significant, and diversity is key to ensuring peer-to-peer learning. Burhan Azeem ('19), a Sloan student, was quoted as saying: "Building a startup can feel lonely at times, but at the Center you see other students on the same path as you, who can even help as a resource for you, and that sense of being in this together is energizing."[6]

PROGRAMS

Besides its programmatic and coordinating activities, the Trust Center also directly manages a number of specific programs. The Trust Center's programs are organized over the academic year in a gradual path, starting with introductory courses and programs (see figure 7.1). These offerings are followed by more rigorous and demanding courses that build on the earlier learning experience. There is also a customizable aspect to the programs,

FIGURE 7.1
The gradual path of the student experience at the Trust Center.
Source: 2018 Annual Report—Martin Trust Center for MIT Entrepreneurship (Cambridge, MA: MIT, 2018), http://entrepreneurship.mit.edu/annual-report/ (accessed July 20, 2018), 29.

aimed at meeting special interests, such as in health care. In addition, there is a sequence of extracurricular workshops, pitch contests, and other activities over the months, such as t=0, StartMIT, and Fuse (most of which will be discussed next), and ending with delta v, the Trust Center's capstone activity, which runs the entire summer. It is a circular process that is renewed each year with a new generation of students. Of course, students whose tenures last longer can participate several times in most of the Trust Center's activities.

T = 0 FESTIVAL OF INNOVATION AND ENTREPRENEURSHIP

In 2011, the Trust Center organized the first weeklong t=0 festival of entrepreneurship, which is held at the very beginning of the academic year in September.[7] In typical MIT "geek speak," t=0 means "the time is now." The impetus for t=0 was the observation that students often waited until late in their tenure to get involved in entrepreneurship, and as a result, they miss out on most of the support that MIT can offer. This series of events is designed to encourage students to start "driving up that start-up ramp" from their first day on campus.[8] During the 2018 edition of t=0, two dozen campus groups showed the myriad ways for students to get involved with entrepreneurship at MIT. That same year, as with prior years, students from other Boston-area universities were invited to participate.

DELTA V

As mentioned previously, delta v is the Trust Center's twelve-week summer accelerator.[9] It started in 2012 and serves as the Trust Center's capstone initiative at the end of the academic year.[10] Through a competitive process, the Trust Center selects the best student teams from across the Institute and provides them with space, money in the form of fellowships, and training to help them create impactful, innovation-driven ventures aimed at changing the world. In 2019, delta v included one of its largest cohorts to date, which featured twenty-four teams formed by 100 students covering fifteen industries. The training that the students received during the summer is based on the methodology of "disciplined entrepreneurship" by managing director Bill Aulet ('94).[11] From June to early September, student teams are allocated space in the coworking part of the Trust Center or the MIT NYC Startup Studio in Manhattan. Teams clarify their target market, conduct primary market research, and collect insights from their potential clients, with whom they test key assumptions about their product. Building a supportive and efficient founding team is also a critical objective.

The delta v program includes mentorship and coaching, peer learning, mock board meetings, guest talks, and seminars, which draw extensively on alumni volunteers and on the broader Boston entrepreneurial community. The program also provides access to prototyping tools and lab space. The Trust Center reported the participation of 232 board members in 2018. Trish Cotter, the associate managing director of the Trust Center, explained that the objective of delta v is not only to provide assistance to the students' businesses formation, but to give them a strong foundation in the fundamentals of entrepreneurship. "We're an educational accelerator, not Y-Combinator," Cotter says, referring to a famous Californian incubator. "This allows the students to take on big business challenges within the security of an educational environment." She goes on to stress that, in line with MIT's culture, what is expected from the teams taking part in delta v is to provide solutions to pressing global problems. "I'm not looking for someone to deliver my food faster or get a date quicker; that really isn't the type of problem we spend our resources on," explains Cotter. "I'd rather have students who want to change the logistics of shipping, bring solar energy to developing communities, or improve the transportation infrastructure of Rwanda."[12]

The MIT NYC Summer Startup Studio, which is delta v's first expansion outside of campus, launched in 2016. It allows some teams to be closer to the heart of the ecosystems of certain industries, such as real estate, fashion technology, enterprise technology, media and advertising, and publishing.

The delta v program ends with Demo Day, during which participants pitch their start-up projects. Demo Day is considered the culmination of delta v, as well as of the Trust Center's yearlong educational process in entrepreneurship, as well as the beginning of the next year's activities. They indeed exhibit the achievements of student teams during the prior twelve months and serve to inspire the new cohort that has arrived on campus.

Companies that have emerged from delta v have raised tens of millions of dollars and created hundreds of jobs.[13] LiquiGlide, founded in 2012 by David Smith ('12) and Professor Kripa Varanasi ('02), designed highly slippery custom coatings with multiple applications, including in consumer goods, wherein the coating allows liquids to slide easily out of containers, offering the potential to prevent significant food waste. EverVest, cofounded by Teasha Feldman-Fitzthum ('14) and Mike Reynolds ('14) in 2013 was a data-analytics platform (which has since been acquired by Ultra Capital) giving investors rapid and accurate cash-flow models and financial risk analysis for renewable-energy projects. Emerald, based on the research of Professor Dina Katabi ('99), uses radio signals to create a fall detection system that works without a wearable device and could potentially be very useful for monitoring elderly people in their homes. Leuko Labs, cofounded by Carlos Castro Gonzalez, Ian Butterworth, Aurelien Bourquard, and Alvaro Sanchez-Ferro, has developed an in-home device to monitor white blood cell counts in chemotherapy patients; its use could lower the risk of outpatient chemotherapy and reduce hospital visits to treat infection.[14]

The Trust Center reported in 2019 that three out every four delta v ventures are still in business or have been acquired. The rate of success was even better for ventures run by female chief executive officers (CEOs), of which 90 percent continue to operate. A total of 58 percent of students still work at the start-ups they founded; and 76 percent of those who are no longer with their original ventures work or are founders of new start-ups, which validates the Trust Center's motto, "We don't build startups, we build entrepreneurs,"[15] which it shares with other key members of the ecosystem, such as the MIT Venture Mentoring Service (VMS) and Sandbox Innovation Fund.

Illustrating the richness of the entrepreneurial support ecosystem at MIT and the complementarity of its components, most start-up projects that went through the delta v accelerator have benefited from VMS, Sandbox, and other supporting entities.

NIMA SENSOR

Nima Sensor ("Nima"), a food testing device created to detect allergens, was founded by Shireen Taleghani Yates ('13) and Scott Sundvor ('12) from 2011–2013, when they overlapped at MIT. Nima functions by placing food into a capsule that then goes into a portable device, which runs through a chemical process to detect a protein in allergens such as gluten and peanuts.

For the company CEO, Taleghani Yates, the development of Nima was a personal mission. In college, she found out she was allergic to gluten, eggs, dairy, and soy, and was always getting exposed to food that she was trying to avoid. She wondered if she could just take a sample of food and know what was in it. Given her background in sales and marketing, she knew that she didn't have the technical expertise to realize the product she envisioned. Fortunately, she met Sundvor, who had the mechanical engineering and product design background to bring her idea to life.

While Sundvor worked on product prototyping, Taleghani Yates took advantage of her classes at Sloan to gain the help she needed to refine her initial idea into a viable venture. Specifically, she shared her ideas in her pricing class, iterating with classmates on pricing and demand models. "The result of that was that I found there's a real opportunity here. There's a need and a willingness to pay [for such products]," Taleghani Yates says.[16]

The Nima team continued to utilize the resources at MIT, entering the $100K Entrepreneurship Competition in 2013 and winning the Audience Choice Award. They then joined MIT's Global Founders Skills Accelerator (GFSA), the predecessor of delta v. Sundvor says that participating in the accelerator program gave the team a safe space to pursue the opportunity that it had identified at an intensive pace, while benefiting from the advice of mentors and having just enough money to get by. The team found MIT's community to be immensely helpful early on. "We got a ton of intros from people who really understood what we were trying to do and trying to build. And from that, we got a lot of good connections, with a few of them turning into investors and people who are still supporting us today" says Sundvor.[17]

After GFSA, the Nima team decided to move to the Bay Area, as it provided more opportunities for funding and support in the consumer product space. The team raised a seed round in 2014 and then went on to raise a Series A round in 2016. Nima released its gluten sensor that same year and sold thousands of them. The company continued to innovate. By 2019, it had rolled out its next sensor, designed for people with peanut allergies.

COLLABORATION

The Trust Center is increasingly involved in a web of collaborations with other initiatives supporting entrepreneurship on campus, especially as they have multiplied since the early 2010s. Collaborations have multiplied notably with the School of Engineering, notably through a growing number of joint courses with the Sloan School of Management and an increasing number of student teams from the Department of Electrical Engineering and Computer Science applying to the delta v program. In 2018, the Trust Center also provided advice and a home to more than thirty student clubs with a direct or indirect link to MIT.[18] Further, the Trust Center's faculty and staff members regularly hold outreach activities around the world. Through these initiatives, and by making its content (such as its publications and methodologies) available to all, the Trust Center aspires to be a thought leader in its field and increasingly broadens its footprint.[19] This open-source content is what it calls its "operating system," a common term used in its various activities and entities, helping them to work together. The Trust Center, in a truly entrepreneurial way, continually experiments with many new forms of support of entrepreneurship, always in the spirit of its educational mission.

VENTURES WHOSE FOUNDERS BENEFITED FROM THE SUPPORT OF THE TRUST CENTER

Many ventures founded by students were nurtured during their time at the Trust Center, including Kurion (2008), founded by Gaëtan Bonhomme ('08) to isolate nuclear waste from the environment for safe disposal, the most challenging technical problem associated with nuclear energy. Kurion was the only American firm and the only start-up involved in the cleanup operations following the Fukushima nuclear disaster in Japan in 2011. The firm was bought in 2015 by the French multinational Viola. In 2012, Natalya Bailey, PhD ('15), and Louis Perna ('09) cofounded Accion, which develops revolutionary, inexpensive satellite propulsion systems the size of pennies using ion beam technology, which allows small satellites to have a propulsion system. Frederick Kerrest ('09) cofounded OKTA, an enterprise software company that securely connects its clients across software platforms and devices, which went public on NASDAQ in 2017. Alex Wright-Gladstein ('15), Chen Sun ('15), and Mark Wade cofounded OptiBit (which would become Ayar Labs), based on Professor Rajeev Ram's research on optoelectronic chips. The company produces chips that decrease energy usage by up to 95 percent in chip-to-chip communication and increases bandwidth ten times more than copper-based products.[20]

SKILLS-BUILDING ACTIVITIES

Some programs and entities set up by students, alumni, the Trust Center for MIT Entrepreneurship, and other stakeholders across MIT focus on building entrepreneurial skills. The large majority of these entities take the form of extracurricular activities and training and mentoring opportunities, and all have a strong experiential learning component. Among the entities promoting skill-building activities, the most noteworthy are VMS and Sandbox. (For more information, see appendix 7.1, "List of Active Extracurricular Support Structures Designed to Build Extracurricular Entrepreneurial Skills as of 2020," at the end of this chapter.)

VENTURE MENTORING SERVICE

VMS, founded in 2000 (see chapter 3), matches aspiring and existing entrepreneurs from the MIT community, including students, alumni, faculty, and staff in the Boston area, with experienced volunteer mentors drawn mostly from the MIT alumni community.[21] Mentors are selectively curated so as to match their expertise and interests with the specific needs of the aspiring entrepreneurs. Their skills as advisors are also an important component in the selection, as is their motivation to give back to the community. Mentors need to adhere to principles avoiding conflict of interest and controlling financial involvement with the mentees and their company, which assures the mentees of the impartial and unbiased nature of the advice. Coaching is practical and hands-on, covering a wide range of topics related to launching and growing a venture, including product development, marketing, intellectual property law, finance, human resources, and issues between the founders. Over the years, VMS has developed a unique methodology of team-based mentoring. Aspiring entrepreneurs often contact VMS at a very early stage before they have a business plan, a strategy, or even a team, let alone funding. Applicants must demonstrate a serious commitment to their venture project. VMS stresses that its services are educational only, saying: "Success is not only defined by starting a profitable company, but in the learning experience that mentees can receive from their mentor team,"[22] and "We don't screen to pick winners; rather, VMS's mission is to use any plausible idea as the focus for practical education on the venture creation process."[23]

In 2019, VMS's website stated that it had over 165 mentors who had assisted more than 2,500 mentees belonging to 1,450 ventures. They raised more than $1.44 billion in investment and grant money. Among the projects were numerous start-ups mentioned in this book, such as Accion Systems, Akselos, Cogito, CoolChip Technologies, Leuko Labs, mSurvey (renamed Ajua), PlenOptika, and SmartCells.[24] In 2018, *Slice of MIT,* a publication of the MIT Alumni Association, reported that at that time VMS was working with about 250 ventures at various stages of development.

BOUNCE IMAGING

When the Haiti earthquake hit in 2010, Francisco Aguilar ('12) knew that rescuers could not easily find people trapped in the rubble with their complicated fiberoptic cameras and thought that there had to be a better solution. That is when he came up with the idea of a throwable, ball-shaped camera, which would turn out to have applications not only in rescue operations, but also for first responders in general, such as police and firefighters. The team of Aguilar and David Young ('13) applied twice to compete in the $100K Entrepreneurship Competition but were not selected. However, they won the 2013 IDEAS Global Challenge (renamed IDEAS Social Innovation Challenge) and the 2012 MassChallenge Competition with their idea. Although Aguilar and Young credit several MIT entities, such as the Trust Center for MIT Entrepreneurship, the $100K Entrepreneurship Competition, and the Media Lab, as being helpful in launching their start-up, they laud VMS especially for contributing to their early development. Leading the VMS mentoring team was Jeffrey Bernstein ('84), a computer scientist and serial entrepreneur who had founded PictureTel. "VMS mentors helped Bounce Imaging navigate, for roughly two years, in funding and partnering strategies, recruiting a core team of engineers and establishing its first market—instead of focusing on technical challenges. 'The particulars of the technology are usually not the primary areas of focus in VMS . . . You need to understand the market, and you need good people,'" said Bernstein.[25] Three years later, Aguilar and company were still regularly consulting their VMS mentors for advice. (Young left Bounce in 2014.) Aguilar stresses that another useful resource was start-ups that had previously been mentored by VMS. Over the years, he has called on them for advice on a number of issues, including manufacturing and funding. "It is such a powerful list, because MIT alumni companies are amazingly generous to each other," said

(continued)

Aguilar.[26] VMS's expertise and contributions have been recognized by numerous prizes. Another significant source of support, and perhaps the more influential one, according to Aguilar, was the MIT Angels of Northern California, one of Bounce Imaging's first funders. At this time, the angel investor group is run by Rojon Nag ('91), a serial entrepreneur and the founder of Lexicus (which was sold to Motorola in 1993) and Cellmania (which was sold to Research in Motion in 2010). Nag currently serves on the board of Bounce Imaging.[27]

SANDBOX INNOVATION FUND PROGRAM

While delta v is the capstone extracurricular program at the end of the academic year, available to the best student entrepreneurial projects, the Sandbox Innovation Fund Program (known as "Sandbox" for short) is, according to Dr. Jinane Abounadi ('90), its executive director, the wide end of the funnel to other types of support for entrepreneurship on campus.[28] It operates year-round and provides mentoring, customized training, and seed funding from $1,000 to up to $25,000 for new ideas in order to facilitate access to hands-on entrepreneurship experience and to accelerate more advanced projects.[29] The threshold for receiving initial financial support is low, and students can apply for additional funds as they meet specified milestones, such as conducting primary market research, building a prototype, meeting with potential clients, and demonstrating market potential. Students must attend at least four workshops while participating in the Sandbox and are required to meet regularly with experienced mentors. They are eligible for the program during their whole tenure at MIT and can always reapply.

Abounadi and Dean Ian Waitz explain that the $1,000 initial level is really the Sandbox's way of inviting students to explore and learn, and it is a time when they can use resources and funding to decide if their idea is worth pursuing. Students are also encouraged to learn about the various entrepreneurship frameworks. If an idea doesn't succeed, it is not viewed as failure, but rather as a natural entrepreneurial learning process. The students might pivot, pursue a totally different idea, or perhaps step back from the program to take relevant classes and develop important skills that would enable them to tackle more complex problems with a much better appreciation for the processes that lead to successful technology commercialization. Several students reported that learning about markets and customers helped them become better researchers.

In a three-year period from 2016 to 2019, the Sandbox had funded over 1,000 ideas and awarded about $5 million to about 2,000 aspiring entrepreneurs. It is estimated that after three years the inaugural cohort of about 110 teams had founded and was operating about twenty-five start-up companies.[30] Some of the projects initiated in the Sandbox have progressed to more advanced stages of development. For instance, Kytopen, founded in 2017 by Paulo Garcia and Professor Cullen Buie, was one of the ideas presented to the Sandbox and subsequently became one of the first ventures in which The Engine invested (see chapter 8). It is a genetic engineering firm that accelerates the process of introducing deoxyribonucleic acid (DNA) or other molecules into cells. Multiply Labs, launched in the spring of 2017 by Joe Wilson ('16), Alice Melocchi, Tiffani Kuo ('16), and Fred Parietti ('16), invented a three-dimensional (3D) printing technique to create personalized dietary supplements. In the spring of 2018, Escher Reality, an augmented-reality start-up founded by Ross Finman ('13) and Diana Hu, was acquired by Niantic, an augmented-reality game-developer giant. Other success stories include ReviveMed, cofounded by Leila Pirhaji ('16), as described in chapter 4; FarmWise, cofounded by Sebastien Boyer ('16), an autonomous robotic machinery that improves productivity, crop health, and yields of cultures; and Yellowstone Energy, cofounded by Samuel Shaner ('14) and Matt Ellis ('17), which has developed a lower-cost nuclear fission reactor.[31]

CONTESTS AND PRIZES

Contests take the form of business plan competitions, pitch challenges, and, more recently, hackathons. Most were initiated by students and remain student run. The contests highlighted in this section are some of the most visible and long-running among all those offered at MIT. (For a full list of contests and prizes, see appendix 7.2, "List of Active Contests and Prizes as of 2020.")

$100K ENTREPRENEURSHIP COMPETITION
Launched in 1989 by a small number of MIT students to promote interest in the Entrepreneurs Club (E-Club), which had formed a year earlier (as described in chapter 2), the $100K Entrepreneurship Competition was a pioneer of this model of contest and has been emulated around the world

since then, to the extent that it was labeled the "granddaddy of business plan competitions" by the *San Francisco Chronicle*.[32]

By 2019, the $100K was organized as one competition, divided into three independent contests running throughout the academic year, Pitch, Accelerate, and Launch, with each contest trying to develop specific skills in the candidate entrepreneurs. First, in the Pitch phase, finalists have ninety seconds to pitch their start-up idea—with no slides or other reference materials allowed—to a panel of judges and a large audience. At stake is the chance to win $5,000. Accelerate helps the teams develop their business idea with the support of experienced entrepreneurs and industry professionals, venture capitalists, and attorneys. The Accelerate phase ends with a Demo Day/ Product Development Showcase, wherein teams can introduce their companies to the entrepreneurial community. All teams are eligible for an audience choice award of $10,000 and being fast-tracked to the Launch Finals. The top three Demo Day/Product Development Showcase teams are chosen by the audience.

In Launch, participants prepare their venture for the marketplace by presenting a full-fledged business plan. Semi-finalists receive funding and are assisted by mentorship. The finalists present their business plan onstage to a panel of judges and a live audience of 1,000 people on the MIT campus. The ultimate grand prize winner receives $100,000. The $100K Challenge mobilizes a large number of alumni and of other members of the Boston and Cambridge entrepreneurial ecosystem, who donate their time to help as judges or mentors. The participants in addition benefit from more than $300,000 in nondilutive funding and from media exposure. In 2019, the competition received 310 submissions across Pitch, Accelerate, and Launch. Of those, 40 semifinalists and 8 finalists were selected for Launch.[33]

While not every start-up project presented at the $100K Competition turns into an actual company, the educational experience that the contest offers is beneficial to all participants for their personal development and the nurturing of their teams. The competition is indeed an educational exercise, and the student organizers have to keep this focus. William Sanchez ('05), the CEO of CoolChip and winner of the 2011 Clean Energy Prize (CEP), emphasized this point when he argued that the role of such competitions is as tool-builders that equip individuals with the skills and resources needed to become entrepreneurs, which are difficult to obtain only in a classroom. The competition, says Sanchez, "requires the contestants to articulate their thoughts effectively and concisely. Communicating ideas and inspiring support is a critical skill in multiple business sectors—and is a skill that competitors develop while writing and pitching their plans." He adds, "The role of competitions and the university environment is to provide a structured environment for unstructured pursuits; to provide a safe environment for exploratory endeavors; and to spawn well-equipped entrepreneurs who in turn spur innovative enterprises."[34]

CLIMATETECH & ENERGY PRIZE

The CEP has become the oldest and largest student-run, clean-energy business plan competition in the US.[35] The CEP competition starts in the spring with a two-month mentorship, during which teams are paired with technology, business, and legal mentors, and culminates with a finale where teams compete in four categories—generating energy, improving energy usage, delivering energy, and energy for developing economies—for more than $200,000 in nondilutive funding. Illustrating another common trend in MIT entrepreneurship, CEP grew beyond the MIT campus. It was originally limited to members of the MIT community but later became open to students from any university across the United States. In 2018, it was available to candidates worldwide for the first time.

Recent winning teams from MIT include UPower in 2013, a start-up developing a nuclear generator to be used in places off the power grid instead of diesel generators. A 2013 finalist, SunHub, educates homeowners so that they can make better choices when buying solar-energy systems. The 2014 winner was United Solar, whose integrated chip restores lost power to partially shaded solar panels; a 2016 winner, Heila Technologies, develops a universal control hub that automatically monitors and manages disparate microgrids; and Infinite Cooling was a winner in 2017 for its plan to reduce water consumption at power plants, which are the largest consumers of freshwater in the United States. (Infinite Cooling also won the grand prize of the $100K Entrepreneurship Competition in 2018.)[36]

IDEAS SOCIAL INNOVATION CHALLENGE

The IDEAS Social Innovation Challenge defines itself as "an annual innovation, service, and social entrepreneurship competition."[37] Run by the Priscilla King Gray Public Service Center, IDEAS gives teams of MIT students the opportunity to address quality-of-life issues, generally in the developing world. Finalists are evaluated for their innovation, feasibility, and community impact by a panel of experts. Teams compete in nine categories: water and sanitation, education and training, agriculture and food, health and medical, emergency and disaster relief, infrastructure, energy and environment, mobile devices and communication, and finance and entrepreneurship. During the academic year, student teams receive training, attend workshops, and get feedback and advice on their initial proposals to prepare for their final pitch at the end of the spring semester, during which they compete for up to $15,000 in grants to implement their project during a fifteen-month grant period. IDEAS is just one example of an MIT program focused on social impact, often with international outreach, that aims to educate and prepare students while solving important local and global problems. (For more on how projects resulting from IDEAS have impacted the developing world, see chapter 9.)

Even after the contest, a number of IDEAS projects compete in other entrepreneurship competitions on campus, such as the $100K Entrepreneurship Competition, and take advantage of other resources supporting entrepreneurial projects. For instance, the 2017 IDEAS grand prize winner, Hey, Charlie, started as a project imagined during the 2016 Hacking Medicine hackathon (described in the section entitled "Hackathons," later in this chapter).[38] Hey, Charlie aims to change the social networks and behavior of people struggling with opioid addiction.

WECYCLERS

Wecyclers,[39] a social entrepreneurship venture, is another good illustration of the synergy between the various pieces of the entrepreneurial ecosystem and the breadth of resources available to aspiring student entrepreneurs. During the Development Venture class, Belikiss Adebiyi ('12) and a classmate, Alexandra Fallon ('12), imagined a solution for recycling plastic waste in Nigeria that would also provide valuable goods to its citizens. Their idea hinged on the placement of pubic kiosks where Nigerians would bring recyclables in exchange for points that can be redeemed for food and consumer goods via text messages. The recycled materials would then be turned into pellets that could be sold in recycling facilities in China. With a grant from MIT's Public Service Center (PSC), they tested this concept, but it turned out that after a

---

(continued)

long workday, Nigerians would not go to a remote kiosk to deliver recyclables, even with the incentive of getting a reward. Adebiyi and Fallon revised their model and came up with Wecyclers, a fleet of cargo bikes that collects waste door-to-door and delivers it to processing centers. "Before people just saw plastic as being useless. . . . Now they say, 'This is money,'" said Adebiyi to the *Washington Post* in 2017.[40] With this iteration of the model, they won a prize at the 2012 IDEAS Competition (which is what the IDEAS Global Challenge [later renamed IDEAS Social Innovation Challenge] used to be called).

The same year, Adebiyi and Fallon took part in the inaugural MIT Founders' Skills Accelerator Program (now delta v). However, after founding Wecyclers in 2012, Adebiyi and Fallon realized that their bikes were inadequate. Therefore, D-Lab sent engineering students to build what became modified tricycles. They removed the back wheels from the bikes and attached a wagon with two wheels to each frame. D-Lab students returned to Nigeria several times to fix issues with the bikes.

The involvement of D-Lab is an example of the synergy between student entrepreneurs and the initiatives that support them, which in this particular case included the student entrepreneurs providing real-world challenges and avenues for innovation to D-Lab students. The Wecyclers founders earned a Legatum seed grant, and Adebiyi was selected as a Legatum Fellow. Wecyclers also won a Carroll L. Wilson Award and prizes from the MIT $100K Entrepreneurship Competition as well as from the MIT Sloan Africa Entrepreneurship Competition.

Wecyclers is, however, still facing huge challenges. The supply of the electricity needed to turn plastic bottles into pellets is unreliable in Lagos. When China's demand for recycled plastic suddenly dried up when it declared a new policy against "foreign garbage," it forced WeCycler to find ways to turn the recyclable material into new items such as plastic furniture.[41] What will never go away are the skills that Fallon and Adebiyi learned, and Adebiyi has become a major voice for entrepreneurship in Nigeria today.

E14 FUND

From its earliest days in 1985, the Media Lab has been a hot spot of entrepreneurship.[42] Since 2013, the Media Lab's E14 Fund has supported the entrepreneurial projects of its students, faculty, staff members, and alumni. Among the more recent promising ventures that the fund has supported is ThruWave, founded by Matt Reynolds ('03), which is revolutionizing manufacturing and e-commerce by using human-safe millimeter wave signals to see through packaging material to provide item count and picking accuracy. Wise Systems, founded by Chazz Sims ('13), optimizes deliveries by automatically scheduling and adjusting the routes of fleet of vehicles in real time through machine learning. Its customers, which belong to various industries, typically experience 10–15 percent mileage reductions, better fleet utilization, and a decrease in late deliveries of up to 80 percent. Tulip, founded by Rony Kubat ('01) and Natan Linder ('11), has developed a customizable manufacturing software that increases employee production rather than automating it away by connecting people, machines, and sensors to optimize processes on shop floors. In 2019, it had multiple Fortune 500 clients and was operating in thirteen countries.[43]

HACKATHONS

Hackathons became popular in the mid-2000s—especially among communities of programmers[44]—with student-led events such as HackMIT, which attracted over 1,000 students from MIT and other schools to the campus for a weekend, and MIT Reality Hack, which focused on virtual reality. The hacking concept was first adapted to entrepreneurship at MIT by MIT Hacking Medicine, and soon after by Hacking Arts. The idea behind Hacking Medicine,[45] a student-run initiative founded in 2011 by Elliot Cohen ('13), Allen Cheng ('13), and Priya Garg ('15), with the supervision of Senior Lecturer Zen Chu as faculty director, is "to disrupt the silos that are prevalent in healthcare by applying MIT's hacking ethos to create innovations," according to Garg.[46] Hacking Medicine takes place over the course of a weekend, at the beginning of which participants present problems in health care that they have experienced in their work or as customers. Multistakeholder groups then form based on shared interests. Next, the participants interview people experiencing the specific problem and search for solutions. Mentors, sponsors, and customers test the design and check the assumptions on which the solutions are developed. The groups build prototypes that try to solve the problems, and finally, they compete for endorsement from mentors and judges. "Everything is so multidisciplinary now that you need to know where you run short of expertise and complement your skillsets through collaboration," says Christopher Lee, a scientist at the David H. Koch Institute for Integrative Cancer Research at MIT.[47]

Andrea Ippolito ('12), a codirector of Hacking Medicine, attributes the interest in Hacking Medicine "to its fast pace of innovation, the passion and talent of the people involved, and the relatively low cost of sponsoring a weekend full of MIT students doing what they do best." And she adds, "Where else could you create that many innovative solutions based on pizza money?"[48]

Some of the ventures that have participated in Hacking Medicine include PillPack (prescription adherence), CAKE (end-of-life care), Augmented Infant Resuscitator (improved bag-valve-mask for newborns), Perfect Latch (improved breast pump design), and Podimetrics (diabetic foot ulcers). Smart Scheduling (later known as Arsenal Health), with doctors and clinics scheduling patients and prediction of no-shows, is another example.[49] PillPack, founded by T. J. Parker and Elliot Cohen ('13), is the best-known project that was born at Hacking Medicine. It addresses the problem of poor drug adherence (i.e., the fact that people tend not to take their medications correctly). This problem causes 10 percent of hospitalizations per year, 125,000 deaths per year, and as much as $289 billion in additional medical costs per year. PillPack's solution allows customers to order their medication online. PillPack then mails the medication in presorted plastic wrappers printed with the date and time at which they should be taken instead of sending separate bottles of each medication. This frees the customers from the headache of sorting, scheduling, and refilling their prescription medications. In June 2018, Amazon announced that it was acquiring PillPack.[50]

Hacking Medicine has distributed $500,000 in prizes since 2011. In addition, according to Zen Chu, a cofounder of Hacking Medicine and a senior lecturer at the Sloan School of Management, $200 million has been invested in ventures originating from the Hackathon and his class, Healthcare Ventures.[51] However, the benefit of participating in the contest lies in the mentoring and networking opportunities, such as when the participants have the opportunity to pitch to representatives of hospitals or to firms in the health care sector. Ippolito also stresses the power of these hackathons, not only in the many ventures and innovative solutions that have come out of them to make an impact in health care and medicine, but also in their educational role. They act as a training ground to expose engineers, designers, scientists, and clinicians to the health care innovation arena. For instance, Ippolito applied the knowledge that she gained from Hacking Medicine, as both an organizer and a participant, to launch the Department of Veterans Affairs Innovators Network as a Presidential Innovation Fellow based in the White House Office of Science and Technology Policy and General Services Administration.[52] Hacking Medicine also led her to become a lecturer at

Cornell University, teaching entrepreneurship. Freddy Nguyen, coorganizer in 2020, also stresses the importance of the impact in terms of community and ecosystem building. "We want to be a convener, a nucleation point," says Nguyen.[53]

Hacking Medicine was so successful right from the outset that it expanded into helping health care technology groups and institutions design accelerators and incubators and helping hospitals and pharmaceutical companies host internal hackathons. Similar to other student initiatives related to entrepreneurship, it also expanded globally. By 2020, it had organized approximately 200 hackathons around the world.[54] The organizers also started to focus on improving the percentage of teams that pursue their projects after the hackathon. They are trying to achieve this by providing mentoring to the teams, with the help of partners in the health care community, including executives in charge of innovation in local hospitals, accelerators, and seed funds.

Hacking Arts[55] was founded in 2012 by MIT Sloan students Kathleen Stetson ('14) and Catherine Halaby ('14) to bring together artists, scientists, and engineers, as well as students with an interest in entrepreneurship, to take on challenges in fields such as visual arts, music, performing arts, design, fashion, film/video, gaming, and virtual reality. MIT students were a fertile ground to develop activities at this intersection. Indeed, a little-known fact is that around half of them join MIT with a serious musical practice. In a typical academic year, more than 1,500 students enroll in music courses, and music is among the most popular of the Institute's forty-two minors. In addition to the projects and start-ups that emerged from Hacking Arts, the initiative—along with the $15K Creative Arts Competition[56]—serves to close the gap between science, technology, and the arts.

One example of a social entrepreneurship start-up that emerged from Hacking Arts and the Creative Arts Competition, as well as other structures supporting entrepreneurship on campus, is Roots Studio.[57] The venture, founded by Rebecca Hui ('18), installs computers and scanners in rural villages in developing countries such as in India, which allow local artists to digitize their arts and upload the creations to Roots Studio's cloud. In turn, Hui and her team license the designs to clients around the world, including global fashion companies, while splitting the profits with the artists and their villages. The goal is to provide additional income to those artists by connecting them to clients from around the world, and to keep secular artistic tradition alive. It also slows the rural exodus to overcrowded large cities and contributes to keeping the social fabric of remote villages.

In spite of the monetary prizes and the inevitable focus on venture projects that succeed commercially, the spirit of these contests, business plan competitions, and hackathons is education. This was well summarized by Maddie Thoms ('17), copresident of the MIT Sloan Healthcare Club, which organized the Sloan Healthcare Innovation Prize. In 2016, she explained that the aim of these competitions is to help all the entrepreneurs further refine their ventures: "It's not just about one or two teams walking away with a good prize. We're hoping to push a bunch of teams forward in their endeavors."[58]

The Trust Center's Bill Aulet reinforced this point of view by insisting that the process of starting a commercial venture and building a team is, in some ways, more valuable than winning a competition. "As you go through this, you're going to face many challenges," he said. "If you lose, you went through a great process. How's your team taking this? What have you learned? If you choose to go forward, that will be infinitely more valuable than $25,000. In a real sense, the pursuit of the prize is the incentive to accelerate their educational process . . . and it works whether they get the prize or not."[59]

Che-Chih Tsao ('95) recalls being a finalist in the 1991 $10K Business Plan Competition with Zhen Hong Zhou ('91), and the subsequent years growing ACT Research Corporation, the start-up that commercialized a volumetric 3D display that was the idea at the heart of the pitch of their business plan: "I think most of us were, and many still are, driven by dreams of achieving something different and significant in technology or in business. You sense this urge and spirit most strongly from people and their activities at MIT. And this sense changed us, made our lives more plentiful, and continues to shape our works."[60] At the time of this writing, Tsao was serving as an assistant professor of engineering at the National Tsing Hua University in Taiwan.

NETWORKING AND COMMUNITY- AND CAREER-BUILDING INITIATIVES

Networking and community- and career-building initiatives are another important form of support for entrepreneurship at MIT. Student clubs play a key role in all of these areas. (For a full list of these initiatives, see appendix 7.3, "List of Active Networking, Community- and Career-Building Resources as of 2020.")

MIT VENTURE CAPITAL AND PRIVATE EQUITY CLUB

The MIT Venture Capital and Private Equity Club (VCPE) is one of the early student clubs related to entrepreneurship.[61] The VCPE was founded in 1995 by Sloan students just as the internet era was spreading, and it quickly became one of the largest clubs at Sloan. The mission of the VCPE is to educate its members about the venture capital and private equity industries, to help them prepare for a career or an internship in those industries, and build connections with professionals. The main vehicle to achieve these goals is the organization of conferences that facilitate links between the venture capital and private equity industries and students. The VCPE's signature event is the annual MIT Sloan Investment Conference. The venture capital conference includes an Entrepreneur Showcase, where early-stage companies have the opportunity to show their products to the audience. Besides these conferences, the club also hosts a speaker series, training courses, networking events, case competitions, and recruiting events. In his thesis, Joost Bonsen ('90) recalls that over the years, the VCPE club has played a useful role in establishing cross-campus links among entities dealing with entrepreneurship. Its members reached out to Professor Edward Roberts and the Deshpande Center for Technological Innovation with the idea for the I-Teams course and worked with the Venture Mentoring Service (VMS) and the Science and Engineering Business Club (SEBC) to organize VentureShips. According to Bonsen, the club has also played incubator to the MIT Energy Conference.[62]

STARTIAP

The student-founded and -run StartIAP defines its mission as connecting MIT engineering undergraduates and alumni to resources related to entrepreneurship on and off campus.[63] It helps undergraduate engineering students start companies and build connections to the Boston entrepreneurial ecosystem. It has been a very dynamic club, sponsoring numerous events, including Startup Bootcamp at the beginning of the academic year. It is a one-day event during which experienced entrepreneurs and venture capitalists talk about how to start a company. The objective is to deliver the message that "if they can do it, so can you."[64] Another event is StartIAP, a miniaccelerator program founded in 2012 that takes place during MIT's four-week break in January, called Independent Activities Period (IAP). Start-IAP aims to take the ideas of its student participants from concept to company and to get teams of students used to working at "entrepreneur speed." StartIAP was renamed MIT Fuse in 2018, and is fully managed by the Trust Center. StartIAP expanded beyond campus in 2017 with InnovateEDU, a semester-long venture competition across local universities that includes Boston College, Boston University, Emerson College, Northeastern University, and MIT.[65]

MIT SLOAN ENTREPRENEURSHIP CLUB

The student-run MIT Sloan Entrepreneurship Club aims at triggering interest in entrepreneurship in the Sloan community, organizing networking events, offering access to inspiring successful entrepreneurs, innovating companies through a speaker series, and providing access to internship and career opportunities. Since 1999, the MIT Sloan Entrepreneurship Club has provided internships with companies such as TripAdvisor, Locu, SCVNGR, OnChip Power, Curisma, MOBEE, Dplay, Forecast, Revolution Foods, ThriveHive, Ginger.io, KyaZoonga, and InsightSquared. The club also organizes treks to entrepreneurial clusters such as Silicon Valley, New York, and Boulder, Colorado.

OUTREACH AND ENTREPRENEURIAL ECOSYSTEM DEVELOPMENT

Following interest from around the world in the $100K Entrepreneurship Competition, the student-led organizers of the $100K Competition initiated the MIT Global Startup Workshop (GSW) in 1997. The first conference of business plan competitions, the objective of the GSW was to share best practices in starting and operating similar competitions to the $100K contest worldwide.[66]

Another early example of an outreach and entrepreneurial ecosystem building project is the student-founded Global Startup Lab (GSL),[67] which was launched in 2000 by three MIT undergraduates from Africa to combat the gap between the knowledge in information technology (IT) in the developing world and in the US.

For selected students who follow MIT's online course Entrepreneurship 101: Who Is Your Customer?[68] MIT Bootcamp offers the opportunity to participate in an intensive, one-week on-campus training for participants who excelled in the MITx online course. It offers them the opportunity to turn what they learned in the class into an entrepreneurial project.[69] It is the brainchild of Erdin Beshimov ('11), an MIT lecturer who also cocreated online courses in entrepreneurship that have been attended by hundreds of thousands of people.

Although such outreach efforts aim at spreading entrepreneurial skills around the world and developing entrepreneurial ecosystems, the learning goes both ways. GSL also has great educational impact on MIT students, who get the opportunity to learn by teaching. MIT students also gain additional knowledge and perspective from local participants and improve their understanding of how to operate in developing countries, which often have sparse access to electricity and the internet. The MIT Entrepreneurship and Maker Skills Integrator (MEMSI),[70] a two-week hardware start-up boot camp for students of MIT and of the University of Hong Kong, is another example of reciprocal learning experience. Nathan Monroe ('13), an MIT graduate student in electrical engineering who took part in the inaugural edition of MEMSI, commented on this aspect when he said, "Exposure to the size and scale of manufacturing in the [Shenzhen and the Pearl River Delta] region is invaluable. Too many hardware system startups fail because it is massively difficult to go from a single prototype to hundreds of thousands. You don't learn that in school. You learn it on the ground."[71]

ACADEMIC SUPPORT: COURSES AND PROGRAMS

By 2019, MIT offered more than sixty courses on or related to entrepreneurship in its five schools. It had thirty-five affiliated faculty members and thirty-five lecturers.[72] The Sloan School offers an MBA track in entrepreneurship and innovation targeted at students who have a strong commitment to entrepreneurship. Sloan and the School of Engineering jointly offer an undergraduate minor in entrepreneurship.[73] The School of Engineering offers a number of courses specifically targeting students of engineering. The Media Lab has its own entrepreneurship program,[74] and the School of Architecture and Urban Planning offers MITdesignX,[75] a specialized program to accelerate entrepreneurial projects that address urgent challenges in cities by making them more sustainable, intelligent, and responsive to their inhabitants. Chapter 10 will delve into more details about the teaching of entrepreneurship.

CONCLUSION

The broad set of extracurricular and academic activities promoting entrepreneurship offers a fairly exhaustive and integrated menu of resources, in spite of the fact that it was not built as part of a grand plan, but rather organically and with little coordination—until recently, in a very typical MIT way. The result is an ecosystem that can cater to a range of interests in entrepreneurship, thanks to its focus on the learning experience rather than on the number of start-ups churned out, which has been stressed several times in this discussion. It caters to those who just want an introduction to the topic and to those who are serious about launching a company. It offers value to those who want to acquire entrepreneurial skills to use them in corporate, nonprofit, or other organizational settings, and to those who want to promote entrepreneurship in accelerators and other supportive structures or to exercise their sills in policymaking. This large set of resources also allow each student team to find its ideal pathway because each one pursues a particular challenge and builds a unique solution that has never been explored before.

Whatever the outcome of their experiences building their entrepreneurial skills at MIT, students keep the learning experiences that become useful to them in a variety of settings. This is illustrated by the case of Gridform's founding team, which won an IDEAS Global Challenge (later renamed IDEAS Social Innovation Challenge) prize in 2014 with a project developing software to optimize microgrid installations in rural India. One of the cofounders, Brian Spatocco ('15), says, "We are no longer together, but the impact of IDEAS actually continues on in our team. One team member became a professor of social good at Carnegie Mellon University, while another stayed in India to build a new startup." Spatocco now works at an agriculture start-up making fertilizer affordable throughout the world.[76]

Figure 7.2, an illustration from the Trust Center for MIT Entrepreneurship, represents the ecosystem of support for entrepreneurship available to students, although of course it does not include the entire supportive structure. It stresses the cumulative complementarity of these structures and the fact that the entrepreneurial projects of students who go through the whole process should be ready to hit the market at the end.

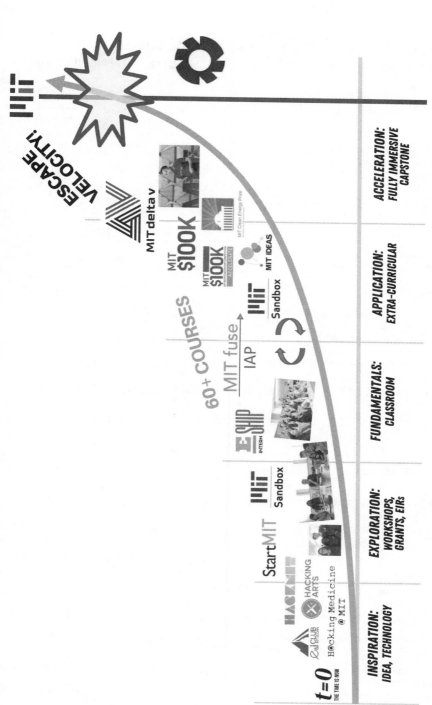

FIGURE 7.2

The MIT entrepreneurial ecosystem for student entrepreneurship.

Source: Trust Center for MIT Entrepreneurship.

APPENDIX 7.1. LIST OF ACTIVE EXTRACURRICULAR SUPPORT STRUCTURES DESIGNED TO BUILD EXTRACURRICULAR ENTREPRENEURIAL SKILLS AS OF 2020

Name	Year Started
Venture Mentoring Service (VMS)	2000
D-Lab	2001
Legatum Center Fellowship	2007
MIT Fuse (formerly StartIAP)	2011
delta v	2012
StartMIT	2014
Entrepreneurship Internship	2016
Sandbox Innovation Fund Program	2016

APPENDIX 7.2. LIST OF ACTIVE CONTESTS AND PRIZES AS OF 2020

Name	Year Started
MIT $100K Entrepreneur-ship Competition	1990
Goldberg Grand Prize of the $50K Entrepreneurship Competition	1996
Global Startup Workshop (GSW)	1998
MIT IDEAS Social Innova-tion Challenge	2001
Patrick J. McGovern Entre-preneurship Award	2001
Adolf Monosson Prize for Entrepreneurship	2005
MIT ClimateTech & Energy Prize (CEP)	2006

(continued)

Name	Year Started
Building Global Innovators	2010
Hacking Medicine	2011
MIT-CHIEF Business Plan Contest	2011
Hacking Arts	2012
$15K Creative Arts Competition	2013
Eddie Awards	2014
Fintech Conference's Startup Competition	2015
InnovateEDU	2016
Innovation@ONE	2016
MIT Inclusive Innovation Challenge (IIC)*	2016
Sloan Healthcare Innovation Prize	2016
MIT Water Innovation Prize	2019
RaboBank—MIT Food and Agribusiness Innovation Prize	2019

* Discontinued

APPENDIX 7.3. LIST OF ACTIVE NETWORKING, COMMUNITY-, AND CAREER-BUILDING RESOURCES AS OF 2020

Name	Year Started
MIT Cambridge Enterprise Forum	1978
Nationwide MIT Enterprise Forum	1981
MIT Entrepreneruship Club (E-Club)	1988
Global MIT Enterprise Forum	1991
MIT Venture Capital and Private Equity Club	1995

(continued)

Name	Year Started
Sloan Entrepreneurs for International Development	2001
Sloan Entrepreneurship Club	2002
Innovation Week	2003
Energy Club	2006
Entrepreneurs Walk of Fame	2011
MIT-CHIEF Conference	2011
StartLabs	2011
t=0	2011
Discover Entrepreneurship and Leadership (DEAL)	2012
Startup Exchange (STEX)	2014
Innovation Mentors	2018

8 ENTREPRENEURSHIP FOR TECHNOLOGY TRANSFER

Most entrepreneurs start with a problem that they hope to solve, but some paths to entrepreneurship at MIT start with a research breakthrough that does not have an immediate use. Technology transfer "is the movement of knowledge and discoveries to the general public."[1] In universities, it can take various forms, including graduating students who go to work in industry, consulting, publishing, event production, and other contexts, and via start-ups that license the intellectual property of a university to commercialize it (often referred to as "spin-offs" or "spin-outs"). University spin-offs are atypical start-up companies. In addition to their reliance on cutting-edge science and engineering, they are often founded at a very early stage of that technology. "Unlike the typical seed-stage startup company, the typical university spin-off begins with technology that has not yet been reduced to practice, has no business plan, no management, and a need for capital to create the company that would need to bring these things together," wrote Scott Shane in his book *Academic Entrepreneurship*. Shane also quotes Lita Nelsen ('64), the director of the MIT Technology Licensing Office (TLO) from 1993 to 2016, who distinguished these spin-offs from early-stage companies by calling them "minus two-stage" companies, in order to stress how early-stage they are. The market for the products from these spin-offs is often not obvious. Whereas ordinary start-ups usually identify a need and develop a solution to satisfy it, university spin-off ventures have created a solution and/or a technology, but then need to look for a problem to solve for which there is a profitable market (i.e., a market opportunity). As a business angel once said of such spin-offs: "We looked at a lot of MIT technologies . . . they were more of a solution looking for a problem. Somebody had a solution, but I wasn't clear there was a real need for that."[2]

Often the initial performance of the new technology is either lower than that of existing solutions or not high enough to justify the switching cost for potential clients.[3] As a result, established companies often don't see the potential of new academic technologies.[4] Moreover, in the few cases when the technology's advantage is obvious or clearly promising, established companies are often concerned lest they cannibalize market share from their existing technology—a technology in which they have invested time and money and around which they have built whole supply chains and other infrastructure.

It is estimated that an investment equal to 10 to 100 times the cost of the academic research is needed to bring an academic technology to market.[5] This process also requires patience and perseverance. It can take at least two to three years for a patent to get issued once it is filed. When a company finally licenses a technology, it might take an additional five to ten years before it generates revenue.[6] All in all, the uncertain performance of developing academic inventions, the associated costs, and the time lag between invention and revenue generation make investing in embryonic academic inventions extremely unattractive.

This does not mean that large firms never license patents from universities, but more often, inventors are the only ones to understand and to believe in the commercial potential of their technology. They are, therefore, frequently the only candidates interested in founding (and sometimes funding) a company to commercialize their technology. This process involves obtaining a license for the patent or patents based on their invention from their university, since, following the Bayh-Dole Act of 1980, the university owns the intellectual property of government-funded research. The edge that inventors have is the extensive and unique knowledge that they have accumulated through their research efforts and exposure to industry over the years.[7]

This chapter will explore the various entities at MIT that assist faculty members and researchers in removing the risk behind the process of commercializing academic research by securing MIT's intellectual property, helping them devise a go-to-market strategy, incorporating insights from industry and about customer needs, and structuring deals that incentivize investors to invest in high-risk endeavors. While these entities, such as the TLO, are not unique to MIT, their being embedded in the MIT culture and their focus on impact rather than on monetizing intellectual property have made MIT one of the most prolific universities in spinning off ventures based on academic research.

AMBERWAVE

Throughout his career at AT&T's Bell Labs, his academic life as a professor of materials science and engineering, and his involvement in several start-ups, AmberWave Systems founder Eugene "Gene" Fitzgerald ('85) was focused on building new, high-performance semiconductors using strained silicon, which would revolutionize the performance of silicon-integrated circuits. It is an example of the kind of "tough tech" that takes significant time and resources to go from lab to market. In 1996, Fitzgerald became convinced that his innovation needed to move beyond research. At that time, support for technology transfer through entrepreneurship was scant compared to today, and it was limited to the assistance provided by the TLO. As is typical of ventures trying to commercialize academic research, however, there was still a gap to bridge to make the technology marketable. That led Fitzgerald to found AmberWave Systems to produce prototypes for market applications. The challenge was more than just a matter of building a better mousetrap. Fitzgerald and his team had to learn to adapt the technology for specific applications and customer needs. AmberWave eventually secured its first contracts with Motorola and the Small Business Innovation Research (SBIR) program of the National Aeronautics and Space Administration (NASA). Fitzgerald stressed that he and his colleagues learned a lot during this period of commercial development from their interactions with clients and with the industry's supply chain. Being armed with industry-specific, practical knowledge allowed AmberWave to innovate further and to identify new applications for strained silicon.

However, external or market-related events often interfere with such endeavors. In 1999, the company faced a crisis when Motorola missed its adaptation from analog to digital technology and had to cancel its contract with AmberWave. This unfortunate development led the company to turn to venture capitalists for several rounds of funding. According to Fitzgerald, however, tensions soon developed between AmberWave and the venture capitalists who wanted to make a fast return and pressed AmberWave to shift its efforts toward capturing the most promising short-term applications. AmberWave went public successfully in 2001 in an initial public offering (IPO).

In 2003, another stumbling block appeared. Intel made it known that it was pursuing a parallel innovation track using compressive strained silicon.

(continued)

From 2002 to 2007, AmberWave and Intel litigated over whose intellectual property it was, but they finally settled, and Intel licensed AmberWave's technology. Prior to the settlement, however, Fitzgerald resigned his position at AmberWave in 2003 because of disagreements with his investors about the direction of the company. He subsequently launched several other start-ups focusing on the same technology of strained silicon, including one involved in solar cells, an opportunity that AmberWave did not want to pursue.

In his book about innovation and commercialization, *Inside Real Innovation*,[8] Fitzgerald stressed that breakthrough innovations do not just require a long-term vision and significant resources—in fact, they will not be achieved by one individual and one organization, but rather by several in succession and sometimes in partnerships over many years, as his own career illustrates.

Notwithstanding scientific and technological challenges, the path of such ventures is fraught with challenges, from the business decisions made by its executives, to the unpredictable evolution of the markets over long periods, to finding the proper financial and strategic partners. As the journey of Amber-Wave illustrates, there are many reasons why such technologies as the one that AmberWave was dealing with are tagged as "tough tech." Today, such entrepreneurial projects benefit from the support of multiple resources, most of which did not exist at the time that AmberWave was launched, including the Deshpande Center for Technological Innovation and The Engine, dedicated specifically to such tough tech start-up projects that require longer development time and more patient capital than other start-ups.

TECHNOLOGY LICENSING OFFICE

The TLO[9] defines its mission as "moving innovations and discoveries from the lab to the marketplace for the benefit of the public and to amplify MIT's global impact."[10] It achieves this by conducting many activities, such as receiving inventions; assessing with inventors whether the inventions have the potential of being commercialized; protecting the inventions by filing patents; finding licensees—large firms as well as start-ups; and negotiating and managing the licenses. If the spin-off ventures create revenue, the TLO receives royalties for the license and distributes that revenue back to inventors, academic departments, labs, and centers across MIT, as well as to coowners of the patent (such as other academic institutions or companies).[11]

As mentioned in chapter 2, MIT's technology licensing follows the mandate of the Bayh-Dole Act, which gave universities ownership of patents of inventions developed with federal funds. Since 1980, MIT has owned inventions made by its employees and its students that were made in the context of sponsored research or while using significant financial resources or facilities from MIT. At MIT, technology transfer and all related activities are administered by the TLO, which is overseen by the Office of the Provost.

Based on the averages for patents and licenses issued, licensing income generated, and start-ups created between 2012 and 2015, MIT ranked as the eighth-best university for technology transfer in the United States, according to the 2017 Milken Institute report *Concept to Commercialization: The Best Universities for Technology Transfer.*[12] That same year, MIT also came in second in Reuter's annual ranking of the world's most innovative universities for the third straight year.[13]

The TLO stated that as of fiscal year 2018 it had received approximately 800 invention disclosures each year, resulting from $1.7 billion in research expenditures that same year (for both the MIT campus and Lincoln Lab).[14] An invention disclosure is filed by researchers when they believe that their work could have an impact on the world through commercialization. When a patent is filed, it generally takes two to three years for it to be issued. In 2018, the US Patent and Trademark Office issued 425 new US patents with MIT as assignee, and an additional 331 patents were issued from all over the world. The TLO manages a growing portfolio of over 10,000 issued and pending US and foreign patents. In 2018, MIT received $45.9 million from over 500 revenue-generating licenses.[15] MIT has spun off an average of 22 companies per year since 2001—including 32 in 2018 (see figure 8.1).[16] These are start-ups to which MIT has licensed patents. There are many more ventures involving MIT faculty and students that are created each year without MIT licensing. It is difficult to pinpoint an exact number, but the estimate is approximately 100 new firms per year created by students and more than 1,000 firms per year created by alumni worldwide.[17] The TLO has experienced a 40 percent increase in technology disclosures received over the last ten years (2009–2019).

In an effort to build on these impressive records, the TLO has embarked on significant structural and programmatic improvements since 2017, under the new leadership of its director Lesley Millar-Nicholson—including a streamlining of the start-up licensing process.

Among many other things, the TLO's formal role in licensing technology to start-ups consists of working with entrepreneurs (potential licensees)

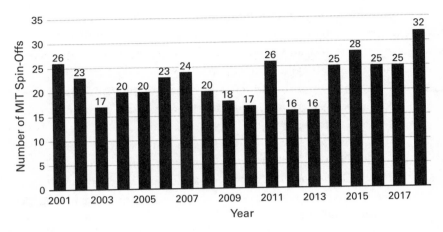

FIGURE 8.1
Number of MIT spin-offs started by fiscal year 2009–2018.
Source: MIT TLO, *An MIT Inventor's Guide to Startups for Faculty and Students* (Cambridge, MA: MIT, 2010), http://web.mit.edu/tlo/documents/MIT-TLO-startup-guide.pdf (accessed November 3, 2019).

to understand the business model for the start-up, strategically filing patents, and negotiating and subsequently managing the license agreements with the licensee companies. The financial terms of a license agreement with a start-up specifies annual fees, royalties, repayment of patent costs, a small minority equity stake in the venture, and, depending on the technology and industry applications, perhaps milestone payments (such as in therapeutics). University licensing agreements typically have low cash requirements during the first few years of a company's existence in order for it to maximize its chances of survival and growth. The agreement recognizes the fact that start-ups have limited financial resources and will take years to develop products and services that will generate positive revenue returns. The nonfinancial terms of a licensing agreement include the degree of exclusivity of the license, which could be nonexclusive, exclusive, or limited to a field of use. When it is exclusive, the technology will not be licensed to another party. When a license is field-of-use limited, for instance, one company could develop products limited to human therapeutic use while another could develop products for animal or other nonhuman uses. A critical part of the license agreement to ensure that progress is made on developing products and services consists of the milestones that the companies will need to achieve, such as raising minimum amounts of capital and making progress in product development.

It is important to the TLO to make sure that an invention is actually being commercialized for public benefit and that it will provide a reasonable financial consideration to MIT. If a licensee does not meet prescribed milestones, the license will revert to MIT. (MIT's nightmare would be to license a cure for cancer, only to have it sit on the licensee's shelves, undeveloped, with the cure never reaching its potential to help the world.) To the best of its ability, MIT wants to ensure that everything it licenses is developed to its full potential, not just commercially but for the betterment of society. Through the Bayh-Dole Act requirements, universities also have obligations to report annually on the utilization of intellectual property for which it has elected to retain title.

The TLO also plays a more informal role at MIT, a role that is much broader than patenting and licensing. The office's staff members meet with inventors, students, and faculty alike in order to educate them on patenting and licensing, taking time to understand their ideas for commercializing an invention; provide insights into the licensing process; and guide them through it as necessary. They also provide introductions to consultants who can help inventors devise an appropriate business strategy and find sources of capital, such as private angel investors and venture capitalists.

However, the TLO does not incubate the ventures, nor does it invest in them with funding, though as part of a start-up license, MIT may take a small equity stake. Similarly, TLO staff, acting on behalf of MIT, do not get involved in a management role and are not on any company's board. This practice aims at maintaining a separation between the company and the Institute and allows it to concentrate on its mission of basic discovery research, dissemination of knowledge, and education. The strong support of MIT's senior leadership and its understanding of technology transfer are key to the effectiveness of the TLO. Staff members who are "bilingual" (i.e., having experience in both science and industry) are also critical.

MIT is committed to avoid conflicts of interest in the process of spinning off start-ups and has developed many relevant policies. For example, policy spells out that the first responsibility of professors is the education of their students.

Policies do not allow faculty members to use students for research and development (R&D) related to a start-up in which that professor has equity, nor may students be employed by such a start-up.[18] A start-up in which a professor has an interest is not allowed to fund research in that professor's lab. Similarly, a professor is not allowed to conduct federally funded research in collaboration with such a start-up, with the exception of SBIR and Small Business Technology Transfer (STTR) funding. A start-up venture may not be located in a lab. Employees of a professor's start-up may not be involved in the research activities of the professor's lab. Research in the lab may not be influenced by a professor's other professional activities. A faculty member's full-time employment at MIT prohibits significant managerial responsibilities in a start-up.

Many universities expect their technology transfer activities to be profitable and bring in revenue.[19] Although MIT is one of the most successful and experienced universities in terms of technology transfer, its experience shows that this kind of financial gain is a misleading expectation. "Any university that counts on its tech transfer to make a significant change in its finances is statistically going to be in trouble," said Nelsen.[20] To that end, her motto during her tenure as head of the TLO was, "Impact, not income."

The TLO does not work in a vacuum; it is instead a piece of a wider system. When asked what the success factors of MIT's technology transfer have been, Nelsen cited the high quality of research and the top-notch abilities of faculty and students sustaining that research. She also cited MIT's desire to have an impact on the real world and the university's long-established tradition of collaborating with industry. MIT's willingness to take measured risks is also key. "Failure is a learning experience, not a black mark," insisted Nelsen.[21] MIT's deep experience with spinning off ventures from MIT's labs built over decades is another factor in success. Nelsen also refers to the local entrepreneurial infrastructure, including private venture investors (i.e., business angels), venture capital firms, lawyers, and other specialized service providers. Role models are also key. Students and faculty at MIT frequently encounter people who have started companies whose experience can inspire. That is, over time, the entrepreneurial ecosystem on campus has made a significant contribution by educating members of the community about entrepreneurship. MIT's model of the TLO is one of an organization with decades of experience operating in a vibrant entrepreneurial ecosystem.

Spinning off a venture from an academic lab is a multistage process, as illustrated by the six steps below. At the start of the process is, of course, academic research, MIT's primary mission alongside teaching. Researchers are encouraged by the TLO to disclose inventions as soon as possible after discovery. From these disclosures, the TLO assesses the disclosure to ascertain if it may be protectable (it may be patentable or copyright material). Not all inventions are pursued: some may be intellectual property already in existence, or there may not be viable markets for the discovery. If intellectual property protection is secured, the TLO will work with the faculty member and others to market the technology and try to license it. Because of the uncertain value of the emerging technologies, only some catch the interest of industry or may be pursued through start-up companies. US universities in general license only half of their patents.[22] To date, MIT has licensed 42 percent of its issued US patents and 85 percent of its issued foreign patents. The winnowing process that the research projects go through as the TLO evaluates their commercial potential means that the amount of research required to generate a spin-off is considerable. In a document titled *MIT Inventor's Guide to Startups for Faculty and Students*, the TLO summarizes the steps leading to a spin-off as follows:[23]

1. *Talk to the TLO.* We encourage you to contact the TLO early in the process to discuss your invention, how to protect the intellectual property, and your thoughts about a start-up company.

2. *Protect intellectual property.* In a start-up, a major source of value, and thus a major tool for attracting investment, is intellectual property (usually one or more patents or substantial software code). Engage with the patent attorney contracted by the TLO to get a patent application filed on your invention before you make any public disclosure or communication of it, because early disclosure may limit your ability to get a patent, particularly outside the US.

3. *Seek input and network.* MIT provides a wealth of resources for inventors looking for help starting a company. The MIT Entrepreneurial Ecosystem can shepherd MIT inventors through all the facets of the start-up process—from writing a business plan, to meeting like-minded entrepreneurs and investors, to attracting board members, to securing funding to demonstrate an invention's commercial viability.

4. *Plan the business.* A formal business plan may or may not be part of this phase, but you'll need to develop an understanding of market potential, competition, funding needs, and how you plan to develop the product and attain the revenues to sustain and grow the company.

5. *Negotiate the license or option agreement.* The TLO will negotiate with a representative of the company to grant a license to the start-up. In some cases, a short-term option agreement may precede a license so that your company can demonstrate to potential funders that it has secured the right to negotiate for a license to the technology.

6. *Pursue funding.* Commercializing technology is typically a capital-intensive process. You will need to present your opportunity to people with the funds to help you make it happen: venture capitalists, angel investors, and perhaps in the initial stages, friends and family. Participation in the MIT Entrepreneurial Ecosystem is one way to start the personal introduction process that can help you get the attention of angel and venture capital investors.

Besides the companies described in the boxes in this chapter, the TLO has licensed patents to multiple other start-ups with strong technology components. One of these was Bluefin Robotics, founded in 1997 by engineers from the MIT Autonomous Underwater Vehicle Lab. Over the years, the company has designed numerous models of autonomous underwater vehicles (AUVs) for civilian and military use. One was the Bluefin 21 AUV, which participated in the search for Malaysian Airlines flight MH370, which disappeared in 2014. Siluria, founded in 2007, grew out of the research of Professor Angela Belcher. The company uses methane, a widely available hydrocarbon, to make ethylene and gasoline rather than petroleum. Its product can reduce oil imports and reduce environmental emissions.[24] GVD Corporation is a spin-off based on Professor Karen Gleason's research; it was founded in 2001 by her and her doctoral student Hilton Price Lewis ('98).[25] It has developed a new approach to making ultrathin polymer coatings, with potential applications in the automotive industry, aerospace, gas and oil exploration, and electronic-circuitry protection. In 2009, GVD's first commercial application in tire manufacturing resulted in less waste, higher-quality tires, and a faster production process.

DESHPANDE CENTER FOR TECHNOLOGICAL INNOVATION

The Deshpande Center for Technological Innovation, part of the School of Engineering, aims to help emerging technologies that have the potential for becoming the basis of a company bridge the gap between science in the lab and its applications in the marketplace—a place known colloquially as the valley of death.[26] The Deshpande Center's motto is "From idea to impact." The center helps remove the risk from innovation projects that are initiated in the lab—both at a technical and market level—to the point where they present a level of uncertainty that is manageable for venture investors and corporations.

The challenge of bridging the gap of the valley of death has become more acute over the years, as corporations have increasingly focused on short-term earnings and seed-stage investors such as business angels and venture capital firms have tended to invest in larger and later-stage start-ups.[27] The Deshpande Center does this by selecting the best research projects with the most commercial potential; providing "proof of concept" funding in the form of grants; seeking advice from mentors from industry and venture capital; and providing networking opportunities in a process called "select–direct–connect" by Leon Sandler, the director of the Deshpande Center.[28]

Selection is a key part of the process at the center and is conducted by about thirty people, including two faculty members and individuals from industry and the venture capital world. In a typical year, approximately thirty-five projects are submitted to the Deshpande Center, from which about twelve will receive support. The jury must first be convinced that a candidate is passionate enough to turn the research into a product. Grants are available to MIT's investigators who are conducting research with a potential significant impact or offering solutions to real problems.

The earliest-stage projects will benefit from an Ignition Grant—worth approximately $50,000—to support the pursuit of experiments in order to confirm initial results, develop a proof of concept, or a prototype. "We do everything from medical devices to materials, electronics, software—anything anyone can come up with, as long as it shows signs of being commercially viable. It doesn't have to be proven, but we have to see potential," said Sandler in 2010.[29] If researchers reach their milestones, they then are invited to apply for an Innovation Grant of up to an additional $250,000 dedicated to more advanced projects that have grown beyond earlier stages of development and are closer to commercialization. Researchers should have achieved proof of concept, identified an R&D path, and planned an intellectual property strategy. The objective is ultimately to attract investment funding to start a company that will commercialize a new product or to sell a license to an existing firm.

Money is only one part of the Deshpande Center's formula. Advice on the path toward commercialization is another key feature. Soon after the grant selection process, a multidisciplinary committee—about fifty advisors from both inside and outside of MIT, called Catalysts—provides advice to the grantees. These Catalysts are vetted volunteers from industry and the venture capital world who also have strong technical knowledge and deep domain expertise. They help scientists better understand market needs and commercial opportunities and devise a go-to-market strategy. Their role is also key to the search for funding when the projects are translated into ventures and provide relevant industry introductions. They help researchers navigate the business world, which they generally are unfamiliar with. According to the director of the Deshpande Center, Catalysts are a big part of the "secret sauce" of the value added by the Deshpande Center. They are bound by the center's conflict of interest guidelines and agree to keep all discussions with grantees confidential.

Connections to the industry and venture capital worlds are complemented by an annual Ideastream Symposium, whose objective is to connect MIT researchers to the entrepreneurial community. They have the opportunity at this event to present their work to industry representatives, venture capitalists, and members of the entrepreneurial community in general.

The Deshpande Center is well integrated into the MIT campus's entrepreneurial ecosystem. For instance, the TLO takes part in the grant selection process and collaborates closely with the Deshpande Center and its grantees regarding the disclosure of information about the inventions, filing patents, licensing, and issues related to protection of intellectual property rights in general.

The New York Times commented in 2010 that the Deshpande Center was at the vanguard of a movement underway in a number of universities that were launching similar proof of concept entities. In 2010, Barack Obama's administration proposed to allocate $12 million among several universities to further test these proof-of-concept centers.[30]

AMBRI

Around 2006, the committee members planning the MIT Energy Initiative asked Professor of Material Chemistry Donald Sadoway to take on the challenge of grid-scale energy storage.[31] For a long time, the world has had batteries that can store small amounts of power, such as to power laptops or even automobiles, but it has been a challenge for generations to build batteries on a large scale ("grid level," in professional jargon). Such batteries are now critical to the adoption of clean wind and solar energy. "This is not in the would-be-nice category; this is in the must-have category. You have to be able to draw electricity from the sun even when the sun doesn't shine. And if you can't do that, then solar power is not the answer." says Sadoway.[32]

After months of research, Sadoway and graduate student David Bradwell ('06) received an Ignition Grant from the Deshpande Center, which gives researchers the financial support to pursue experiments and develop a proof of concept. With the first goal successfully achieved, the duo then moved to the next step in the Desphande model, earning an Innovation Grant. Those early funding sources allowed Bradwell to create a working prototype. "Without that initial funding, we all would have moved on to other things," says Bradwell.[33] As is aimed for with the Deshpande Center model, this early success attracted additional funding from Lightspeed Venture Partners, the Chesonis Family Foundation, and the Massachusetts Clean Energy Center. It was followed by more financing by the Department of Energy, the French company Total SA, and Bill Gates.

The research of Sadoway and his team led to the founding of Ambri in 2010 by Sadoway and Bradwell. The venture aims to disrupt the current electricity grid storage solutions with liquid batteries that are big, scalable, and cheap. In the fall of 2013, the company opened a prototype cell manufacturing facility in Marlborough, Massachusetts, with plans to build initial commercialization scale plants in 2014. Unfortunately, the company ran into significant technological issues in 2015 when their battery seals proved unable to handle the heat requirements of the technology. In 2016, Ambri rolled out a redesign of their seals, which now could meet the high temperature needs. In 2018, Ambri revealed a new design that would be even more durable and cheaper than their previous design.

The company's biggest competitor had been natural gas firms, but since 2010, lithium ion batteries have taken over as its biggest challenger, as the prices of such batteries have declined. An ongoing challenge for Ambri is its ability to get to commercial scale quickly enough to compete effectively with lithium ion grid solutions like Tesla. Ambri was supposed to work with the state of Hawaii, a pioneer in clean energy efforts, for one of their first implementations. That plan did not come to fruition, as in 2017 Tesla

(continued)

implemented its grid solution in Kauai with lithium ion batteries. However, in spite of those difficulties, Ambri has proved its resilience in surviving when others in the industry have gone bankrupt. The company's evolution showcases the difficulties of taking promising research and trying to launch it as a full-scale commercial solution with limited capital and rapidly evolving market forces.

In 2020, Bradwell said that Ambri was in the development and verification phase and hoped to move into the commercialization phase within two years.[34] "[It's a project that] we believe will change the world," says Bradwell. Adds Sadoway, "It is science in service of society."[35] It is also a project well in line with the Deshpande Center motto, "From idea to impact."

As of April 2019, the Deshpande Center had funded more than 140 projects with grants in excess of $19 million, of which 40 translated into spin-off ventures.[36] Among the projects that have benefited from the support of the Deshpande Center and translated into start-ups are Firefly Bioworks and Ambri (see the boxes in this chapter).[37] Another example is Brontes Technologies, which is based on Professor Douglas Hart's research on particle imaging velocimetry that eventually translated into a video-rate scanner that could digitally scan three-dimensional (3D) images of the inside of a patient's mouth for applications in the dental industry.[38] Following the suggestion of the Deshpande Center, Hart entered the $50K Entrepreneurship Competition, where he founded Brontes in 2003 with János Rohály ('04) and two Harvard Business School graduate students. After exploring forty potential markets, the founders eventually settled for an application in dentistry, designing and producing various types of dental restorations such as crowns and bridges. Brontes was bought by 3M in 2006. Hart gave credit for the success of Brontes to the seed funding provided by the Deshpande Center and the advice of mentors including Professor Robert Langer ('74) and Krisztina Holly ('89), then-director of the center.[39]

In addition to its impact on commercialization, the Deshpande Center exerts a positive influence on the MIT faculty and students. Their experience with the Deshpande Center does not affect the desire of the researchers to do basic science, but it does encourage them to think earlier and differently about aspects of commercialization. It also affects their teaching, as some of them incorporate economic aspects into their science or engineering courses, giving students a broader perspective and influencing their career trajectory.[40] "The Center serves a really important role, fitting between the National Science Foundation and venture capital. It works not only by helping technical entrepreneurs think through a business plan that can help them land funding, but more importantly, in helping to steer research in a commercial direction where a couple of good results can convince investors to make a larger financial bet," said Stan Reiss ('95), a general partner in the venture-capital firm Matrix Partners and a longtime sponsor of the Deshpande Center.[41]

INNOVATION CORPS

The National Science Foundation (NSF) observed the low success rate for the commercialization of projects that resulted from academic research that had been funded by federal grants. Typically, the challenges to commercialization were not of a technical nature; rather, they occurred because the aspiring entrepreneurs did not give enough consideration to customer needs in the creation of their products.[42] In an effort to improve this situation, the NSF created the Innovation Corp (I-Corp) program in 2011 under the leadership of Subra Suresh ('81), former professor and dean of the School of Engineering at MIT. (Currently, there are ninety-six I-Corp sites nationwide.) The objective of I-Corp was to incorporate more customer insight into the design of products to help scientists and engineers commercialize NSF-funded research. I-Corp offered scientists and engineers introductory entrepreneurship courses and awarded them microgrants of up to $1,500 to explore the potential commercial applications of their technology, including understanding who their potential clients could be.

MIT was selected in 2014 to be an I-Corp site, providing this first module of support to members of its community. The completion of the initial I-Corps program makes participants eligible for a $50,000 grant to take part in a seven-week national I-Corps program and to earn further government grants to pursue their projects.[43] During this period, participants are required to conduct at least 100 interviews with potential users to explore what the best product-to-market fit could be. In 2018, MIT was selected as an Innovation Corps Node by the NSF to support innovation not only at

MIT, but at a regional level in New England and beyond, because it leads the New England Regional Innovation Node. It was the ninth such node that was created by the NSF, with others covering different regions in the US.[44]

It is too early to assess the impact of I-Corps on MIT spin-offs because, as mentioned previously, those entrepreneurial projects require years of development time, including additional R&D, after they are spun off from their academic labs. However, even if it is too early to see the impact of I-Corps at MIT in terms of the commercialization of breakthrough technologies, the process is useful in the short term for identifying early on academic research that does *not* have any real market potential.

Conducting face-to-face interviews with potential clients is a critical part of I-Corp. It may be especially important for scientists in order to help them avoid the temptation of developing entrepreneurial projects in the isolation of their labs as opposed to identifying real-world problems that need a solution. Because few realize that they need to take this step and most are uncomfortable doing it, the process may take them out of their comfort zone. Sandymount Technology,[45] founded by Ronan McGovern ('12), illustrates the value of discovering real market opportunities through interviews with potential customers. Through such interviews, and after a number of iterations, McGovern abandoned his initial target market of seawater purification for industrial and municipal needs. He discovered instead that his technology could remove water from beer without affecting its taste, and could thus provide savings on transportation and more sustainable supply chains in the form of lower fossil fuel emissions. His story exemplifies that best markets are not always the most obvious ones. It also illustrates the need for start-ups to find a beachhead market with a real need to satisfy, as doing so is essential to a company's survival.

I-Corps and Deshpande play a critical role in managing the transition from working in a university lab to launching a start-up. Roman Lubynsky ('89), the executive director of the I-Corps program at MIT, says that in the past, the transition from working in a university lab to launching a start-up was often facilitated by an intermediary period, during which scientists worked at corporate places such as Bell Labs. As these entities have largely disappeared, I-Corps tries to provide such a transition.[46]

FIREFLY BIOWORKS

In the mid-2000s, Daniel Pregibon ('04) was midway through his PhD program in Professor Patrick Doyle's lab in the Department of Chemical Engineering when a failure in an experiment revealed an opportunity. Pregibon found a way to produce hydrogel microparticles that could be used to detect specific deoxyribonucleic acid (DNA), ribonucleic acid (RNA), and protein biomarkers in a novel manner. Furthermore, this opportunity could be commercially viable. Optical liquid stamping (OLS), the technology that Pregibon, Doyle, and Dhananjay Dendukuri ('04) developed based on this discovery, offered the potential of high-multiplexing and high-throughput analyses at a fraction of the traditional microribonucleic acid (miRNA) assay cost.

Pregibon and Doyle reached out to the Deshpande Center for funding and mentoring support. In 2009, when Pregibon presented his OLS technology at the Deshpande IdeaStream symposium, he was approached by Davide Marini ('03), a PhD in mechanical engineering from MIT and a Deshpande grantee as well, who also had a background in finance. After hitting it off initially, the two decided to form a company around OLS; the result was Firefly BioWorks, which they created with Professor Doyle in 2010.

Marini as chief executive officer (CEO) and Pregibon as chief technology officer (CTO), found that by focusing on developing sophisticated hydrogel particles for first-rate miRNA assays, they shifted the onus of intricacy from analysis equipment to their particle, their product. This would prove to be a key business decision; these microparticles were attractive because not only could they be customized easily through user-friendly software and produced and processed rapidly, but they also could be analyzed on standard lab analysis equipment such as low-cost flow cytometers.

MIT's entrepreneurial resources played a huge role in the early stages of the firm, according to Pregibon. The Deshpande Center provided the early grants, but it also offered mentorship, contacts, and business advice. With its support, the company obtained two phase-1 and one phase-2 SBIR grants from the National Cancer Institute, as well as a grant from the Massachusetts Life Sciences Center. "The Venture Mentoring Service, I-Teams, and Concept Clinic were all very helpful as well. While publications validated the science, these groups helped identify and validate the business opportunity," said Perigon.[47]

By 2013, Firefly BioWorks had raised approximately $7 million from SBIR and angel funding.[48] In October 2013, EMD Millipore (Merck's global Life Science division) joined Firefly BioWorks in a partnership to commercialize the Firefly miRNA Assay. In January 2015, Firefly was acquired by Abcam plc, an international heavyweight in the life sciences research industry.

THE ENGINE

In 2015, President Rafael Reif took up the exact points discussed thus far in this chapter in an op-ed article in the *Washington Post* titled "A Better Way to Deliver Innovation to the World," which presaged the launch of The Engine at MIT in late 2016.[49] His argument was that the process of bringing scientific inventions to the marketplace was broken. Corporations had closed their R&D labs for the most part, venture capital had too short a time horizon for science-based ventures to develop, and cash-strapped governments in the West had retreated from large-scale societal projects. The entrepreneur and venture investor Peter Thiel captured the frustration of these circumstances with his now-famous quote: "We were promised flying cars and all we got was 140 characters," referring to "tweets" on Twitter.

As a result of this broken process, many promising technologies are stranded in university labs. The implications are significant: great potential for human progress has been abandoned, and competitive and existential threats can arise in the US in such areas as sustainable energy, water and food security, and health. In the face of these challenges, Reif called for different types of pathways to market for researchers and entrepreneurs of science-based start-ups working on important issues for our society. In his view, it would require "patient capital" to bring ventures that are trying to commercialize "tough science," and they need more time than digital businesses to reach a stage where they are venture capital–ready. Physical space, mentorship, and a coalition of funders from the public, for-profit, and not-for-profit sectors were also required for what Reif called "innovation orchards." He strongly believes that a new public benefit initiative would be in line with MIT's mission statement, which directs the institution "to bring knowledge to bear on the world's great challenges."[50]

The answer that MIT's leadership came up with was The Engine, the creation of which was officially announced in October 2016. The Engine is a for-profit but public benefit corporation, separate from MIT, which is designed to play multiple roles, including as an accelerator for start-ups trying to commercialize "tough tech" and as a venture fund of "patient capital." As a public benefit corporation, The Engine has a double bottom line: it seeks financial returns and it seeks impact. The Engine raised $200 million for its first fund, with MIT contributing $25 million.

According to its CEO and managing partner Katie Rae, the goal of The Engine is to offer three key ingredients to support the commercialization of scientific inventions: capital, infrastructure, and networks.[51] First, it provides long-term financial investment to start-ups. The fund invests from $250,000 to $2 million per venture, and its investments are not exclusive to MIT-related firms. The investment is made with a time horizon of eighteen years, rather than the typical five to eight years given in the case of venture capital funds.

Second, The Engine gives start-ups access to infrastructure, such as expensive, specialized equipment, including some from MIT, that otherwise might represent a barrier to entry to firm foundations. (Indeed, "tough tech" start-ups often have to begin by spending $300,000 or more on specialized equipment, another feature that differentiates them from web-based start-ups.) This equipment, as well as labs, offices, and prototyping and makerspaces are often shared in a cost-efficient formula. The Engine's facility was initially located in 26,000 square feet of space at 501 Massachusetts Avenue in Central Square, Cambridge, with the ambition of expanding to 200,000 square feet through a network of offices, labs, and prototyping and makerspaces a few blocks from Kendall Square.

Third, the new initiative comes with a network of professionals and mentors in the so-called hard-tech space. The support of The Engine focuses on two of the critical developmental stages of start-ups: the initial "proof of product" stage, when an innovative idea is turned into a product and the product-market fit is tested; and a later stage when the venture moves from prototyping to commercial production. The Engine has a board and an investment advisory committee consisting of business leaders, entrepreneurs, venture capitalists, and members of MIT's leadership.

The goal is for The Engine to support around forty locally based start-ups per year, which seek to develop tough technologies in advanced materials, quantum computing, space, energy, biotechnology, and other areas. President Reif made it clear that in the selection process, precedence would be given to ventures that "prioritize breakthrough answers to big problems over early process and early profit."[52]

In September 2017, The Engine announced that it had selected its first seven companies in the fields of aerospace, advanced materials, genetic engineering, and renewable energy, among others. Analytical Space builds high-speed data transmissions for space with applications in agriculture, climate monitoring, and city planning. Form Energy builds energy-storage for renewable energy to turn it into a reliable source of power. C2Sense translates smell into data that can be used in sectors such as food, agriculture, and workplace safety. ISEE is a common-sense artificial intelligence (AI) company building an autonomous driving system. Kytopen tries to make it easier and faster to develop genetically engineered cells. Suono Bio uses ultrasonic technology to deliver therapeutics. Finally, Via Separations builds a more efficient process for the industrial separation of materials used to make food, pharmaceuticals, chemicals, and consumer products, among other applications.

The story of Analytical Space, as reported by the *Boston Globe*, illustrates a piece of the puzzle contributed by The Engine that is otherwise missing in the ecosystem for the commercialization of tough tech. When the founders of Analytical Space tried to raise funding from venture capitalists, they had to spend the first hour of their presentation teaching them physics. As is typical with start-ups tackling complicated technological issues, investors showed interest but did not want to commit capital before the firm had actually launched its product in space—but, of course, Analytical Space couldn't do that without raising money.[53]

Professor Cullen Buie, cofounder of Kytopen, also clearly described the void that The Engine is filling when he said to Fast Company, "I think pre-The Engine, a technology like ours would be likely to fall into this dangerous gap where it's no longer fundamental research–the science is done–it's not software, it's not one of those other areas that's getting venture funding these days. It would be a shame for something like this to kind of die on the vine, but I think for a lot of technologies, that's exactly what happens."[54]

When Jeff Engel of *Xconomy* asked about potential conflicts of interest, such as in the selection of firms for investment, Provost Martin Schmidt said that the way that The Engine is structured should help it avoid many of these issues. Schmidt noted that The Engine would be an entity separate from MIT; a professional fund manager from outside the Institute would be hired to run the fund, and the selection of start-ups and management of the fund would be the responsibility of individuals outside of MIT. In addition, MIT hosted faculty-led working groups addressing this issue and others related to The Engine's relationship with MIT.[55]

In a classic MIT tradition, The Engine followed an objective of local economic development of the Boston area, as reflected in Reif's statement: "We believe this approach can offer exponential growth to regions that pursue it successfully—and we want Greater Boston to lead the way."[56] A related goal, says Rae, was to keep top talents in the local area and its research institutions. In practical terms, it was also designed to encourage start-ups to stay in the Boston area instead of moving to California.[57]

MIT STARTUP EXCHANGE

Established in 1948, the MIT Industrial Liaison Program (ILP) promotes collaborations and partnerships between MIT and corporations globally.[58] More than 200 of the world's largest corporations are partners of the program. Whereas ILP's traditional focus had been on connecting large corporations to MIT's faculty and labs, it broadened its focus in 2014 to include MIT-originated start-ups. This new orientation translated into the creation of the MIT Startup Exchange, aimed at building bridges among established corporations, ILP's traditional "clients," and MIT-related start-ups, building on ILP's expertise in academic–industry collaborations. The shift in focus also included the creation of STEX25, a start-up accelerator with the specific focus on facilitating collaborations among MIT-related start-ups and the large corporations that are members of ILP.

For instance, at one such event, an officer of the ILP introduced Karl Iagnemma ('01), CEO of the MIT spin-off nuTonomy,[59] an autonomous driving venture, to executives of the Samsung Global Innovation Center, which led to Samsung Ventures taking part in a seed round of investment into the venture. Similarly, DropWise Technologies Corporation, a spin-off of the Gleason Lab at MIT that is commercializing advanced industrial coatings and vapor deposition processes, concluded a joint development agreement with Henkel Corporation at a recent event.[60]

PROTO VENTURES PROGRAM

In 2019, the Innovation Initiative launched the Proto Ventures Program under the leadership of professor of engineering Michael Cima, who is also a serial entrepreneur.[61] The Proto Ventures Program is a new approach to venture formation that was at the pilot stage at the time of this writing. The program relies on domain experts in certain fields, the "venture builders" who explore the research being conducted at MIT and evaluate it for its potential to evolve into business opportunities, while also bringing together faculty and students involved in the process. Its objective is to confirm the robustness of a technology and the viability of "proto ventures" that will eventually turn into real ventures.

CONCLUSION

The TLO, the Deshpande Center for Technological Innovation, and the other entities described in this chapter add to the rich network of support for entrepreneurship at MIT in the late 2010s, with a specific focus on entrepreneurship for technology transfer and the peculiarities of the start-up and growth processes of science-based ventures whose technologies originated in the Institute's labs.

IV   IMPACT AND IMPLICATIONS

In this fourth and last part of this book, the discussion moves beyond the details of interest and support for entrepreneurship at MIT and deals with broader themes. It looks at various forms of impact that entrepreneurial projects by members of the community have had locally and internationally. It offers a discussion about teaching entrepreneurship and its implications. Finally, it examines how MIT's dealing with entrepreneurship education and entrepreneurship related to technology transfer could initiate useful conversations at other institutions interested in these topics and in adapting them to their own conditions.

9 THE EXTERNAL IMPACT OF MIT ENTREPRENEURSHIP

Although activities supporting entrepreneurship were originally meant to serve the MIT community, their impact quickly had an influence beyond campus—first locally and then globally. The economic impact of companies founded by MIT alumni has been well documented and evaluated to be approximately equivalent to the gross domestic product of the world's tenth-largest economy. Beyond the impact in terms of revenue and employment, there were other forms as well, such as the emergence of a major entrepreneurial cluster in Kendall Square, next to the campus, where a new industry, biotechnology, emerged. Impacts in the form of diffusion of ideas and practices have also occurred internationally with the replication of the $100K Entrepreneurship Competition all over the world.

Entrepreneurship has thus been a major enabler for MIT to conduct its mission of building a better world. However, the impact and learning from those exchanges has gone both ways and MIT students and other members of the community have gained a great deal from their exposure to other regions and cultures. Operating in developing countries with irregular access to electricity, for instance, has forced students to rethink their assumptions on how to build a company.

ECONOMIC IMPACT

As mentioned earlier in this book, by 2014 MIT's alumni had founded at least 30,000 active companies with revenues of $1.9 trillion and employing an estimated 4.6 million people.[1] These numbers are all the more impressive if we take into account that start-ups are the source of a high percentage of job creation and that new and high-growth firms are responsible for 70 percent of all the jobs created in the US.[2] However, the economic impact is not limited to the US—23 percent of new companies founded by MIT alumni are created in other countries. The trend indicates a growth in alumni entrepreneurs, according to a 2014 survey by Edward Roberts, Fiona Murray, and J. Daniel Kim. The percentage of participants in the survey who had founded a company within five years of graduation rose from 4 percent in the 1960s, to 8 percent in the 1990s, and to 11 percent in the 2010s, after a drop to 7 percent in the 2000s (probably due to the crash of the internet bubble). The figure of 11 percent in the last decade probably underestimates the reality because it naturally does not include alumni who had not graduated yet.[3] The authors of the survey estimated that MIT alumni created 5,300 companies in the 1980s, 8,000 in the 1990s, and 9,100 in the 2010s up through 2014.[4] They expect the figure to correspond to 18 firms per 100 active alumni. It is also interesting to point to the decrease in the median age of first-time founders from thirty-nine years old in the 1940s, to thirty-seven in the 1970s, to thirty in the 2000s. It seems that the figure should be even lower in the 2010s. Finally, 31 percent of respondents indicated that they were named as an inventor on a patent.[5]

In 2015, the Industrial Liaison Program (ILP)[6] built a database of more than 1,500 start-ups with MIT-connected pedigrees, meaning firms founded and/or led by MIT faculty, staff, or alumni, or that were based on MIT-licensed technology. It estimates that 172 MIT professors, or about 17 percent of the faculty, are prolific entrepreneurs.[7]

Besides those impressive aggregate figures, entities supporting entrepreneurship at MIT have also had an impact outside the campus that are more difficult to measure in economic terms, such as employment and revenue. Their influence can be sensed in terms of local economic development, establishment of new networks and partnerships, diffusion of best practices, sensitivity to cultural differences, and diffusion of MIT's model of support to entrepreneurship.

LOCAL IMPACT

Both student-led entities supporting entrepreneurship and official initiatives organized by the Institute itself—either as a whole or its schools, labs, departments, and centers—have had significant impact on MIT's local community.

KENDALL SQUARE

In 2009, the Boston Consulting Group called Kendall Square (the neighborhood bordering MIT's East campus in Cambridge) "the most innovative square mile on earth."[8] This had not always been the case, however. Until the late 2000s at least, Kendall Square was a desolate urban wasteland of industrial factories, open space, and parking lots, nicknamed "Nowhere Square," where it was not safe to walk outside at night.[9] It had suffered the decline and the exodus of older industries, some of them dating from the Industrial Revolution.

The origin of Kendall Square's renewal in relation to its interactions with MIT can be traced to the 1970s. At that time, groundbreaking scientific advances in recombinant deoxyribonucleic acid (rDNA) were allowing scientists to document and alter genomes of organisms in new ways. However, research on rDNA triggered fears in Americans about potential health and environmental issues, and research was not allowed to be conducted in the US. In an effort to clarify rDNA research and overcome the public's fears, MIT and Harvard faculty and administrators reached out to wider local stakeholders, including the city of Cambridge and civic groups of citizens by organizing multiple events in which they explained their work in the plainest terms.[10] "We made every effort we could to demystify this whole thing," said Professor Philip Sharp of MIT.[11] This approach turned out to be critical in winning the support of the community. Once an ordinance stating that research on rDNA was allowed in Cambridge was passed in 1977, making the city the first place in the US allowing this kind of research, MIT was in a good position to make progress in rDNA-dependent research. From the early days of rDNA, it appeared that it had significant commercial potential for the emerging sector of biotechnology.

The successful research on rDNA convinced philanthropist Jack Whitehead to found the Whitehead Institute in Kendall Square in 1982 as an affiliate to MIT. The research made possible by Cambridge's regulatory framework in the form of the ordinance allowing research on rDNA also attracted venture capitalists who sensed the commercial potential of the new field. One of them, Ray Schaefer ('32), started talks with MIT professor Philip Sharp and Harvard University professor Walter Gilbert, along with a number of scientists in Europe, which led to the founding in 1978 of Biogen, an early biotech firm. Biogen would develop one of the first treatments for hepatitis C, as well as the vaccine given for hepatitis B, before becoming a dominant player in treating multiple sclerosis. Biogen is today one of the giants of the biotech industry.

In 1982, Biogen relocated near MIT and kicked off the biotech revolution in Kendall Square. The choice of location was motivated by its proximity to MIT and the opportunity that it provided to recruit excellent scientists.[12] Another emblematic local biotech company with MIT ties is Genzyme, which was founded in 1981 with the involvement of MIT faculty members Charles Cooney ('67), Harvey Lodish, ChoKyun Rha ('62), William Roush, Anthony Sinskey ('66), Graham Walker, and George Whitesides (see chapter 3). In the 1980s and 1990s, as Cambridge was emerging as one of the global centers of biotechnology, a growing number of companies also chose to settle in "Gene Town," as it was sometimes called. These firms included Genetics Institute, Millennium, and Vertex, as well as the MIT spin-offs Verastem, Fidelity Biosciences, Courtagen, and Aclara. Kendall's rundown neighborhood became a strength, as the vacant industrial buildings in the area provided space for start-ups to expand into. Although it did not end up settling in the Kendall Square area, Genentech was another biotech pioneer with ties to MIT. The future industry giant was cofounded by Bob Swanson ('69) in 1976.

Kendall Square's emergence as a high-tech cluster was dominated by biotech,[13] but it was not exclusively about the life sciences. In fact, one of the companies most responsible for Kendall Square's revitalization was Lotus Development Corporation, a successful software company (see chapter 3). After cofounding Lotus in 1982, Mitch Kapor, a former student at the Sloan School of Management, chose Kendall Square for the Lotus headquarters, attracted by the area's low rents and access to public transportation.[14] The location was not an obvious choice, given that most information technology (IT) companies at the time were located on Route 128, the peripheral highway circling the Greater Boston area. Lotus's status as one of the great success stories of the personal computer era brought renewed cachet and a bigger workforce to Kendall Square, prompting growth and prosperity.[15] Years later, Akamai (1998) and Hubspot (2006) would become anchor IT companies in the region. They would all produce numerous spin-offs.

Soon Kendall's reputation for innovation attracted multinational pharmaceutical companies struggling with the poor productivity of their own research labs. In 2002, Novartis moved its research division from Basel, Switzerland, to Kendall Square (a major move) to be closer to MIT and the other universities and hospitals of the Boston area. Following Novartis, other larger biotechs and pharmaceutical companies soon joined the start-ups in Kendall Square, such as Amgen, AstraZeneca, Sanofi, Pfizer, Johnson & Johnson, and Merck. Locating their laboratories in Kendall Square gave them a distinct advantage when it came to acquiring the young biotech start-ups established in and around Kendall Square. Meanwhile, MIT grew affiliated interdisciplinary centers of excellence in Kendall Square, like the Whitehead Institute (1982), which played a key role in the Human Genome Project; the Picower Institute for Learning and Memory (1994); the McGovern Institute for Brain Research (2000); the Broad Institute of MIT and Harvard (2004), a biomedical and genomic research center; and the Koch Institute for Integrative Cancer Research (2007).

Former president Susan Hockfield reports that shortly after she joined MIT in 2004 a third of MIT's almost 400 engineering faculty members used the tools of biology in their research.[16] This change reflected the growing integration of life sciences with engineering—a concept represented by the Koch Institute. The integration with IT would also grow, which was probably one of the motivating factors for Google, Microsoft, IBM, and other IT giants to open research facilities in Kendall Square.

However, Kendall Square still lacked the amenities and housing that would make it a real neighborhood. In reaction to that, in 2008, Hockfield asked the MIT Investment Management Corporation to devise a plan to develop Kendall Square. In 2015, MIT presented its Kendall Square Initiative,[17] a $1.2 billion proposal for development that aimed to fill this gap in housing and amenities and to enhance the innovation hub on its doorstep.[18]

Entrepreneurs settle in Kendall Square for the unique dynamic that has developed there through the interaction of MIT, the start-up population, large established companies, accelerators, and investors. Katrine Bosley, the chief executive officer (CEO) and president of Editas Medicine, for instance,[19] told the *Boston Globe* in 2016 that she planned to keep her company in Cambridge, "within blocks of the investors, entrepreneurs, and drug development veterans that keep Kendall ticking. You're going to run into these people all the time and it creates that density of interaction," she said.[20] This "density of interactions" is the oil that facilitates the circulation of information and collaborations, all of which are critical to the knowledge economy of Kendall Square. Similarly, Kevin Bitterman, a partner at the venture capital firm Polaris Partners in Boston, justified his company's choice of Kendall Square for his next start-up in 2015 by saying, "You can't walk two feet there without seeing someone in biotech. That kinetic energy of having everybody squished together—it leads to a lot of advantages you can't get outside the city."[21] Ben Vigoda ('99), a founder of Lyric Semiconductor in 2006, chose to keep his company in the shared office space of the Cambridge Innovation Center in Kendall Square even after his company grew to more than twenty employees, because "from a business perspective, there is a life of ideas that flows into Kendall. We're always hearing about the coolest innovations here. We've met customers, employees, and discovered new technologies here [that have] had a substantial impact on the growth and development of this company," he said. "We're not leaving. We want to stay close to the fire hose,"[22] referring to the famous quote of MIT president Jerome Wiesner: "Getting an education from MIT is like taking a drink from a fire hose."[23]

Bosley, Bitterman, and Vigoda were referring to the power of serendipitous interaction among various parties that Kendall Square offers, or what Bob Krim, a historian of innovation in the Boston area, called the power of "bump and connect,"[24] which was so supportive of innovation. It echoes what the English economist Alfred Marshall wrote: that in such dense clusters "the mysteries of the trade become no mystery but are, as it were, in the air."[25]

Kendall Square may have become a victim of its own success. Office rents in the area are the highest in the country and housing prices are increasingly prohibitive as well. This reality seems to benefit other parts of the Cambridge and Boston area that are experiencing a renewal, as people and companies who are priced out of Kendall move farther from the center.

THE MULTIPLYING EFFECT OF SHARED OFFICE SPACES AND ACCELERATORS

In the early days of MIT entrepreneurship, MIT alumni not only founded start-ups, but a number of them launched accelerators and shared office spaces, some of which will be described in this chapter. They have had a multiplying effect in terms of start-up creation. As early as 1999, Tim Rowe ('99) launched Cambridge Innovation Center (CIC), a new concept of shared office spaces in Kendall Square (better known as "coworking spaces" nowadays) that today has more than 5,000 alumni companies.[26] In such spaces, various companies share common facilities, thus cutting down on the expense of a traditional office.

Start-up accelerators are intensive entrepreneurship development programs offered to a cohort of venture founders and are aimed at speeding up the launch and growth of start-ups through mentoring and various forms of support. John Harthorne ('07) and his cofounders, Akhil Nigam and David Constanine, launched MassChallenge in 2009 as a nonprofit[27] in reaction to the recession triggered by the financial crisis, with the aim of connecting high-impact entrepreneurs with the resources they needed to succeed. MassChallenge was initially a business plan competition inspired by MIT's $100K Entrepreneurship Competition, which Harthorne had won in 2007, but it later evolved into the largest accelerator in the world, with sites around the globe. MIT graduates are the largest source of finalists in MassChallenge. Its impact has been significant: 2,458 start-ups were created as of 2020, and $6.2 billion has been raised by the participating companies, which had $3 billion in combined revenue and had created over 157,000 jobs.[28] MassChallenge's nonprofit status sets it apart from other major accelerators.

Techstars, one of the two most recognized for-profit accelerators, was cofounded in 2006 by Brad Feld ('87) and grew by 2018 into forty-four separate programs covering six continents and a large number of industry verticals (programs specific to industries), as well as corporate-backed accelerators.[29] Techstars–Boston was one of the most successful programs, with 155 ventures graduating from its program by 2019. Techstars accelerated 2,157 start-ups that had raised $9.3 billion by 2020 and had a market capitalization of $26.8 billion.[30] Its most famous MIT-related graduate is PillPack, founded by Elliot Cohen ('13) and TJ Parker; it was sold to Amazon in 2018, reputedly for close to $1 billion.

CIC, MassChallenge, and Techstars have all been pioneers of shared offices and accelerators and are nowadays major players in these fields. More recent accelerators have applied the concept to specialized domains. Jason Hanna, Sam White, Sorin Grama ('07), Jeremy Pitts ('10), and Adam Rein ('10) founded Greentown Labs in 2011, which became the largest clean-tech incubator/accelerator in the US, with 120 ventures accelerated by 2019.[31] That same year, Jean Hammond ('86) founded LearnLaunch[32] in

Boston, an accelerator specializing in technology-based start-ups focusing on the educational sector; it had accelerated 58 companies by 2019, according to Hammond.[33]

ALUMNI AS BUSINESS ANGELS AND VENTURE CAPITALISTS

MIT alumni have been active as venture investors (known as "business angels") and some alumni have launched groups specifically aimed at financially backing start-ups. One of the earliest of these investment groups was Common Angels in Boston, founded in 2000 and managed for many years by James Geshwiler ('00). Around the same time, Charlie Cameron ('79) and David Verrill ('87) founded the Hub Angels Investment Group. In more recent years, Castor Ventures and MIT Alumni Angels were formed.[34] Each of these groups have funded numerous start-ups, many of which related to MIT. Hub Angels, for instance, claims that in 2019 it managed a portfolio of more than forty companies across six funds and that it and its members had invested more than $40 million in a broad range of sectors.[35]

Some alumni founded venture capital firms that operated both in the US and abroad. Among those founded in the US are Zero Stage Capital, started in 1981 by Gordon Baty ('61), Jerry Goldstein ('64), Paul Kelley, Arthur Obermayer ('56), and Professor Edward Roberts ('57), and was according to the latter the first seed fund in Boston; Morgenthaler Ventures, founded by David Morgenthaler ('40); Kleiner-Perkins, cofounded by Thomas Perkins ('53); IDG Venture Capital, founded by Patrick McGovern ('60); Flagship Ventures (now named Flagship Pioneering), founded by Noubar Afeyan ('87); and Mobius Capital and Foundry Group, cofounded by Brad Feld ('87). IDG Venture Capital was a pioneer venture capital firm in China and other emerging economies.

MIT'S IMPACT ON STANFORD UNIVERSITY AND THE EARLY DAYS OF SILICON VALLEY

MIT can claim to have involuntarily played a role in the development of Stanford University, and of Silicon Valley as well. Frederick Terman ('24) was a PhD graduate whose advisor was the influential MIT professor and dean of the School of Engineering—and cofounder of Raytheon Corporation—Vannevar Bush ('16) (see chapter 1). When Terman returned to Stanford after World War II, he transferred MIT's model of science-based economic development from academia to Stanford. He organized research centers modeled after the famous wartime Rad Lab of MIT (see chapters 1 and 5). He cultivated relationships between Stanford's School of Engineering and local industries. Spinning off new firms and encouraging them to stay nearby were also built into the model, which Terman facilitated by creating the Stanford Industrial Park, one of the first such complexes in the country. Terman famously encouraged his students William Hewlett ('36) and David Packard and lent them money to form their firm, Hewlett-Packard, in Palo Alto based on their invention of a resistance-tuned oscillator.[36] HP, as it is now known, is considered the symbolic founder of Silicon Valley.

INTERNATIONAL IMPACT

In typical MIT fashion, the expansion of programs, entities, and extracurricular activities beyond the borders of the United States has occurred on a mostly ad hoc basis, outside any grand strategic plan. This is particularly true of the earliest forms of international expansion, in contrast to the entities that emerged late in the 2010s, when MIT leadership adopted a more overarching, strategic approach to the global impact of its entrepreneurial expertise.

MIT'S FORMAL INTERNATIONAL COLLABORATIONS WITH OTHER REGIONS

In the last two decades, MIT's formal international collaborations with other countries or regions have had a growing entrepreneurship component to them that has had various levels of local impact within those countries or regions. The Singapore-MIT Alliance for Research and Technology (SMART),[37] which launched in 2007, is a research partnership established by MIT with the National Research Foundation of Singapore (NRF). It is MIT's largest such partnership. From the outset, SMART included an innovation center inspired by the Deshpande Center for Technological Innovation (see chapters 3 and 8) to reduce the technology risk and establish a go-to-market strategy. This orientation toward entrepreneurship and innovation is not surprising when taking into account that Institute professor Tom Magnanti, a former dean of the School of Engineering and a key player in the origin of the Deshpande Center, was instrumental in establishing this partnership.[38] As a result, a number of start-ups have spun off from SMART. The first one was Visterra in 2010. It is a biotechnology company set up for the discovery and development of new therapies, diagnostics, and vaccines for infectious diseases, including influenza and dengue fever.[39] Another SMART research project lead to the launch of Visenti in 2011 by professor of mechanical engineering Kamal Youcef-Toumi ('81) and professor of civil engineering Andrew Whittle ('87). The company's goal is to increase the world's water supply by decreasing water loss through leaks (10–40 percent of water loss in developed countries is due to leaks; those figures are higher in developing countries). In order to achieve this, the company deploys swimming robots to place sensors in a city's water pipes. These sensors relay information to control centers aboveground. The robots can even fix the leaks. By 2015, Visenti had installed sensors across Singapore and was expanding to other countries.[40] nuTonomy, an autonomous driving start-up, spun off from SMART in 2013, first as a driverless car consulting company and then as a driverless taxi service provider in Singapore.[41] In October 2017, Aptiv (known previously as Delphi Automotive) acquired nuTonomy for over $400 million. In 2019, SMART announced a commercially viable way to manufacture integrated Silicon III-V chips that have potential for intelligent optoelectronic and 5G wireless devices.[42] Given SMART's entrepreneurship and innovation orientation, it is perhaps not surprising that professor of engineering Eugene Fitzgerald ('85) was appointed SMART CEO and director in 2019. Fitzgerald is a serial entrepreneur and specialist in high-performance semiconductors using strained silicon, which revolutionizes the performance of silicon integrated circuits (see box about Amber-Wave in chapter 8). As mentioned by Professor Charles Cooney, SMART has been an important experiment in both university building and in a new paradigm for education revolving around innovation.[43]

The MIT Portugal Program is a multiyear, multifaceted collaboration between MIT and the government of Portugal launched in 2010. It has an entrepreneurship component called Building Global Innovators, which put in place a contest modeled after the MIT $100K Entrepreneurship Competition[44] and entrepreneurship boot camps in Portugal and on the MIT campus. It offers mentoring and other support to its alumni ventures for up to five years after the completion of the program. By 2019, it had accelerated 133 ventures from 64 countries, 80 of which were still active and which had raised €201 million of capital.[45]

In 2011, MIT started the MIT Skoltech Initiative,[46] a four-year collaboration (later extended for four additional years), to assist Russia's Skolkovo

Foundation in building the Skolkovo Institute of Science and Technology ("Skoltech"), a new private university based in a suburb of Moscow. From the outset, the project had a strong emphasis on innovation and entrepreneurship. The Russian partners said that they chose MIT as their main international partner because of the Institute's strong record in start-up creation and industrial impact. MIT helped Skoltech design an entrepreneurship and innovation (E&I) program that included an academic curriculum, a translational research program, a technology transfer office, and other pieces of an innovation ecosystem.[47]

The Madrid-MIT M+Visión Consortium[48] was formed in 2011 by the Community of Madrid (the state of Spain that includes its capital of the same name), the Fundación Madrid+d para el Conocimiento, and MIT—specifically, its Institute for Medical Engineering and Sciences[49]—to strengthen Madrid's health care innovation ecosystem and position it as a global center for biomedical imaging innovation. Translational research and entrepreneurship have been central components of M+Visión as well. A key component of the consortium was the fellowship in biomedical imaging (later renamed M+Visión Catalyst). From the outset, fellows, known as Catalysts, needed to identify unmet medical needs and explore possible new solutions. At each stage of development, the teams reduced the risk of their project by focusing on proven feasibility and by narrowing their efforts down to the most promising solutions.

Among the ventures founded by Catalysts is Leuko Labs, cofounded by Carlos Castro Gonzalez, Ian Butterworth, Aurelien Bourquard, and Alvaro Sanchez-Ferro, which builds an optic-based medical device that can see through the skin and count blood cells.[50] It can be particularly helpful for patients going through chemotherapy, for whom counting white blood cells serves as an indicator of the health of their immune system. The traditional solution is to rely on blood tests performed in a hospital. With the Leuko Labs device, patients themselves could monitor their response to the treatment on a daily basis and as a result decrease their visits to the hospital and risk of infection.[51]

When the Innovation Initiative was launched in 2013 by MIT's leadership, it announced its intention to create global innovation nodes, with the aim of fostering innovation communities beyond campus to expand the Institute's footprint into regions with strong entrepreneurial ecosystems. This intention began to materialize in 2016 with the opening of the first such node in Hong Kong. The Hong Kong node is a collaborative space to facilitate the connection between the MIT community, Hong Kong, and the neighboring Pearl River Delta's unique resources, notably in manufacturing. It is not surprising that Hong Kong was MIT's first choice for setting up a global innovation node, given its role as a gateway to China, its thriving entrepreneurial scene, and the growing economic prominence of the entire region. MIT's interest in the role of manufacturing in the process of innovation was an important pull toward investing in the region.[52] There is probably no place in the world that can compete with Shenzhen and the Pearl River Delta in terms of low-volume manufacturing, rapid prototyping, and scale-up.

The signature event of the Hong Kong node is the MIT Entrepreneurship and Maker Skills Integrator (MEMSI), which was organized in partnership with the Trust Center.[53] MEMSI is a two-week hardware start-up boot camp for students of MIT and from various universities in Hong Kong that is held twice per year. Students form mixed teams working on building rapid prototypes that they showcase at the end of the period. During the program, they also take part in workshops, experience the vibrant Hong Kong start-up scene, and are exposed to product design and manufacturing processes in facilities in China. Nathan Monroe ('13), an MIT graduate student in electrical engineering who took part in the inaugural program, commented on the effects of the experience. "Exposure to the size and scale of manufacturing in the region is invaluable. Too many hardware system startups fail because it is massively difficult to go from a single prototype to hundreds of thousands. You don't learn that in school. You learn it on the ground."[54]

In 2017, the first joint start-up, Aavia, was launched by Aagya Mathur ('18), Alex Wong of Hong Kong University, and Aya Suzuki ('18), who also participated in the delta v accelerator program on the MIT campus.[55] In 2018, the Hong Kong node initiated its second boot camp, the MIT Entrepreneurship and FinTech Integrator, building on Hong Kong's strong financial sector.

Other international collaborations are the Cambridge–MIT Institute launched in 1999 (a partnership between Cambridge University in the UK and MIT) and the MIT & Masdar Institute Cooperative Program in Abu Dhabi started in 2007. Both had an important entrepreneurship and innovation component.

All of these programs, achieved through institution building, attest to MIT's international impact, particularly in the areas of entrepreneurship and innovation.

REPLICATION OF THE $100K ENTREPRENEURSHIP COMPETITION

The $100K Entrepreneurship Competition was a great success from the outset. Although the organizers of the competition have not kept rigorous records about its history, its archives mention that from 1990 to 2019, the $100K Competition has given birth to over 160 companies, created over 4,600 jobs, and received more than $1.3 billion in venture capital.[56] These numbers are not hard data and require further examination; however, they do indicate the potential impact of the contest. In 2019, the market capitalization of Akamai and Hubspot alone, both $100K participants, was around $20 billion.

Several international MIT students have tried to replicate the model in their home countries. For instance, Victor Mallet ('02) and several fellow Ghanaian undergraduate students founded the Ghana New Ventures Competition in 2001 after returning home. Dmitry Repin ('02), a postdoc, started the Business Innovation Technology challenge after returning home to Russia. Filipino MIT students created the Philippines Entrepreneurial Startup Open.[57] In 2004, Miguel Palacios ('99) organized a $100K-type competition called ActúaUPM at the Universidad Politécnica de Madrid. By 2019, 260 companies were created by the participants of the competition, whose companies raised €10.2 million, mostly from private investors.[58]

The MIT $100K also triggered considerable interest from third parties from around the world who wanted to replicate it in their home countries. This led the student organizers of the $100K to launch the Global Startup Workshop (GSW) in 1997 in order to share best practices in organizing business plan competition. Since then the GSW has grown into a major annual event involving a business plan competition, a conference, and a start-up showcase. Since 1998, twenty international workshops across six continents have been organized that have attracted participants from over seventy countries.[59]

IMPACT OF OUTREACH ACTIVITIES
OF THE VENTURE MENTORING SERVICE

As discussed in chapters 3 and 7, the Venture Mentoring Service (VMS) matches aspiring entrepreneurs of the MIT community with selected experienced volunteer mentors. Following numerous requests from third parties, the VMS developed an outreach program in 2006 consisting of training representatives of other institutions in establishing and growing similar mentoring programs. In 2019, the VMS's website claimed that it had helped launch more than 100 such programs in the US and across the world, encompassing economic development organizations, business accelerators and incubators, and approximately forty colleges and universities,[60] including Barcelona Activa in Barcelona, Spain; O3NL in Amsterdam; the University of Alberta in Edmonton, Canada; the University of Missouri in Columbia, Missouri; the Universidad Anahuac Mayab in Mérida, Mexico; and the Harvard Innovation Lab.[61] VMS also trained the Chicago Innovation Mentors program, sponsored by local universities and research organizations, which now has 180 mentors working with seventy-five ventures that focus specifically on biomedical and health care.[62]

The VMS Outreach Program usually initially takes the form of a two-and-a-half day Immersion Training Program, during which VMS staff and volunteers teach the basic principles of VMS's mentoring formula, including its cornerstone concept of team-based mentoring. It also includes discussions about governance, vetting mentors, and scaling. After this training on campus, VMS follows up with the programs at clients' locations. One important focus is the vetting process, which involves strict screening of mentors, who need to be willing to operate in a team-mentoring environment. This onsite follow-up also includes a stakeholder workshop, during which VMS members conduct meetings with representatives of the local community to increase program credibility. Officials from universities that went through the VMS Outreach Program said that it can make a difference in the communities surrounding their campuses. For instance, Michael Chambers of the University of South Alabama declared: "What's great for smaller communities like ours is that all this [meeting and learning in groups] means you are building infrastructure. All of a sudden you have an organized network of mentors, and they become aware of all these other local companies, and they become cheerleaders for those companies when they're out in the community."[63]

MIT–CHINA INNOVATION AND ENTREPRENEURSHIP FORUM
In 2011, the MIT–China Innovation and Entrepreneurship Forum (MIT-CHIEF) was set up by MIT students as a nonprofit student organization dedicated

to connecting entrepreneurial communities in the US and China.[64] Its main events are its annual conference, MIT-CHIEF Business Plan Contest, and trip to China. MIT-CHIEF has grown into a significant event attracting hundreds of participants each year from all over the US and China. In its first eight years, more than 31,500 people have participated in its various activities. MIT-CHIEF's organizers claimed in 2019 that the program had grown into the largest Sino-US start-up community on the East Coast, and they had collaborated with more than 200 corporations, more than 100 incubators, and more than 230 investors.[65] Some company projects that have competed in MIT-CHIEF's business plan contest have experienced notable success. For instance, Smarking (2013), cofounded by Wen Sang ('14) and Maokai Lin ('14), was selected to participate in the famous accelerator Y-Combinator and was funded by Khosla Ventures.[66] It provides data analytics to the parking industry enabling automatic dynamic pricing. XTalPi, founded by Jian Ma ('12), Lipeng Lai ('12), Shuhao Wen ('13) applies artificial intelligence to drug discovery and development. The Google-backed start-up raised more than $300 million.[67]

INCLUSIVE INNOVATION CHALLENGE

The Inclusive Innovation Challenge (IIC) exemplifies the growing interest in social entrepreneurship at the Institute.[68] The IIC, founded in 2016, also highlights the concern that MIT's leadership has about some of the technologies that the Institute has helped to create, such as digital technologies in general and, more specifically, automation, robotics, and artificial intelligence (AI)—as well as the negative impact that those technologies have had on certain social groups. The incomes and upward mobility of low- and middle-income workers have stagnated in recent decades in the US, and the situation of these workers in general has become more precarious, in part due to digital technology. According to MIT Sloan professor Erik Brynjolfsson, the grand challenge of our era "is to use digital technologies to create not only prosperity, but shared prosperity."[69] Therefore, the IIC promotes the use of technology to improve skills and empower workers at the bottom and middle of the skill spectrum using a crowdsourced approach. It celebrates entrepreneurs and innovators who use technology to improve economic prospects for targeted groups. From an initial focus on the US, the IIC quickly expanded its scope and opened the competition to candidates beyond MIT, even internationally. By 2019, the IIC had awarded $3.5 million, with $250,000 going to each of the grand prize winners. Three thousand submissions have been proposed from 100 countries since its inception. By 2019, the winners of the IIC had raised more than $1 billion in venture capital, served more than 350 million people, and created 7,000 jobs in 43 countries.

A 2016 winner of this contest was Iora Health, a company that manages primary care services for patients with chronic diseases, using technology to make sure that they regularly check their blood pressure, follow their diets, and exercise. Medical outcomes improved and costs declined by 15 percent to 20 percent due to a lower rate of hospitalization of patients.[70] The company employed approximately 250 coaches in 2016, with starting salaries between $35,000 and $45,000. Laboratoria is another company that took top honors in the 2016 edition of the IIC. It is a six-month coding boot camp that trains women in Latin America as developers and then matches them with job opportunities in the technology sector. The training includes not only technical skills, but also so-called soft skills that are key to success in every job market. A total of 80 percent of graduates find jobs that pay three times what they earned before.[71]

Jana Mobile won the first Technology Access prize of the 2016 IIC.[72] The company was founded by Nathan Eagle ('06) in 2009, based on his research in Professor Sandy Pentland's Wearable Computer Group at the Media Lab, with the goal to make the internet free for 1 billion people by 2020. In developing countries, where most people earn low wages, they buy expensive prepaid mobile phone cards for communication and browsing the internet. Jana assessed that mobile connectivity consumes on average 10 percent of their wages and that three hours of work bought one hour of data. Mobile phones have become affordable, but not data plans. As a result, the majority of smartphone users in developing countries don't connect their phones to the internet because it is unaffordable. With mCent, Jana's app, mobile users download ads and sponsored apps and they receive credit that they can use to buy more data. Jana offers people the opportunity to engage with a brand, whose sponsors then subsidizes the user's total internet access. The sponsors pay for the data, and Jana Mobile takes a cut. "This is the world's largest compensation platform," said Eagle.[73] By 2015, the company had partnered with 237 mobile operators in 102 countries, and by 2016, the app had 35 million users.

GLOBAL STARTUP LAB

Some initiatives supporting entrepreneurship were conceived with a focus on developing countries.[74] An early example of this type of initiative is the student-founded Global Startup Lab (GSL), launched in 2000 by three MIT undergraduates from Africa: Paul Njoroge ('01), Martin Mbaya ('00), and Solomon Assefa ('01). With the GSL, MIT student teams led entrepreneurship workshops in developing countries. By 2017, GSL had created sixty-eight workshops in twenty-two countries: Algeria, Brazil, Colombia, Ethiopia, Germany, Ghana, India, Indonesia, Kenya, Malaysia, Mauritius, Mexico, Mongolia, Nigeria, Peru, Philippines, Russia, Rwanda, Senegal, South Africa, Sri Lanka, and Zambia. "It is so amazing to see some of the early GSL alumni who got to know about entrepreneurship through the program completely change their professional outlook and become successful entrepreneurs in their country. Some are now leading companies with million dollar revenue and hundreds of employees," said Saman Amarasinghe, a professor of electronic engineering and computer science who serves as GSL's faculty advisor.[75]

GSL has had a number of success stories over the years. One example is Enhanzer, a firm founded by Lashan Silva, a 2013 GSL alumnus from Sri Lanka who also serves as the company's CEO. Enhanzer enhances the efficiency of businesses via cloud data storage, automated processes, and enterprise resource planning consulting services. It processes 11,000 transactions a day. Another example is 4Axis Solutions, a mobile-app start-up founded by Dumindu Kanankage of Sri Lanka. In 2015, four years after Kanankage graduated from GSL, 4Axis was listed nineteenth in the productivity category on iTunes. It had revenues of $1 million and 16 million downloads worldwide. PrepClass, founded by Olumide Ogunlana and Obanor Chukwuwezam from Nigeria, is another success story. PrepClass is an online portal for students preparing for standardized tests in Nigeria. In 2014, it was named one of *Fast Company's* Top 10 Most Innovative Companies in Africa.

In 2018, GSL's website listed seventeen companies that were created following the program. However, the program's impact can be measured by more than just revenue and employment created. For instance, its impact on how local students view the world is major, as reflected in testimonials such as the one from Silva, the founder of Enhanzer: "At that time we didn't have any entrepreneurship-related programs in our country. The GSL program helped me a lot to change my track from a traditional engineer to an entrepreneur."[76] GSL also facilitates new local networks. "If not for the MIT-GSL instructors who came to Nigeria, the team would not have pursued entrepreneurship, met, or built PrepClass," said Ogunlana in 2014.[77]

D-LAB

As discussed in chapter 3, D-Lab supports the development, design, and dissemination of technologies and sustainable solutions adapted to the developing world.[78] It was founded by Amy Smith ('84) and grew out of the Priscilla King Gray Public Service Center. It encompasses a number of programs, including twenty courses, fieldwork opportunities for students, research and evaluation programs, conferences, and K–12 outreach. Experiential learning, real-world projects, community-led development, scalability, and ability to make a global impact are central to D-Lab.

Over the years, D-Lab has developed and perfected a number of technologies, such as community water testing and treatment systems, human-powered agricultural processing machines, medical and assistive devices for global health, and clean-burning cooking fuels made from waste. Although its main focus was not on entrepreneurship, from the onset it saw entrepreneurship as an important tool to scale the dissemination of its technologies. In that spirit, D-Lab launched the Scale-Ups program in 2012 in order to leverage transformative innovations through scalable business models that can accelerate positive social change in the developing world. "No matter how good the technology, if there is not a strong enterprise behind it, it's probably doomed," said Saida Benhayoune, director of the Scale-Ups program, in the *Wall Street Journal.*[79]

By 2015, D-Lab Scale-Ups fellowships had raised $5.2 million, creating more than 200 direct and 1,240 indirect full-time jobs, and directly improved the lives of over 420,000 people. By 2016, D-Lab Scale-Ups fellowships had supported twenty-seven fellows working in sectors including agriculture, energy, water, health care, housing, mobility, recycling, education, and personal finance.

For instance, Karina Pikhart ('09) cofounded 6dot Innovations to market a handheld Braille labeling device that helps blind people to print custom adhesive labels in Braille to allow them to identify medicines and other bottled products, as well as appliances and file folders. A total of 3.5 billion people suffer from vision loss in developing countries, and with little access to medical treatment and other forms of assistance, technologies like 6dot can be an important way to improve quality of life and safety for the blind.[80]

Surgibox[81] addresses the fact that, according to a 2015 study published in the *Lancet*, 5 billion people don't have access to safe, clean surgical care. Their device is a collapsible tent that creates a sterile space around the portion of a patient undergoing surgery. The motto of the company is: "Surgibox, the operating room in a backpack." It was designed by Debbie Lin Teodorescu, a doctor and a D-Lab research affiliate, and was later produced by Teodorescu, D-Lab's workshop manager Dennis Nagle, D-Lab alumna Madeline Hickman ('11), David King of Massachusetts General Hospital, and Sally Miller ('16), as well as MIT professor Daniel Frey ('97). They aim at selling Surgibox for less than $100. The Surgibox team won numerous awards, including one from MassChallenge in 2018. That same year, the team was poised to seek approval from the US Food and Drug Administration (FDA) once the testing phase of the product was completed.[82]

Arun Cherian was a Scale-Ups fellow in 2016. He is trying to develop a solution to help the 26 million people in India who suffer from disabilities that affect mobility in many cases. Existing prosthetic legs were either free and inefficient for walking or good, but too expensive for most people. Rise Legs, Cherian's social enterprise, is in the process of creating prosthetic legs made of cane from local forests, which are four times lighter than existing products. The use of cane has the added bonus of providing income to cane artisans. With his fellowship, Cherian conducted a pilot clinical trial in 2016, prototyped a course in India on assembling the product, and explored the potential to introduce it in Africa. "We are looking into becoming a multiproduct-and-service company, thereby being able to affect the lives of more people worldwide," said Cherian.[83]

LEGATUM CENTER'S FELLOWSHIPS AND OTHER PROGRAMS

The Legatum Center for Development and Entrepreneurship is built on the notion that entrepreneurs are key to improving economic and social progress in developing countries, a philosophy that is in opposition to the traditional support for a more top-down perspective.[84] The virtual circle that the Legatum Center tries to achieve is based on the assumption that sustainable and scalable business models provide not only jobs, but long-term solutions to poverty and, in some cases, systemwide solutions that complement international aid. The Legatum Center's capstone initiative is its Fellowship Program. Founded in 2007, the program accounted for twenty to twenty-five fellows per year in its first ten years. The program provides fellows with tuition, support for travel and prototyping, and special seminars, as well as access to the resources of MIT's entrepreneurial ecosystem.

In 2017, on the tenth anniversary of its founding, the Legatum Center reported that it had distributed $7 million in fellowships to 213 fellows since the Fellowship Program began. It had 58 active Legatum entrepreneurs operating in the developing world, who had collectively raised $79 million and created approximatively 15,000 jobs, which affected the lives of 600,000 people.[85] Legatum has also managed Open Mic Africa, a selection process leading to the Zambezi Prize that recognizes African entrepreneurs who are working on promising solutions to encourage financial inclusion.[86] In 2018, the grand prize was awarded to South Africa's fintech Wala (founded in 2015), which uses blockchain technology to allow zero-fee micropayments.[87] It also provides a cryptocurrency wallet, transactional banking, remittances, loans, and insurance.[88]

mSurvey is a successful representative venture founded by a Legatum fellow.[89] During a trip to Kenya funded by a Legatum seed grant, Kenfield Griffith ('06), a 2010–2011 fellow, experienced how challenging it was to access consumer data in developing countries because most developing economies are informal (i.e., cash based and not recorded). In Africa, for instance, 66 percent of the economy is informal. After graduating in 2012, Griffith founded mSurvey, which allows clients to create survey conversations using multiple-choice and open-ended questions with a text message–based survey tool, with Louis Majanja. Consumers are incentivized to participate with mobile rewards. The company's clientele included 21 million people in Kenya alone in 2018. Its clients might use the surveys to brand products, for instance. If consumers indicate that they buy yogurt because it is healthy, the client might underscore this quality in advertising campaigns. A key feature of mSurvey is collecting data in real time and at scale. In 2017, mSurvey was growing its operations in Kenya, the Philippines, Jamaica, Trinidad and Tobago, and other locations in Africa, the Caribbean, and the US.[90]

A more recent venture that has not yet had time to fully scale—but whose impact seems very promising—is ClimaCell. ClimaCell, which was founded in 2015 by two 2016–2017 Legatum fellows, master's of business administration (MBA) students Rei Goffer ('17) and Itai Zlotnik ('17), along with Shimon Elkabetz,[91] repurposes wireless communication networks as sensors to increase the accuracy of weather forecasts. Most current weather forecasting models are based on technology primarily developed fifty years ago, which relies on radar tracking systems, costly satellite technology, or both. ClimaCell's technology has the advantage of being scalable because it does not need to install additional hardware—a particular boon in developing countries. CEO Elkabetz said in 2017 that an average of 3,400 people die each year in India due to flash floods and that "Developing countries like India don't have sufficient weather infrastructure, like radar and weather stations, to ensure public safety and serve the private sector."[92] He added, "Our technology helps developing countries leapfrog from no weather data to granular data using software. ClimaCell can issue alerts about flooding, including warnings to citizens and information for rescue teams."[93] With such information, farmers could also better forecast rainfalls and thus improve their yield.

IDEAS SOCIAL INNOVATION CHALLENGE

Since its founding in 2001 until the present day, the IDEAS Social Innovation Challenge (formerly IDEAS Global Challenge) has awarded over $1 million to more than 170 teams that have implemented innovative service projects in forty-four countries, affecting hundreds of thousands of lives.[94] (For more on the formation of IDEAS and the way that it operates, see chapters 3 and 7.) These teams have secured more than $65 million in additional funding, with many having a substantial impact around the world. Nearly 50 percent of IDEAS projects are still active in some form today.[95]

The 2018 IDEAS grand prize winner was Umbulizer, which is developing a low-cost, portable medical ventilator to serve patients in rural areas of developing countries where the medical infrastructure is unreliable. The team was composed of Moiz Imam ('18), a senior in mechanical engineering, Sanchay Gupta, a Harvard Medical School student, and Hamza Khan, a Harvard Business School student. The ultimate objective of the team is to produce the device locally and mass-manufacture it. Loop,[96] another 2018 winner, is the creation of two MIT mechanical engineers, Sarah Tress ('19) and Shannon McCoy ('19), who are trying to prevent the pressure sores that often afflict those who use wheelchairs. In some developing countries, the life expectancy for people with spinal cord injuries can be as low as one year due to such infected sores. Loop has created an air cushion that is made of cheap bicycle inner tubes that are looped through a grid of holes in a plastic base. It aimed at producing it for as low as $5 (in contrast with the $400 cost of existing cushion products) once they reached manufacturing scale.[97]

The Kanchan Arsenic Filter, winner of the 2002 IDEAS competition, was coinvented by MIT Department of Civil and Environmental Engineering senior lecturer Susan Murcott and her student Tommy Ngai ('02).[98] The filter removes arsenic from potable water. After winning the IDEAS Global Challenge, Kanchan gained financial support from the World Bank, the Asian Development Bank, and other prominent development agencies. As of 2014, their filter had reached 350,000 Nepalis.[99]

Assured Labor, a spin-off of the Media Lab cofounded by David Reich ('08), Joe Bamber ('08); Siddhartha Goyal ('99), and Ximena Fernandez Ordoñez, was a 2008 winner of the IDEAS Global Challenge. Assured Labor made the labor market much more efficient by enabling job seekers in developing countries find jobs using their cell phones. Using their method, it only took employers seven days to hire someone, as opposed to the thirty-five days that the process took with classified ads. Assured Labor specializes in recruiting mid-to-low-wage positions, such as cashiers, salespeople, and security officers. By 2014, it was a multimillion-dollar employment resource company in Nicaragua and Mexico, with plans to expand in other countries.

NONDEGREE EDUCATIONAL PROGRAMS

The growing interest in MIT's entrepreneurship achievements from around the world led to the development at the Institute of a few nondegree education programs that have had significant impact on their participants and their local entrepreneurial ecosystem. The Entrepreneur Development Program (EDP),[100] launched in 1999, is a one-week executive education program dedicated to the process of starting, growing, and scaling businesses following a structured and disciplined approach. It is aimed at ambitious entrepreneurs from ventures with international potential and "intrapreneurs" from corporations, as well as university staff and regional development professionals interested in stimulating their entrepreneurial ecosystem (ideally in combination with local entrepreneurs). It is rooted in a team-based, hands-on, action learning approach combining lectures, live case studies, and hands-on experience in developing a business plan. EDP exposes participants to the Greater Boston entrepreneurial ecosystem and to a global entrepreneurial network.

In some cases, EDP partners with regional entities to stimulate their entrepreneurial ecosystem on a longer-term basis, such as in the case of Scotland and Northern Ireland. There is, for example, the case of Dr. John Breslin, director of TechInnovate and a senior lecturer in electronic engineering at the National University of Ireland (NUI) Galway, who organized several initiatives at NUI that were based on what he learned at EDP. He created intensive boot camps for NUI's PhD candidates and postdocs that focused on how to launch start-ups and how to teach intrapreneurship to the staff of local large companies. He also secured European Union funding, with other European partners, to teach researchers and innovators in research and development (R&D) organizations across Europe how to create start-ups,[101] illustrating the leveraged impact of EDP across the world. A total of 2,205 persons have participated in EDP since 2000 and, in the program's 2018 edition, there were more than twenty industries and thirty countries were represented.

The Regional Entrepreneurship Acceleration Program (REAP)[102] was launched in 2012 at the instigation of Bill Aulet, then senior lecturer and director of the Trust Center, and professors Fiona Murray, Edward Roberts, and Scott Stern of the Sloan faculty. Their initiative came in response to the growing number of delegations from around the world visiting MIT to try to understand the inner workings of its success in spinning off start-ups. In response to this interest, REAP is a two-year educational program aimed at representatives of regions dedicated to promoting their entrepreneurial ecosystem. Each region taking part in the program must be represented by delegates of five categories of stakeholders: government policymakers, risk capital providers, academic institutions, corporations, and the entrepreneurial community, all of whom must collaborate. MIT REAP admits up to eight such teams every year, representing regions of 1 to 10 million people. Each team needs to conduct an assessment of its region's strengths, weaknesses, and potential; what the region's needs are; and how to implement its strategy most effectively. Participants do this through a combination of workshops at MIT and remote sessions from their local bases.

As of 2019, forty-five teams from around the world have been through the REAP program, including Scotland, Ghana, Ecuador, Thailand, Saudi

Arabia, Singapore, Central Denmark, and China, all of which are part of the MIT REAP Global Network of alumni of the program. Measuring the impact of REAP in economic terms is tricky and will probably only be tangible over time, but the cohorts of teams from all over the world that sign up for the program is a success in and of itself.[103]

For instance, Scotland was part of REAP's first cohort in 2012. The multi-stakeholder teams assembled to take part in the REAP program identified that, although Scotland had a rich fabric of small and medium-sized enterprises (SMEs), they invested little in R&D. While there was no lack of entrepreneurial spirit, there was a lack of aspiration to grow on the part of those firms compared to other innovative regions. Scottish universities were centers of innovation, but transforming that innovation into businesses that could compete at an international level was a challenge.

As part of the action plan based on this analysis, the REAP team from Scotland launched three actions. First, the REAP team established, in collaboration with the two major economic development agencies in the region, a three-year Entrepreneurship Support Program with a budget of 3 million British pounds, aimed at enabling established entrepreneurs with the potential to think more globally. A Can-Do-Scale program was also created to promote innovation-driven entrepreneurship, in reaction to a lack of support for entrepreneurs aspiring to scale globally. A competition called Scottish EDGE was also set up, with the objective of identifying and supporting the next generation of entrepreneurial talent.[104]

MIT Global Entrepreneurship Bootcamp[105] started in 2014 in typical MIT fashion, as an experiment in blended learning, building on MIT's online course Entrepreneurship 101: Who Is your Customer?[106] Out of the 54,856 students who enrolled in the course that year, 47 were selected from 22 countries to participate in the inaugural Global Entrepreneurship Bootcamp at MIT, where they were challenged to start a company in one week. The motto of the boot camps is "One semester condensed into one week." At the end of the week, nine teams pitched their plans to a panel of judges. In 2019, the MIT Bootcamps website claimed that more than 800 alumni who represented more than seventy countries participated, with more than 100 new ventures formed and more than $70 million raised.[107]

When Yen Pei Tay of Malaysia joined MIT Global Entrepreneurship Bootcamp in 2017 (after taking the online entrepreneurship courses), he hoped to validate his proposal for enabling mobile phone users to sell their unused data to other users and to figure out how to bring it to market. The feedback from mentors led him to reorient his customer target from businesses to individuals, which translated into an app called Simplify. Within a few months of its release, *Fast Company* named Simplify one of the world's 50 Most Innovative Companies.[108] The Office of Digital Learning that runs the boot camp argues that the program was founded to support visionaries like Tay, who have the potential to make a breakthrough but need just a little help to make it happen. The impact of MIT Bootcamps is measured not only in metrics such as number of start-ups created, but also by the more intangible energy and motivation that it conveys to its participants, as exemplified by the participant Iman Urooj's quote: "This bootcamp gave me the necessary injection of inspiration to go back to Pakistan with newfound enthusiasm and energy and a desire for change."[109]

CONCLUSION

As this chapter shows, MIT entrepreneurship has had a substantial impact across the world in terms of wealth and employment creation, health care improvements, applications of new technologies to the marketplace, local economic development, and better understanding across cultures. This impact also goes both ways, such as when MIT students learn to operate in developing countries, where they must learn to navigate irregular electricity and internet services, or when they get exposure to rapid prototyping in the Pearl River Delta in China.

10 EDUCATING ASPIRING ENTREPRENEURS

This chapter will dive specifically into how entrepreneurship education at MIT is conceived and taught. Education is the preeminent function of the initiatives and entities of the Institute that are dedicated to promoting entrepreneurship—with the exception of those committed to technology transfer. Although start-up launches and successes are celebrated, the objective of MIT's set of training resources is not to simply churn out start-ups, but to educate students and members of the MIT community at large, as members of the MIT leadership regularly stress. For instance, when Professor Ian Waitz, the dean of the School of Engineering, announced the launch of the Sandbox Innovation Fund Program in 2016, he emphasized its educational mission, insisting that it is not a competition, nor is it about picking winners. Rather, it is about creating opportunities for MIT students "interested in learning about innovation through doing, about developing people."[1] Bill Aulet ('94), managing director of the Martin Trust Center for MIT Entrepreneurship, argues that it is extremely important that educators stay 100 percent educators—that they not be tempted to play other roles, such as becoming investors or substituting themselves as policymakers. "Incentives almost immediately are at cross-purposes, and the students figure this out quickly. Do the students look at us as educators who are there for their personal development or as investors who have a vested interest in a positive outcome? Should they be open and honest with us, or should they try to impress us so they convince us to become investors? What happens to those we do not invest in, and what signal does that send to the broader market? The moment that we are something other than 100 percent educators is the day we lose our 'honest broker' uniqueness," says Aulet.[2]

FROM CURRICULAR AND EXTRACURRICULAR TO COCURRICULAR

There is still a debate today in society as to whether entrepreneurship is innate or can be taught. MIT clearly stands on the side of those who believe it can—and should!—be taught as a key engine to feed innovation. Critical to this teaching was moving past the way that entrepreneurship was discussed in the classroom in the early years, which consisted largely of successful entrepreneurs reliving the highlights of their journeys to glory. The current approach contains more traditional pedagogical elements aimed at providing the students with effective tools combined with opportunities of experiential learning that are often in extracurricular settings—hence the use of the word "cocurricular" lately. By 2019, MIT offered more than seventy-four entrepreneurship and innovation classes across its five schools.[3] The Trust Center's annual report divides them into categories according to the development phase of a start-up: the nucleation phase, product definition, and venture development (see figure 10.1). First are courses about the nucleation phase that touch upon topics such as ideation, team building, and career choices. Second come courses that focus on product definition, with subjects such as defining product-market fit, primary market research, and strategy. The third group includes courses grouped under venture development themes, including product design, finance, business models and pricing, scaling the business, human resource management, and industry-specific courses. There are also practice-oriented courses offering in-company experiences, such as the MIT Entrepreneurship Lab (E-Lab) and the Global Entrepreneurship Lab (G-Lab), discussed in previous chapters.[4] (For more information, see appendix 10.1, "Course Offerings, 2019–2020," at the end of this chapter.)

Some of these courses are part of specialized programs, such as the minor in entrepreneurship and innovation offered to undergraduate students jointly by the School of Engineering and the Sloan School of Management. The objective of this minor is to provide students with knowledge about each step in the innovation process, from conception to the designing of a solution to the launch of a funded organization. The students are also provided with tools to acquire the necessary interpersonal skills to engage

NUCLEATION PHASE 1		PRODUCT DEFINITION PHASE 2	VENTURE DEVELOPMENT PHASE 3			
CORE ENTREPRENEURSHIP-SPECIFIC SKILLS						
Career Choice	Ideation	Defining & Refining Product-Market Fit	Key Founders Decisions	Sector Deep Dives	Business Model & Pricing	HR
	Team Building I		Basics of Finance	Product Design	Scaling: Manufacturing	Leadership & Culture
		Primary Market Research	Legal	Product Development	Scaling: Process & Infrastructure	Work-Life Balance
		Strategy	Customer Acquisition	Product Management	Financing	Corporate Entrepreneurship
						Building Eship Systems
ESSENTIAL SKILLS FOR ENTREPRENEURS (SEMI-CUSTOMIZED)						
Soft Skills			Sales	Communication	Dealing with Adversity	Negotiations
GENERAL SKILLS VALUABLE TO ENTREPRENEURS						
				Project Management	Corporate Strategy	

FIGURE 10.1
Entrepreneurship courses offered in 2019–2020.
Source: *2020 Annual Report—Martin Trust Center for MIT Entrepreneurship* (Cambridge, MA: MIT, 2020), http://entrepreneurship.mit.edu/annual-report/ (accessed December 14, 2020), 6.

with team members and stakeholders and the frameworks to understand entrepreneurship and innovation in their societal context.

The Sloan School of Management offers an Entrepreneurship and Innovation Track (E&I) within its master's of business administration (MBA) program. The track is focused on teaching students with a strong interest in entrepreneurship how to launch and develop emerging technology ventures, and it leads to a certificate in entrepreneurship and innovation in addition to the MBA degree. The track's curriculum emphasizes teamwork and focuses on real-world entrepreneurial projects, balancing theory and practice. After an introductory course during the first semester, the students participate in a one-week Silicon Valley study tour during the Independent Activities Period (IAP) in January, during which they have the opportunity to meet the owners of local start-ups and venture capitalists in California. During subsequent semesters, E&I students can choose among a number of elective courses focusing on entrepreneurship and innovation. They are also required to take part in at least one team of the MIT $100K Entrepreneurship Competition or an equivalent undertaking.[5]

As mentioned in earlier chapters, the Media Lab also offers a specialized Entrepreneurship Program, as does the School of Architecture and Urban Planning with their MITdesignX initiative. The School of Engineering does not offer a specific program in entrepreneurship, but in recent years, it has multiplied its offering of courses in entrepreneurship catering specifically to engineering students. It has also launched extracurricular initiatives for the wider student population that have an educational objective, such as the Sandbox Innovation Fund Program and StartMIT (described in chapters 4 and 7).[6]

MIT also offers three online courses in entrepreneurship through its edX platform: Entrepreneurship 101: Who Is Your Customer?, Entrepreneurship 102: What Can You Do for Your Customer?, and Entrepreneurship: Show Me the Money.[7] In addition, the Sloan School of Management offers various executive education courses in entrepreneurship and innovation.[8]

The courses in entrepreneurship are complemented by experiences that students gain in dozens of extracurricular activities, as documented in previous chapters. The need, particularly in entrepreneurship, to go beyond skill building in classes and to learn by doing has blurred the lines between curricular and extracurricular skill building to the extent that MIT increasingly talks about cocurricular training. The Sandbox Innovation Fund Program, which facilitates access to a hands-on entrepreneurship experience and helps accelerate more advanced projects with funding and mentoring (as described in chapter 7), is a good example of this phenomenon.

The teaching of entrepreneurship at MIT presents a number of characteristics worth mentioning; we will do so next.

THE SEARCH FOR RIGOR

Consistent with its identity as a research university and its tradition of excellence, MIT has tried to bring rigor and discipline to the teaching of entrepreneurship. Indeed, it had traditionally been taught in most institutions primarily through storytelling by outside professionals, such as entrepreneurs or venture capitalists acting as outside lecturers, rather than by regular, tenure-track academics. This state of affairs was a reflection of the fact that there was very little scholarly work on entrepreneurship until the early 2000s; it was also indicative of the commonly held perception that entrepreneurship was considered to be a professional domain rather than a disciplinary field. A first attempt at overcoming this limitation at the level of teaching was in the creation of Sloan's dual-track teaching model, which consists of classes being taught in tandem by both an entrepreneurship professional and an academic. The professionals bring relevance and the tenure-track faculty contribute scholarly rigor, consistent with the *Mens et Manus* (mind and hand) motto of MIT.

As mentioned earlier, there was very little scholarly work in entrepreneurship, which was not recognized as a credible disciplinary field, for a long time. Academic quality in teaching and research was also made possible by the fact that MIT faculty members generally pursue research in their disciplinary fields—such as economics, finance, strategy, or sociology—but include exploration of the entrepreneurial terrain as part of their research. For instance, a professor with a PhD in finance would publish an article about venture capital—a topic relevant to entrepreneurship—but in a finance journal rather than in an entrepreneurship journal, which has less recognition in his or her discipline. This arrangement was reflected in the joint appointment of those faculty members teaching entrepreneurship both in the group within the Sloan School in charge of entrepreneurship and in the group of their discipline. In other words, the same scholarly rigor was pursued in research related to entrepreneurship as it was in other parts of MIT. This approach was an important consideration when MIT started to hire tenure-track faculty members with a double affiliation in their disciplinary group (such as finance, economics, or marketing) within the Sloan School and in the Management of Technological Innovation and Entrepreneurship group. This approach to scholarly rigor takes its roots in the early research conducted for the National Aeronautics and Space Administration (NASA) in the 1960s by Professor Edward Roberts (see chapter 1).

Since the late 1990s, MIT tenure-track faculty members have developed and taught several new subjects in entrepreneurship, based upon their own PhD training and scholarly research,[9] which has provided a disciplinary rigor in the teaching of entrepreneurship. Examples of such classes include Entrepreneurial Finance, Entrepreneurship Strategy, and Innovation Strategy.

Bill Aulet made an important contribution to the goal of bringing rigor to the teaching of entrepreneurship with the publication of two books: *Disciplined Entrepreneurship: 24 Steps to a Successful Startup* and *Disciplined Entrepreneurship Workbook*,[10] whose framework is used in a number of courses, as well as in the delta v summer accelerator program discussed in several chapters of this book. These books propose an analytical process for starting a company through a number of questions, such as "Who is your customer?" "What can you do for your customer?" and "How does your customer acquire your product?" In trying to reconcile the tension between rigor and relevance, Aulet argues convincingly that entrepreneurship should be framed as a craft as opposed to a science or an art. Like a craft, it is built on fundamental concepts. A potter, for instance, needs to master the basic mechanical and chemical principles of his craft. Knowing those does not guarantee success, but they considerably improve the chances. Like a craft, entrepreneurship is best learned through apprenticeship, or learning by doing, rather than relying only on lectures or manuals. "On the theory side, entrepreneurship education must focus on building a robust body of knowledge that codifies a common set of fundamental concepts designed to increase our students' odds of success. We must validate these concepts using the rigorous research techniques of social sciences. Simultaneously, we must develop craft-like training programs in our schools for how to apply these concepts using an apprenticeship model," writes Aulet.[11] He argues that we should aim to bring entrepreneurship to the level of rigor of medicine, law, or architecture.[12]

ACTION LEARNING

The apprenticeship learning model is prevalent in the teaching of entrepreneurship at MIT, particularly in the practice-oriented "Lab" classes at the Sloan School of Management. Founded in 1996, The E-Lab course was the first of this kind of lab class, providing students with opportunities to solve real-world problems for high-tech start-ups in the Boston area. E-Lab was followed in 2000 by G-Lab, which offered students the chance to get involved with start-ups in developing countries. The pedagogy was very much in line with the learning-by-doing philosophy so dear to MIT, but in this case it was being applied to entrepreneurship and framed as action learning. G-Lab was "an innovative course that fundamentally changed the learning landscape at MIT Sloan. G-Lab became MIT Sloan's flagship Action Learning course and has served as a model for establishing several similar classes," according to Sloan.[13] By 2019, there were thirteen action learning labs at the Sloan School of Management that encompassed topics beyond entrepreneurship. In lab courses, students work in teams with actual companies to solve real-life problems. In G-Lab, for instance, student teams are paired with entrepreneurial ventures in developing countries. Students first interact remotely from campus with the firms to research a problem. They then spend the month of January on site with the companies. All along, student teams work under the guidance of both a faculty content mentor, who provides industry expertise, and a process mentor, who helps with team dynamics. Students need to tackle unfamiliar business problems, most of the time in resource-scarce environments, and solve issues in real time. Students are faced with issues requiring cultural sensitivity, intense teamwork, and a willingness to challenge theoretical assumptions about management. Reflection is emphasized as a learning method throughout the action learning process. Students are encouraged to reflect not only at the end of the project, but also before the project starts and while they are working on it. Journal writing, team processes, mentor coaching, and formal public presentations are all considered helpful tools in the reflection process.

Another real-world-focused class worth mentioning is Innovation-Teams (I-Teams),[14] because of its uniqueness and because its practice orientation and mixed-team feature have been replicated by many other classes.[15] In I-Teams, mixed teams of students from Sloan and the School of Engineering explore over the course of one academic year a "go-to-market" strategy for research conducted in MIT's labs. The students aim to reduce or eliminate the risk of what Luis Perez-Breva ('99), the course's lead instructor, called "deep-tech projects" by examining various possible commercial applications of the technology and by planning for scale. The objective, according to Perez-Breva, is "to take a technology from lab to society to solve a meaningful problem."[16] This effort is operated in coordination with the principal investigator, usually a professor, leading the research. Between 2008 and 2019, I-Teams students had devised a path to commercialization for over 200 research projects. Although creating start-ups is not an objective in and of itself for I-Teams, some forty companies have emerged from this effort, including Arctic Sand, EyeNetra, Lantos Technologies, LiquiGlide,

Lux Labs, and ReviveMed.[17] Most of these start-ups also used other resources available to aspiring entrepreneurs on campus. The I-Teams course has had a significant impact on the teaching of entrepreneurship by initiating a new formula: the deliberate teaming of students of management with students of engineering to work on potentially viable commercialization projects.[18] This formula would later be applied to numerous other classes involving mixed business and technical student teams working on real-world commercialization of technologies, as discussed next.[19]

MIXED TEAMS OF SCIENCE AND ENGINEERING STUDENTS WITH BUSINESS SCHOOL STUDENTS

There is a strong belief at MIT that entrepreneurship is a team sport. It is based on the evidence that teams of founders tend to perform better than individual founders[20] and that complementary teams tend to do better than homogeneous teams. Following on the heels of the I-Teams class, nowadays, most teams in entrepreneurship-related courses or contests are required to be composed of a mix of engineering or science students with management students. This has become an important feature and a great strength of entrepreneurship training at MIT. Both groups benefit from each other's contributions. Engineering and science students discover the market dimensions of the projects with the help of their peers from the business school and learn that it is not enough to build a better mouse-trap, while the latter benefit from scientific and engineering insights. Both groups are forced to deal with cultural differences and with more complex team dynamics than what occurs in homogeneous teams. The results are stronger teams and more effective projects.

The teaching of entrepreneurship at MIT, whether through classes or cocurricular activities, covers various phases of the formation of an entrepreneurial project and does not, as is often the case in other institutions, focus only on the formulation of business plans. First, there are efforts aimed at creating awareness of the entrepreneurship resources available so that students become engaged in entrepreneurship as early as possible during their tenure at MIT. An important tool for creating early awareness is t=0, the festival of entrepreneurship that is held at the beginning of the academic year. Second, there are introductions to entrepreneurship through courses such as

The Founder's Journey and Introduction to Technological Entrepreneurship, which are offered through StartMIT, a two-and-a-half week introductory program, as well as the student-run StartLabs' Entrepreneurship Experience and its Entrepalooza, an event showcasing entrepreneurship at MIT.

Foundational entrepreneurship courses are followed by progressively more specialized ones that provide students with specific skill sets. These courses are complemented by concentrated training during the IAP period with MIT Fuse, a three-week microaccelerator aimed at making students function at "entrepreneurial speed."[21] There is also the Nuts and Bolts of Business Plans course during IAP. Students can confirm and solidify their commitment to entrepreneurship through more advanced courses, as well as by exposing their training to the real world through internships and involvement in action learning labs such as E-Lab and G-Lab, and by moving through the stages of mentoring and selection leading the finale of various contests. Sandbox's financial and advisory resources stay available for more advanced entrepreneurial projects that have overcome earlier hurdles. The most committed teams with the best projects, who want to embrace the entrepreneurial career path, could be selected to participate in the delta v summer accelerator, whose objective is to prepare the teams of founders to launch their companies in the real world after completion of the program. Prizes earned from participating in contests, such as the $100K Competition, the IDEAS Social Innovation Challenge, or the ClimateTech & Energy Prize (CEP), help the winners seed the early phases of their companies. Once companies have been launched after graduation, the MIT Venture Mentoring Service (VMS) is available to provide ongoing mentoring. MIT Startup Exchange (STEX) connects MIT-related startups with established companies, principally members of the MIT Industrial Liaison Program (ILP), which are potential customers, partners, and investors. The Media Lab's E14 venture fund offers the lab's graduates fellowships that allow them to benefit from a six-month runway to establish a venture and provides equity seed investment as well. The entrepreneurial projects dealing with more complex technologies requiring longer development time can apply to The Engine, which was set up specifically to assist such start-ups. Learning, mentoring, and benefiting from introductions do not stop with graduation either, thanks to the networking with alumni and the entrepreneurial community at large that graduates gain through their participation in curricular and cocurricular activities. Many of them, once they have become accomplished entrepreneurs, return to campus to share their expertise with students.

ENTREPRENEURSHIP EDUCATION CATERS
TO VARIOUS TYPES OF MOTIVATIONS

Of course, not all MIT students will become entrepreneurs. Therefore, training in entrepreneurship is tailored to students with a variety of motivations, from the curious ones to those who come to MIT with the clear idea of starting a company. In between, there are students who feel more comfortable joining an existing start-up rather than launching one. Some feel their calling is to be intrapreneurs in a large corporation, conducting innovation within a larger entity. Still others fulfill their aspirations by becoming entrepreneurship amplifiers, who build infrastructures that foster entrepreneurship in a region, including accelerators or educational programs. The description of the minor in entrepreneurship and innovation in the course catalog states this clearly: "The Minor in Entrepreneurship and Innovation (E&I Minor) educates students to serve as leaders in the innovation economy with the knowledge, skills, and confidence to develop, scale, and deliver breakthrough solutions to real-world problems. They will be prepared to do so within a range of organizational contexts: an entrepreneurial start-up of their own, as key members of a founding team, or as an entrepreneurial member of a large organization."[22] Aulet often says, "We want to teach our students not just how to launch businesses; we want to teach them how to think like entrepreneurs."[23] In doing so, he stresses the educational dimension of entrepreneurship at MIT.

The outcomes of teaching students how to think like entrepreneurs are diverse and can take students to some surprising places, not only in start-ups, as the following examples illustrate. Dave Danielson ('08), a cofounder of the MIT Energy Club (see chapter 6) went on to serve as assistant secretary of the US Department of Energy's Office of Energy Efficiency and Renewable Energy for four years under President Barack Obama, where he led the largest government agency for clean energy innovation funding in the world.[24] As mentioned in chapter 7, Andrea Ippolito ('12) states that she went from Hacking Medicine to cofounding Smart Scheduling (later known as Arsenal Health), to being a Presidential Innovation Fellow of the

Innovators Network at the US Department of Veterans Affairs, to teaching entrepreneurship at Cornell University.[25] Thomas Massie ('93), discussed in chapter 6, was the winner of the 1995 Lemelson-MIT Student Prize and of the 1995 MIT $10K Business Plan Competition, and he also was the cofounder of SensAble Technologies. In 2010, he was elected to the office of judge executive of Lewis County, and in 2012 he was elected to Congress as the US representative for Kentucky's Fourth Congressional District.[26]

INTEGRATION OF ENTREPRENEURSHIP TEACHING INTO THE BROADER CURRICULUM

Training in entrepreneurship is well integrated within the broader curriculum to form a new educational experience. As Lita Nelsen ('64), the former director of the Technology Licensing Office (TLO), explains: "It's not 'you go and learn how to be an entrepreneur'; it's you learn biology or chemistry or electrical engineering or computer science, but you also learn how entrepreneurship and innovation and moving technology out into the marketplace works—rather than having to learn that after you graduate."[27] This approach is rooted in the realization that entrepreneurship has become a credible career pathway for students. It is also a valid path to innovation at a time when the US innovation system is broken, with the disappearance of large corporate labs and the short-term focus of most corporations. The minor in entrepreneurship and innovation represents integration into the broader curriculum, as well as the fact that MIT's leadership, with the Innovation Initiative, embraced entrepreneurship explicitly.

CUSTOMER FOCUS

When we look at Aulet's Disciplined Entrepreneurship methodology, the Deshpande Center for Technological Innovation's process of moving academic research from the lab to real-world impacts, the Innovation Corps (I-Corps) methodology, and the many practice-oriented courses at MIT, we see that all of these entities at the Institute share the goal of satisfying real needs. They also emphasize the necessity of talking to potential customers to validate the market early on. For instance, as already mentioned, the first stage of Aulet's methodology is "Who is your customer?" Participants in the I-Corps program need to conduct 100 interviews with potential customers because experience and research have proved that the market is usually not where we think it is, and would-be company founders tend to build products that customers don't need. This extreme due diligence may also be a reaction against the critique that MIT-related entrepreneurs have tended to be excellent technologists but poorer marketers.[28] Aulet argues in favor of accelerating the process of customer feedback so that entrepreneurs can discover as early as possible the flaws in their business model. He also believes that it is best for potential founders to fail early in order for them to learn from their mistakes and to be in a better position to subsequently improve their projects. He argues that projects under pressure to accelerate their development end up on a steeper growth path than projects that are not under such constraints and thus tend to stagnate.[29] Luis Perez-Breva, the leader of I-Teams, puts the bar even higher by advocating removing the risk of commercialization by examining not one, but multiple, commercial applications of a technology.[30]

FOCUS ON INNOVATION-DRIVEN ENTERPRISES

Entrepreneurship courses at MIT don't deal with just any type of entrepreneurship, but rather focus on what Aulet and Murray call "innovation-driven entrepreneurship," or the creation of innovation-driven enterprises (IDEs), which they define as "the pursuit of global opportunities based on bringing to customers new innovations that have a clear competitive advantage and high growth potential. By innovation, we mean new-to-the-world ideas in the technical, market, or business model domain."[31] They stress that they do not call it "technology-driven" entrepreneurship because while innovation can originate from technology, it also can come from other types of sources, including business processes and models. They contrast it with small business entrepreneurship, or the creation of small and medium-sized enterprises (SMEs), which are a form of self-employment "serving local markets with traditional, well-understood business ideas and limited competitive advantage" (see figure 10.2).[32] This is not to say that SMEs are unimportant to an economy, but they do offer on average lower wages and benefits compared to IDEs and large companies, and SMEs are less good at creating jobs because they stay small. It is new IDE companies (i.e., five years old or less) that generate most of the jobs.[33] The two types of entrepreneurship are thus very different. IDEs are likely to raise external

SME Entrepreneurship	IDE Entrepreneurship
Focus on addressing local and regional markets only.	Focus on global markets.
Innovation is not necessary to SME establishment and growth, nor is competitive advantage.	The company is based on some sort of innovation (tech, process, business model) and potential competitive advantage.
"Non-tradable jobs"—jobs generally performed locally, e.g., restaurants, dry cleaners, service industry.	"Tradable jobs"—jobs that do not have to be performed locally.
Most often family businesses or businesses with very little external capital.	More diverse ownership base including wide array of external capital providers.
The company typically grows at a linear rate. When you put money into the company, the system (revenue, cash flow, jobs, etc.) will respond quickly in a positive manner.	The company starts by losing money, but if successful will have exponential growth. Requires investment. When you put money into the company, the revenue/cash flow/jobs numbers do not respond quickly.

FIGURE 10.2

SME versus IDE entrepreneurship.

Source: William Aulet and Fiona E. Murray, "A Tale of Two Entrepreneurs: Understanding Differences in the Types of Entrepreneurship in the Economy," in *SSRN Electronic Journal*, 2013, https://doi.org/10.2139/ssrn.2259740 (accessed December 14, 2020).

capital to develop a competitive advantage, whereas SMEs generally need little capital and their founders typically want to keep control of their enterprises. IDEs are also more inclined to be created by teams of founders with members with higher levels of education, rather than a sole founder as in the case of SMEs. Of course, IDEs are risky and many fail, but those that succeed have a disproportionate impact on the economy in terms of jobs and wealth creation, as well as innovation, as the examples of MIT-related companies such as Akamai, Analog Devices, and Biogen illustrate, as discussed in previous chapters.

ENTREPRENEURSHIP SITUATED IN A BROADER CONTEXT

The teaching of entrepreneurship at MIT makes sure that students realize that entrepreneurship is a team sport, but also that it does not happen in a socioeconomic vacuum. Aulet told the *Wall Street Journal* that "entrepreneurs create an organization that didn't exist before. They have a scarce amount of resources with which to do that. They are the underdog."[34] It echoes Harvard Business School professor Howard Stevenson's widely accepted definition of entrepreneurship as "the pursuit of opportunity beyond the resources you currently control."[35] As a result of not controlling resources, entrepreneurs rely on others to access them and need to use their social capital to ask for favors and reciprocities and convey trust and gratitude. They also need to employ personal relationships and networks, in order to succeed. It is with the goal of making students realize this early on that the large majority of classes include field projects, are complemented by labs and internships, or are entirely practice-oriented.

A number of classes also teach that entrepreneurship is not only about entrepreneurs. Successful entrepreneurship also relies on an ecology of other stakeholders, such as government entities putting in place adequate regulations, enforcing the rule of law, and funding basic research, just to name a few examples. It also requires efficient capital markets intermediating the flow of savings to the funding needs of start-ups. Corporations are also critical as customers, investors, and partners. This perspective is very much present, for instance, in the design of the minor in entrepreneurship and innovation, which aims notably at providing students skills in "a range of global contexts for entrepreneurship and innovation, including variations in the interface with key stakeholders whose interests have the potential to enable or limit the potential effectiveness of innovation and entrepreneurship."[36]

This broader perspective on entrepreneurship also includes a number of courses grouped under the category E&I, which aim to understand the role of entrepreneurship in various contexts, and its contribution to economic prosperity and its impact on the environment. The graduate-level course Innovation Ecosystems for Regional Entrepreneurship-Acceleration

Leaders provides a framework to understand this broader perspective on entrepreneurship, as does the Regional Entrepreneurship Acceleration Program (REAP), by analyzing the strengths and weaknesses of entrepreneurship regionally and exploring how to reinforce the local entrepreneurial infrastructure.[37] MIT professor Scott Stern and colleagues—more recently Jorge Guzman ('11), now a professor at Columbia University—have conducted research on the more macro and policy aspects of entrepreneurship. So have Fiona Murray, Phil Budden, and Anna Turskaya ('17).[38]

Of course, classes and cocurricular activities focusing on social entrepreneurship do provide a broader perspective on entrepreneurship through their focus on social needs and impact, as this book highlighted in previous chapters. It is the case, for instance, with courses offered by D-Lab, as well as training provided by the Legatum Center for Development and Entrepreneurship. The integration of this broader societal perspective also lies at the heart of MITdesignX, the School of Architecture and Urban Planning's entrepreneurship program, which aims to accelerate entrepreneurship that addresses urgent challenges in cities by making them more sustainable, intelligent, and responsive to their inhabitants. "When you're in the complexity of a city, you're trying to invent with so many different stakeholders at once. You're dealing with people's lives. The vision for [MITdesignX] is to create a place that's inventive and creative from a design focus, but that's also grounded in responsible entrepreneurship,"[39] said Andrea Chegut, a research scientist in the MIT Center for Real Estate and director of the MIT Real Estate Innovation Lab.

Finally, entrepreneurship at MIT is viewed within its original mission of local economic development, which has recently grown to achieve the ambition of having a positive impact globally given the major challenges, such as climate change, that the world is facing.[40] The Trust Center's mission statement reflects this as well: "Our mission is to advance knowledge and educate students in innovation-driven entrepreneurship in a manner that will best serve the nation and the world in the 21st century."[41]

As this chapter shows, entrepreneurship education is imprinted by MIT's culture of excellence, a commitment to learning by doing, the embracing of interdisciplinarity, a desire to have a positive impact, and a willingness to experiment. In just a few years, entrepreneurship has moved to the core of the MIT curriculum. It is not a distraction from chemistry or biology, but rather a desired complement in a world where the center of gravity of innovation has moved to start-ups now that most corporations have shut down their research labs and most governments restrict public funding of fundamental research. In this evolving economic and political landscape, MIT's entrepreneurship education prepares students for career paths where they will be agents of innovation and betterment, whether through start-ups or in other organizational settings.

APPENDIX 10.1. COURSE OFFERINGS, 2019–2020

CORE COURSES
Nucleation Phase:
VENTURE ENGINEERING

INTRODUCTION TO TECHNOLOGICAL ENTREPRENEURSHIP
Product Definition Phase:
NEW ENTERPRISES
Strategy:
ENTREPRENEURIAL STRATEGY
Venture Development Phase:
ENTREPRENEURIAL FOUNDING AND TEAMS

SCALING ENTREPRENEURIAL VENTURES

ENTREPRENEURIAL SALES

ENERGY VENTURES

HEALTHCARE VENTURES

FINTECH VENTURES

STRATEGIC DECISION MAKING IN LIFE SCIENCES

ENTREPRENEURSHIP FOR COLLABORATIVE INTELLIGENCE

CORPORATE ENTREPRENEURSHIP

ENTREPRENEURSHIP LAB

INTRODUCTION TO MAKING

DESIGN FOR 3D PRINTING

BUILDING AN ENTREPRENEURIAL VENTURE: ADVANCED TOOLS AND TECHNIQUES

SHORT, INTENSE COURSES

Nucleation Phase:

STARTMIT

MIT FUSE

NUTS AND BOLTS OF BUSINESS PLANNING

Venture Development Phase:

DISCIPLINED ENTREPRENEURSHIP LAB

AFFILIATED COURSES

Nucleation Phase:

ENTREPRENEURSHIP IN ENGINEERING

INTRODUCTION TO DESIGN

ENGINEERING INNOVATION AND DESIGN

INTEGRATED DESIGN LAB I

INTEGRATED DESIGN LAB II

ENGINEERING LEADERSHIP LAB

MANAGEMENT IN ENGINEERING

Product Definition Phase:

INNOVATION TEAMS

PRODUCT DESIGN AND DEVELOPMENT

LISTENING TO THE CUSTOMER

EXECUTING STRATEGY FOR RESULTS

INNOVATION STRATEGY

Venture Development Phase:

ENTREPRENEURSHIP, INNOVATION STARTUPS AND THE LAW

ESSENTIAL LAW FOR BUSINESS

PATENTS, COPYRIGHTS, AND THE LAW OF INTELLECTUAL PROPERTY

SCIENCE AND BUSINESS OF BIOTECHNOLOGY

SOFTWARE AND INTERNET ENTREPRENEURSHIP

INNOVATING FOR IMPACT

MEDIA VENTURES

DEVELOPMENT VENTURES

MEDICAL DEVICE DESIGN

BIOMEDICAL ENGINEERING SEMINAR SERIES

ENTREPRENEURSHIP IN CONSTRUCTION AND REAL ESTATE DEVELOPMENT

GLOBAL BUSINESS OF ARTIFICIAL INTELLIGENCE AND ROBOTICS (GBAIR)

IMAGING VENTURES: CAMERAS, DISPLAYS, AND VISUAL COMPUTING

INNOVATION AND COMMERCIALIZATION OF MATERIALS TECHNOLOGY

PRINCIPLES AND PRACTICES OF DRUG DEVELOPMENT

REVOLUTIONARY VENTURES: HOW TO INVENT AND DEPLOY TRANSFOR-
MATIVE TECHNOLOGIES

STRATEGIC OPPORTUNITIES IN ENERGY

DEVELOPMENT OF MECHANICAL PRODUCTS

THE PRODUCT ENGINEERING PROCESS

ENGINEERING SYSTEMS DESIGNS

DIGITAL PRODUCT MANAGEMENT

PRICING

EFFECTIVE BUSINESS MODELS IN FRONTIER MARKETS

D-LAB: DESIGN FOR SCALE

PROFESSIONAL SEMINAR IN GLOBAL MANUFACTURING INNOVATION
AND ENTREPRENEURSHIP

MANUFACTURING PROCESSES AND SYSTEMS

DESIGN AND MANUFACTURING

MEMSI: MIT ENTREPRENEURSHIP AND MAKER SKILLS INTEGRATOR

ENTREPRENEURIAL FINANCE AND VENTURE CAPITAL

MONEY FOR STARTUPS

LEADING CREATIVE TEAMS

REGIONAL ENTREPRENEURSHIP ACCELERATION LAB

MANAGEMENT IN ENGINEERING

NEGOTIATION AND INFLUENCE SKILLS FOR TECHNICAL LEADERS

MULTI-STAKEHOLDER NEGOTIATION FOR TECHNICAL EXPERTS

GLOBAL ENTREPRENEURSHIP LAB (G-LAB)

MODERN BUSINESS IN CHINA: CHINA LAB

ISRAEL LAB: STARTUP NATION'S ENTREPRENEURSHIP AND INNOVATION ECOSYSTEM

HOW TO MAKE (ALMOST) ANYTHING

11   LESSONS LEARNED

Every year, groups of visitors from around the world come to MIT's campus to try to understand its vibrant entrepreneurial ecosystem and its positive impact on the local economy. These visitors—policymakers, university administrators, and other executives—usually spend from a day to a week in Cambridge, but they often return home with an insufficient understanding of what they came to study and few actionable plans. This outcome is not surprising given that, as this book has shown, the phenomenon is so complex, multifaceted, and rooted in MIT's history and culture.

This chapter highlights lessons that others may find useful from the case of MIT—without, however, any presumption of presenting a model that will work for everyone. Instead, I identify what seems to have worked well for MIT. Readers will consider if any of these ideas, or some variation of them, may be useful in other contexts and should keep in mind, while devising their own plans to promote entrepreneurship in their institutions, that what we observe at MIT today in terms of entrepreneurship is the result of at least seventy-five years of organic developments, with significant highs and lows along the way.

CULTURAL FIT

It is clear that entrepreneurship at MIT has thrived in part because of its fit with its culture. This has allowed the Institute to be an effective link between idea generation and invention on the one hand and commercial innovation on the other. Changemakers in other academic institutions who would like to devise a plan to promote entrepreneurship in a different context will wish to review their own culture and to build initiatives and entities supporting entrepreneurship that fit that culture—or at least don't go against it.

Sometimes the broader national culture of an institution is not supportive of entrepreneurship. In France and in Spain in the 2000s, for instance, polls revealed that 70 percent of the students wanted to become civil servants. In such cases, efforts to promote entrepreneurship may need to focus on a minority of early adopters who will, over time, become role models who may inspire others. Changing cultures may be difficult, and at a minimum one must plan for a long-term endeavor.

At MIT, entrepreneurship and entrepreneurs have indeed been celebrated, at least in the last two decades. Every culture needs its heroes, so it likely is a good idea for academic and other institutions that want to promote entrepreneurship to celebrate entrepreneurs, especially those to whom its members can relate. Such celebration may be a successful first step in influencing an existing culture.

COMMITMENT TO PRIMARY MISSION OF RESEARCH AND TEACHING

MIT has a great interest in the application of science and engineering and a real impact on the world, but it also has an unwavering commitment to fundamental scientific research. Basic research has been important in fueling marketable innovations—sometimes years after the initial research was conducted. As a famous example, US government funding for the war on cancer and investment by MIT in molecular biology in the 1970s served as a basis for the emergence of the biotech industry. Universities wishing to promote technology transfer through entrepreneurship should note that basic research is at the start of the funnel leading to innovations in the marketplace and should relentlessly lobby their governments and other funding sources, which otherwise may give priority to shorter-term objectives.

At MIT, spin-off ventures licensing the Institute's intellectual property are not a core objective in themselves for the university, but rather a coincidental by-product of academic research. It is, however, necessary to have a licensing infrastructure in place to support spin-offs when opportunities appear.

AVOID CONFLICTS OF INTEREST

We saw that MIT tries hard to avoid conflict of interest in every element of the entrepreneurship process. However, this does not mean that MIT's record has always been spotless on this front. For instance, the Bose Corporation was started in 1964 in Building 20, which had hosted the legendary Radiation Laboratory (Rad Lab), something that would be unimaginable today.[1] Avoiding conflicts of interest is obviously a core value for a university looking at promoting entrepreneurship. It is a complex issue with various facets. These include regulations about the technology transfer process and monitoring the relationship between faculty members and start-ups spun-off from their labs, in order to ensure that mentors have only the best interest of the aspiring entrepreneurs in mind, as mentioned in previous chapters.

The topic can be particularly delicate in cases of universities running their own seed funds, when a single entity acts as a licensing office and runs the university's seed fund, or when such a fund has the right of first refusal to invest in the university's spin-offs. A proprietary fund raises the issue of negative selection bias. If a university fund were to invest in some of its spin-off ventures and not others, what message would it send to the market about those in which it did not invest?[2] A proprietary fund also raises potential conflicts of interest. If part of the role of a university is to finance the launch of start-ups, how could this influence what faculty and students it funds and what research it supports?[3]

Of course, the choice could be more difficult for universities located in regions with weak venture investment infrastructures, in contrast to MIT, which is located in the entrepreneurially vibrant Cambridge/Boston area. In some regions with this kind of market failure, propriety funds could sometimes be necessary, but they should be a last resort, coupled with the strongest governance, because they present risks of abuse, conflict of interest, and favoritism. In the absence of private venture investment, government-funded venture funds offer a more arm's-length relationship with universities, but they are susceptible to political interference and the civil servants running them usually don't have the incentive to take risks in order to turn the start-ups that their funds financed into successful growing companies.

The creation by MIT of The Engine seems to contradict this discussion, but the Institute did put in place an arm's-length relationship with The

Engine for the selection of the start-ups projects that it chose to finance. The Engine also has elaborate governance mechanisms, including rules to avoid conflicts of interest. MIT created it in large part to compensate for what it perceived as a market failure to provide early-stage "patient capital" at a time when venture capitalists are focusing on financing entrepreneurial projects with shorter payback periods and higher returns.[4]

As seen in chapter 8, MIT has been an advocate of technology transfer as a service to society, as opposed to a revenue-generating activity. This approach is summarized by the motto "Impact, not income." It is a principled position, but also a pragmatic one because data shows that the odds are against universities making significant money from licensing intellectual property to start-ups. It is sobering that many universities, in continental Europe for instance, still hope to make a fortune from such discoveries by requesting aggressive valuation of their intellectual property.[5] The result is that these universities remove a major incentive for would-be founders, who become more like employees than entrepreneurs when their stake in the firm is diluted to such an extent on day one. It also affects the incentive to grow the venture because that would reduce the founders' stake even further.

Part of the problem is that some universities overestimate the value of their intellectual property and underestimate the time and resources necessary to further develop and commercialize academic technologies. It is estimated that 10 to 100 times the cost of academic research is required to bring academic technologies to market. It is the moral duty of universities to facilitate the transfer of publicly funded intellectual property to society via commercialization, not consider it as an opportunity to make a profit.

Successful management of conflict of interest takes other forms as well. We saw in chapter 10 that MIT is concerned about protecting its students from agents who might have conflicted agendas. Several quotes from students and educators reported in this book reflect the importance of providing for aspiring entrepreneurs a safe space where they can test their ideas, make their early mistakes, and receive honest feedback from unconflicted mentors. The collective belief that professors, staff members, and mentors exist for the benefit of the students is a great strength, but one that could be damaged quickly with one bad example.

As Bill Aulet ('94), the managing director of the Martin Trust Center for MIT Entrepreneurship, stresses repeatedly, it is critical that the educator be an honest broker and that there be clear rules of engagement so the students don't question where the faculty's interests lie.[6] For other universities, following such principles should not be a matter of debate. However, when some ventures with extraordinary potential appear, that inevitably increases the risk that some might compromise their standards. Successful avoidance of conflicts of interest is an ongoing effort. A prominent MIT insider summarized it well when he said that entrepreneurship at MIT (and at universities in general) should be about enhancing the impact of research and not about making money. Entrepreneurship at MIT is part of the life cycle of ideas being translated to have impact in the real world that is spelled out in MIT's "Mens et Manus" motto. Students are engaged in entrepreneurial endeavors, but with the knowledge that those endeavors are about learning and making the world a better place and not about enriching the coffers of MIT or its faculty.

ENCOURAGE A MULTIDISCIPLINARY APPROACH TO ENTREPRENEURSHIP

MIT's multidisciplinary mindset and its commitment to overcoming silos have been key factors in facilitating the emergence of novel solutions based on new combinations of disciplines, technologies, and processes, which is the basis of innovation. The integration of engineering in medical fields is an example highlighted in this book. Beyond overcoming silos, flexibility in the university's structure also played a positive role in allowing experiments with courses and activities supporting entrepreneurship to emerge. Following this example might be a real challenge for universities that are siloed and rigid. MIT professor Michael Cusumano, for instance, recently wrote that in Japan classes mixing students from different schools are rare and sometimes prohibited.[7] A good place to start could be to foster collaborations between students from science and engineering and management. These might take place in entrepreneurship classes, projects, and contests.

Such collaborations have become a key development at MIT, unanimously celebrated. Management students help their colleagues in joint projects to open up to the market dimension of entrepreneurial technology projects; science and engineering students help aspiring managers to work on projects based on defensible, technology-based ideas. If universities are too rigid or slow to implement such changes, perhaps students (in their clubs, for instance) could initiate small changes and nudge their university in that direction. It is what MIT students did in the late 1980s and 1990s (see chapter 2).

CULTIVATE ENGAGEMENT OF ALUMNI

The case of MIT illustrates extensively the important roles that alumni played in developing an interest in entrepreneurship and in supporting it in various forms. Alumni have served as lecturers, mentors, and role models and provided financial support. They are also the privileged channel of universities to industry, government, civic groups, and society at large, all stakeholders that have a role to play in the promotion of entrepreneurship locally. Alumni represent a huge resource to employ, even in countries where there is a weak tradition of philanthropy and weaker tax incentives to make donations.

There is thus a strong argument for a university to develop a well-resourced alumni office and a vibrant alumni community oriented toward entrepreneurship. If the message does not go through at the university level, students and alumni themselves can launch initiatives to build links. As the MIT case shows, even a few motivated individuals can sometimes be catalysts of real change.

Cultivating links with alumni may be difficult in countries where universities have no or weak ties to their alumni. Some universities lose touch altogether with their graduates after they complete their studies. Clearly a major shift in alumni relations will be worthwhile in order to begin engaging with alumni for entrepreneurial projects.

ENTREPRENEURSHIP EDUCATION IS NOT ONLY ABOUT PREPARING STUDENTS TO PITCH A BUSINESS PLAN

In many universities and business schools, training in entrepreneurship is still seen mainly as preparing students to write a business plan or pitch a business idea to a panel of judges. In contrast, MIT offers a kind of life-cycle approach that starts much earlier and ends beyond the stage of pitching a business plan. It includes activities to stimulate various stages of interest in entrepreneurship, and it trains students to deal with the idiosyncrasies of various stages of the start-up process. As seen in chapter 10, MIT starts with creating awareness and inspiration by offering opportunities for students to explore their motivation for entrepreneurship by proposing introductory courses or extracurricular activities. The Institute provides chances to search for opportunities such as hackathons (see chapters 5 and 7). Various levels of courses are part of the process of allowing students to build fundamental and then specialized entrepreneurial skills.

Students have the chance to test themselves in the real world through fieldwork, lab-based courses, and internships, as well as contests. The most advanced and motivated teams can bring their project to the next level through the delta v acceleration program in view of launching real companies and understanding how to scale a business. Resources may be provided to ventures after they have been created, through such entities as the MIT Startup Exchange (STEX) and The Engine.

Chapters 7 and 10 are particularly useful to understanding this phasing-in of entrepreneurship training and support. Of course, an extensive offering is possible only in universities of a certain size that have been involved in training for entrepreneurship for some time, because it is not possible to build such an infrastructure overnight. Smaller institutions, or those with a more recent involvement in entrepreneurship education that do not have the required scale, should perhaps consider pooling resources with others at a local or regional level.

MEETING VARIOUS LEVELS OF MOTIVATIONS RELATED TO ENTREPRENEURSHIP

MIT's attention to meeting various levels of student motivation in entrepreneurship and educating them in developing an entrepreneurial spirit—rather than focusing on turning them all into entrepreneurs—appears to be a valuable insight and orientation. As MIT understood from the late 2000s on, entrepreneurship has become a credible career path for students, while some traditional sources of employment have receded (see chapter 4). It is thus important that universities prepare their students for such a professional future and offer the foundations for future entrepreneurs. At the same time, not all students will become entrepreneurs (nor should they), but they do have various degrees of interest in learning about entrepreneurship.

It is important that universities be able to prepare students who want to start a company. And it is equally important to equip students who will pursue careers in large corporations, in government, in philanthropy, and in the professions to be intrapreneurs. Students can learn to be agents of change and dynamism in all organizations if they are exposed to entrepreneurship during their studies. Finally, virtually all students in today's world need at least a taste of what entrepreneurship is if they want to control their destinies.

THE IMPORTANCE OF LEARNING BY DOING

Aulet's framing of entrepreneurship as a craft, as opposed to a science or an art (presented in chapter 10), is a powerful concept to guide the implementation of adequate training in entrepreneurship. A craft requires learning some basic concepts in a class-type setting, but also opportunities to learn by doing. It is a much more accurate and useful vision than trying to pretend, as some institutions do, that entrepreneurship is a science or a disciplinary area equal to economics or psychology. The craft analogy also opens the door to viewing entrepreneurship as a profession like medicine or architecture.

Practice-oriented courses, particularly lab courses and extracurricular activities, have successfully adapted the principle of learning-by-doing to the training of entrepreneurship at MIT, where there was a long and strong tradition of such pedagogy. It has been a cornerstone of training students in entrepreneurship that other institutions should consider emulating.

It may be more difficult for universities that conduct themselves with a good deal of distance between themselves and the professional world (otherwise known as being in an "ivory tower") or that still operate based on a rote-learning type of pedagogy. Perhaps it would be easier for such institutions to initiate learning-by-doing in extracurricular activities rather than in the academic curriculum right away.

Mixing training through academic curricula with extracurricular activities has worked well at MIT for training in entrepreneurship. The cocurriculum, discussed in chapter 10, may serve as a useful concept for other institutions. The idea is that curricular and extracurricular activities be viewed as components of one learning experience. Traditional classes are suited to learn the fundamental tools of entrepreneurship, but it is not enough to learn them in a vacuum. It needs to be complemented by internships, fieldwork, boot camps, and contests, and other short experiences in the real world in order to promote learning by doing.

Related to real-world relevance, the dual-track teaching model, using both an academic and a practitioner in the classroom, has worked well at MIT. It provides relevance while not giving up academic rigor. Still, training in entrepreneurship in many universities and business schools today is being offered either by academics with little or no real-world experience and no experience with start-ups and the business world in general, or by entrepreneurs or venture capitalists telling war stories about their successes. Of course, a dual-track mode of teaching requires more demanding logistics, including access to a pool of good practitioners willing to offer their time. Again, this is additional motivation for cultivating relationships with alumni and to establish links with industry.

DISTINCTION BETWEEN SUPPORT FOR STUDENT ENTREPRENEURSHIP AND FOR TECHNOLOGY TRANSFER

Although there are overlaps, MIT's case suggests that there should be a distinction between entrepreneurship training for students and entrepreneurship support for technology transfer by faculty. This distinction is often overlooked by many academic institutions. The entrepreneurship projects of students generally have less technology content. Their aim is primarily educational, although some students pursue their project after graduation and launch companies. Their time horizon is different. Students consider projects that can be deployed in a matter of months, while commercializing academic intellectual property usually requires years of capital-intensive scientific research and development (R&D), as well as commercial development. In addition, student projects follow the logic of standard entrepreneurial projects, going from the identification of a need to the building of a commercially viable solution fulfilling this need. In contrast, commercializing academic technology is more akin to having a solution in search of a problem.

It is worth mentioning here that both types of entrepreneurship benefit early on from outreach to potential customers, as discussed in chapters 7 and 8. This insight could be particularly useful to academic institutions that still operate following a rote-learning model, or in engineering schools, where the belief is that all that matters for commercial success is to build a better mousetrap.

SUPPORT FOR INNOVATION-DRIVEN ENTREPRENEURSHIP

As explained in chapter 10, MIT clearly supports what professors Bill Aulet and Fiona Murray call "innovation-driven entrepreneurship," or the creation of "innovation-driven enterprises" (IDEs), as opposed to "small and medium enterprises" (SME), which are primarily a form of self-employment. MIT professor Antoinette Schoar makes a similar distinction, but she talks about transformational and subsistence entrepreneurship. All too often, both universities and policymakers ignore the differences between these two types of entrepreneurship, or else they underestimate them. Most of the time in Europe, for instance, they aspire at generating the next Google, but in reality the types of support mechanisms that they put in place promote SMEs. Government regulations often discourage IDEs, while their rhetoric pretends to favor them. It is common that universities, by trying to extract revenue from their spin-offs and taxing them by requesting huge equity stakes against their intellectual property, incentivize the founders to found an SME instead of growing an IDE. It is thus critical, first of all, for universities and policymakers to understand the differences between those two forms of entrepreneurship and to learn what policy or support structure promotes specific kinds of entrepreneurship. Too many resources are wasted on promoting the wrong type of entrepreneurship.

It is more difficult to promote IDEs in regions with weaker entrepreneurial infrastructure than in the case of MIT, which is located in a vibrant and mature local entrepreneurial ecosystem. It is important that such regions realize that building a supportive local entrepreneurial ecosystem is a long-term endeavor that may require decades of effort.

INVOLVING A VARIETY OF STAKEHOLDERS

An interesting takeaway of the MIT example is that the promotion of entrepreneurship does not happen in a vacuum; it not only is about entrepreneurs but also requires the collaboration of a number of other stakeholders, such as large corporations, providers of risk capital, and government, as the Regional Entrepreneurship Accelerator Program (REAP) preaches (discussed in chapter 9). Universities and policymakers who want to improve their entrepreneurial footprint should examine this argument. Universities could also be the catalysts initiating such collaborations. As MIT professors Richard Lester ('80) and Michael Piore argue in their book *Innovation: The Missing Dimension*, an important role that universities can play is to serve as a public space for local conversations about the direction of technologies and markets.[8] The work of MIT's STEX program (detailed in chapter 8) could serve as a useful inspiration to others as well. It connects MIT-related start-ups and corporations, with the goal of developing potential joint research, procurement and distribution agreements, manufacturing deals, and investments. The complementarity of start-ups and corporations is often misunderstood and underestimated by universities, and as a result, they ignore relationships that have great potential.

MERGING SUPPORT FOR CONVENTIONAL FOR-PROFIT ENTREPRENEURSHIP AND SOCIAL ENTREPRENEURSHIP

Interest in social entrepreneurship has grown a lot in recent years among MIT students. This is probably the case in other institutions as well because many sources attribute this phenomenon in part to the millennial's interest in their own social impact on society. When it appeared in the early 2000s, social entrepreneurship at MIT was treated as a distinct category from conventional entrepreneurship. Over time, however, the two have increasingly merged (as argued in chapter 4), and social entrepreneurship projects now take part in courses, contests, and accelerators alongside other projects. The trend observed at MIT is probably one that other institutions should follow, if only to impose the same standard of excellence to social entrepreneurship projects as applies to conventional ones. Indeed, some social entrepreneurship projects often hide their mediocrity behind the good intentions that motivate them.

INVESTING IN CONTENT, PEDAGOGY, AND LOGISTICS IN A SYSTEMIC WAY

The resources required for launching and conducting an entrepreneurship course, program, or extracurricular activity are often overlooked. Launching and conducting a class, for instance, are too often conceived as hiring a lecturer, reserving a room, and more or less copying and pasting a curriculum from another institution. Most initiatives based on such shallow preparation don't attract a critical mass of participants, and have meager outputs. Behind the success of MIT's many educational initiatives related to entrepreneurship—courses, extracurricular activities, programs, internships, and so on—lie considerable efforts and deep experiential knowledge accumulated over the years in terms of teaching content, pedagogy, and logistics, all of which Aulet calls the "operating system" of the Trust Center, which he shares with others in an open-source mode.[9]

For instance, in the mid-2000s, the need for a course related to energy and entrepreneurship appeared. Aulet and his colleagues realized that it was not enough to create an "Energy Venture" class—they needed to adopt a more systemic approach. They created a mutually supportive series of activities, including an entrepreneurship class, but also other entities addressing fundamental aspects of the energy sector. They built bridges between the School of Engineering and the Sloan School of Management and even reached out to the Kennedy School of Government at Harvard to integrate policy aspects into the offering. They created the ClimateTech & Energy Prize (CEP) and relied on the student-run Energy Club to manage the competition and found external partners in the utility NSTAR (now Eversource) and the US Department of Energy. This systemic approach of building an entrepreneurship curriculum has served as a model for other initiatives since then. This knowledge base is key to keeping a common denominator across silos when expanding the entrepreneurship offering in an institution. It is also useful in getting a new initiative (e.g., a course, a mentoring program, and a contest) related to entrepreneurship off the ground.

The history and evolution of entrepreneurship at MIT are deep and rich. Parts of MIT's entrepreneurial ecosystem are unique to the philosophy and culture that are so prevalent at this institution and may not be easily duplicated at others. However, there are many other parts that can be a source of inspiration to other universities, corporations, and countries that exist in various cultures, environments, and circumstances. At minimum, an understanding of MIT entrepreneurship could trigger other organizations to reflect on their own practices and prompt conversations about their own approach to entrepreneurship. If that happens as a result of reading these pages, this book will have achieved its purpose.

EPILOGUE: MIT'S ENTREPRENEURIAL ECOSYSTEM RESPONDS TO COVID-19

As of this writing in late summer 2020, the COVID-19 pandemic has been ravaging our world and altering our way of life. While it is far too early to tell what the future holds, or to talk about any specific long-term plans and consequences, there are some initial actions on the part of the MIT entrepreneurial ecosystem that shine a light on how those involved are responding to the pandemic, philosophically and pragmatically. These reactions have, unsurprisingly, been in line with the culture underpinnings at MIT that have been discussed extensively in this book.

In the time of COVID-19, MIT's tried-and-true culture has once again been translated into practical initiatives aimed not only at educating entrepreneurs, but also empowering them to do what comes naturally when faced with a challenge: turn it into an opportunity. Examples of such initiatives include D-Lab's COVID-19 Bridge Fund, which was established to help D-Lab Scale-Ups fellows (social entrepreneurs that have set up businesses and serve customers in some of the more underserved markets in the world, as discussed in chapter 9) survive the pandemic. There is also the COVID-19 Rapid Innovation Dashboard, a hub for MIT's COVID-19-related activities, such as an initiative to help low-income K–12 students with school shutdowns and multiple projects aimed at improving access to ventilators. The Martin Trust Center for MIT Entrepreneurship has encouraged students to utilize its Orbit app to connect more easily with the members of the MIT entrepreneurial community, as well as its many resources.

In the spring of 2020, the Trust Center also launched the "Antifragile" entrepreneurship lecture series, which attracted over 20,000 viewers; it featured world experts conveying their knowledge and experience about how to manage and thrive during and after a crisis. This online speaker series is named for a term coined by mathematical statistician Nassim Nicholas Taleb in his book *Antifragile: Things That Gain from Disorder*, which postulates that "some things benefit from shocks; they thrive and grow when exposed to volatility, randomness, disorder, just as entrepreneurs are more able to function in crisis mode than others who are more drawn to reliability and stability." The "Antifragile" series segued into a series of virtual hackathon-style events, such as the MIT COVID-19 Challenge, that the Trust Center sponsored and helped organize, which attracted participants from around the world as well as on campus. These events carried into the summer, when many MIT students had internship offers rescinded due to the COVID-19 crisis. The Trust Center responded to this unfortunate development with an entrepreneurship internship program with summer stipends for master's of business administration (MBA) students. In the fall of 2020, Sloan adopted a system by which students attended classes alternatively in person and online. Students were also offered a new class, "Hacking the Future: The Fall of COVID," taught by faculty from across the Institute.

Many of the COVID-era offerings on campus are in their early stages, and there are surely many more to come. Beyond campus, MIT-affiliated companies have hit the ground running to address the myriad problems resulting from this global health crisis. Biotech company Moderna Therapeutics' mRNA-1273 vaccine was one of the first COVID-19 vaccines to receive emergency use approval and is currently being distributed to people across the globe. Other companies in the biotech and pharmaceutical sphere are also working overtime to develop potential vaccines and therapeutic treatments to mitigate the severity of the virus. Pathr, a start-up that uses data analytics and machine learning to understand how people move through environments, has launched SocialDistance.ai, which utilizes a "spatial intelligence" platform to provide information on how infectious diseases might spread in different scenarios. Another MIT-affiliated start-up, BioBot Analytics (see box in chapter 4), builds predictive health analytics from molecular data present in human waste collected from sewers to predict infectious disease. Since the arrival of COVID-19, it has launched a pro bono virus testing program in collaboration with researchers at MIT, Harvard, and Brigham and Women's Hospital. The team will process sewage samples from plants across the United States in order to determine the presence of the COVID-19 virus.

This information is very valuable in helping communities determine the various sources of the virus and how to react to prevent the spread of the disease.

These are just a few examples of the dozens and dozens of products, resources, and research being developed by MIT-affiliated companies in an effort to combat COVID-19. As time goes on, there will surely be more, just as there are bound to be adjustments to curricula, an evolution of online learning, and new initiatives designed to empower students, faculty, and the administration at such a critical time in world history.

APPENDIX 1   MILESTONES
IN THE DEVELOPMENT
OF ENTREPRENEURSHIP AT MIT
AFTER WORLD WAR II

- 1946: American Research and Development Corporation (ARD) was incorporated with MIT as a cofounder.
- 1961: New Enterprises was the first entrepreneurship course offered by the Sloan School of Management at the instigation of alumnus Richard Morse ('33), who also taught it.
- 1964: The first research on technology entrepreneurship conducted by Professor Edward Roberts ('57) concerning spin-off ventures from MIT laboratories.
- 1969: Members of the Boston MIT Alumni Association organized a weekend seminar titled "Starting and Building Your Own Company," which was later replicated in several cities across the US. Over 2,000 alumni attended the seminars.
- 1978: Members of the Boston MIT Alumni Association launched the Cambridge MIT Enterprise Forum (MITEF).
- 1986: Following the passage of the Bayh-Dole Act in 1980, the Patent, Copyright and Licensing Office was renamed the Technology Licensing Office (TLO) and restructured into a proactive entity helping the commercialization of MIT-owned technology.
- 1987: The TLO begins to license technology to new spin-off ventures in exchange for equity.
- 1988: The first student clubs devoted to encouraging entrepreneurship were founded: the MIT Entrepreneurs Club (E-Club) and the Sloan New Venture Association (SNVA) club.

- 1989: Student leaders of the E-Club and the SNVA launched the $10K Business Plan Competition. In the first edition of the contest, held in 1990, fifty-four teams of students competed.
- 1991: Foundation of the Entrepreneurship Center (E-Center) by Edward Roberts to support entrepreneurship education.
- 1996: First entrepreneurship tenure-track faculty member Scott Shane was hired.
- 1996: Ken Morse ('68) becomes the first director of the E-Center.
- 1997: BankBoston published *MIT: The Impact of Innovation,* a report about the economic impact of companies founded by MIT. It found that MIT graduates had started 4,000 companies generating 1.1 million jobs and $232 billion in sales as of 1994.
- 2000: The Venture Mentoring Service (VMS) was created by Alec Dingee ('52) and MIT professor of engineering David Staelin ('60) to mentor aspiring entrepreneurs of the MIT community and its alumni.
- 2001: Amy Smith ('84) and Sally Susnowitz launch the first social entrepreneurship initiative, the IDEAS Competition, out of the Public Service Center (PSC). (It was later renamed the IDEAS Social Innovation Challenge.)
- 2002: The Deshpande Center for Technological Innovation, which aims to bridge the gap between academic research and marketable products, is founded.
- 2006: Introduction of the MIT Sloan School of Management's Entrepreneurship and Innovation (E&I) Track within its master's of business administration (MBA) program.
- 2006: A program in developmental entrepreneurship is launched by the Media Lab.
- 2009: The first report on the economic impact of firms founded by MIT alumni, *Entrepreneurial Impact: The Role of MIT,* is published by Edward Roberts and Charles Eesley ('09). The study would be updated in further editions in 2011 and 2015.
- 2011: The central administration organizes entrepreneurship seminars for faculty, "From Ideas to Impact: Lessons for Commercialization," at the initiative of MIT president Susan Hockfield.
- 2011: The central administration organizes the Faculty Committee on Innovation and Entrepreneurship at the initiative of President Hockfield.

- 2011: The Entrepreneurship Center was renamed the Martin Trust Center for MIT Entrepreneurship to honor Martin Trust ('58), whose Trust Family Foundation made a significant gift to endow the center.

- 2012: The Committee on Student Entrepreneurship was established by the central administration to examine growing interest in entrepreneurship and its implications.

- 2014: Launch of MIT Innovation Initiative, extending the Institute's mission beyond its primary roles of education and research to entrepreneurship and innovation.

- 2016: A new minor in entrepreneurship and innovation (E&I) for undergraduates is created.

- 2016: The Engine, a new company providing patient capital and access to infrastructure support to start-ups dealing with tough technologies that have the potential for significant societal impact, is launched.

APPENDIX 2 LIST OF INITIATIVES SUPPORTING ENTREPRENEURSHIP (1946–2019)

Initiatives	Year
American Research and Development Corporation (ARD)*	1946
First entrepreneurship class ("New Enterprises")	1961
"Starting and Building Your Own Company" seminar*	1969
"Starting and Building Your Own Company" seminar (national rollout)*	1970
Entrepreneurship Registers*	1971
Development Foundation*	1972
Cambridge MIT Enterprise Forum (MITEF)	1978
"Starting and Running a High-Tech Company," the first Independent Activities Period (IAP) seminar on entrepreneurship	1982
Nationwide MITEF	1985
Technology Licensing Office (TLO)	1986
Sloan New Venture Association (SNVA)	1988
Entrepreneurship Club	1988
$10K Business Plan Competition	1989
Event 128: A Salute to Founders (Boston + Sillicon Valley)	1989
Entrepreneurship Center (E-Center)/Trust Center for MIT Entrepreneurship	1991
$10K Business Plan Competition, Morgenthaler Grand Prize	1990
"Nuts and Bolts of Business Plans," the first student-led Independent Activities Period (IAP) seminar on entrepreneurship	1990
Sloan New Product and Venture Development Track (NPV)*	1994
Venture Capital and Private Equity Club (VCPE)	1995
$50K Entrepreneurship Competition	1996

(continued)

Initiatives	Year
Goldberg Grand Prize of the 50K Business Plan Competition	1996
Paul Gray Technology Breakfast Series	1996
First managing director of E-Center: Kenneth Morse	1996
First entrepreneurship tenure-track faculty member: Scott Shane	1996
First Entrepreneurship Faculty chair endowed	1997
Global Startup Workshop (GSW)	1998
Chairman's Salon*	1999
Venture Mentoring Service (VMS)	2000
Deshpande Center for Technology Innovation	2002
Global Startup Lab (GSL)	2000
Patrick, J. McGovern Entrepreneurship Award	2001
IDEAS Competition (now IDEAS Social Innovation Challenge)	2001
D-Lab	2001
Sloan Entrepreneurs for International Development	2001
Ideastream	2001
MIT Sloan Entrepreneurship and Innovation Club	2002
Innovation Week	2003
Energy Club	2004
VentureShips	2004
Adolf Monosson Prize for Entrepreneurship	2005
Global MIT Enterprise Forum	2005
Ignite Clean Energy Business Plan Competition*	2005
Entrepreneurs in Residence at Trust Center	2006
Sloan MBA Entrepreneurship and Innovation Track	2006
$100K Entrepreneurship Competition	2006
Clean Energy Prize (CEP)	2006
Media Lab Developmental Entrepreneurship Program	2006
Legatum Center for Development and Entrepreneurship	2007
Legatum Center Fellowship	2007
Legatum Conferences	2008
First impact study published by Edward Roberts and Charles Eesley	2009
Education Ideastorm	2009
Music Hack Day @MIT*	2009
Legatum Grants	2009
Silicon Valley Study Tour	2009

(continued)

Initiatives	Year
Building Global Innovators	2010
Entrepreneurship Review (MITER)*	2010
MIT Sloan Africa Business Plan Competition	2010
t=0	2011
Entrepreneurship Walk of Fame	2011
Endowment of the Entrepreneurship Center by Martin Trust	2011
Seminars for faculty, "From Ideas to Impact: Lessons for Commercialization"*	2011
Faculty Committee on Innovation and Entrepreneurship*	2011
D-Lab Scale-ups seed grants	2011
StartIAP (renamed MIT Fuse in 2018)	2011
StartLabs	2011
Hacking Medicine	2011
Regional Entrepreneurship Acceleration Program (REAP)	2011
MIT China Entrepreneurship and Innovation Forum (CHIEF) Business Plan Competition	2011
D-Lab Scale-Ups fellowship	2011
D-Lab Scale-Ups Conference	2011
Beehive Cooperation	2012
Committee on Student Entrepreneurship*	2012
Hacking Arts	2012
Media Lab Entrepreneurship Program	2012
Launch*	2012
Digital Shingle*	2012
delta v	2012
Translational Fellows Program*	2013
$15K Creative Arts Competition	2013
E14 Fund	2013
Innovation Initiative	2014
Innovation Lab*	2014
Trust Center's Sector Practice Leaders	2014
Female Entrepreneurs Pitch Contest	2014
StartMIT	2014
Startup Exchange (STEX) and STEX25	2014
Global Entrepreneurship Bootcamp	2014

(continued)

Initiatives	Year
Entrepreneurship Online classes	2014
Entrepreneurship and Intellectual Property Clinic	2015
Samuel Tak Lee MIT Real Estate Entrepreneurship Laboratory	2015
FinTech Club and Business Plan Competition	2015
Entrepreneurship Summer Internship	2016
The Engine	2016
Innovation@ONE	2016
Inclusive Innovation Challenge (IIC)	2016
Eddie Award	2016
Undergraduate Minor in Entrepreneurship	2016
Sandbox Innovation Fund Program	2016
Sloan Healthcare Innovation Prize competition	2016
MIT Entrepreneurship and Maker Skills Integrator (MEMSI)	2016
InnovateEDU	2016
MITdesignX	2016
PitchtoMatch	2017
MIT Entrepreneurship and Fintech Integrator (MEFTI)	2018
Proto Venture Program	2019
Mission Innovation Program	2019
MIT Water Innovation Prize	2019
RaboBank—MIT Food and Agribusiness Innovation Prize	2019

* Has since been discontinued

ACKNOWLEDGMENTS

I want to extend my deepest gratitude to the multiple members of the MIT community who helped and encouraged me in the creation of this book: faculty and staff members, alumni, and administrative personnel. You accepted with good grace to be interviewed; you directed me to information sources, opened doors, shared your insight as well as your enthusiasm, and fact-checked sections of this book. Unfortunately, there is not enough room or time to list you all by name, but without your goodwill and invaluable assistance, this book would not exist.

I owe a special thank-you to Professor Bill Aulet, who has been encouraging from the beginning, has introduced me to multiple resources and people, and has taken the time in his busy schedule to review various versions of this book. Equally generous with his time was Professor Edward Roberts, the pioneering figure of entrepreneurship at MIT, on whose work I have drawn a great deal. His encyclopedic knowledge of entrepreneurship at MIT has been precious in the final review of the book.

Professor Sandy Pentland provided insights into the early days of entrepreneurship at the Media Lab. Professor Richard Lester provided an important perspective that was very helpful in the early days of this project. I benefited greatly from Professor Charles Cooney's decades of involvement with entrepreneurship across the MIT campus. Lita Nelsen, the director of the MIT Technology Licensing Office (TLO) until 2016, and Lesley Millar-Nicholson, the current director of the TLO, have been invaluably helpful for my understanding the multifaceted role of technology transfer at MIT. Nelsen's thirty years of experience at the core of the entrepreneurship ecosystem at MIT has also been a source of many critical insights. I want to acknowledge the value that the reviewers brought to this book. Ken Morse and Sherwin Greenblatt were especially helpful and supportive. Nora Murphy and Liz Andrews facilitated access to the MIT Archives. Alumni have often provided archival sources, as well as the stories and anecdotes that put a human face on the hard data that I had gathered. A special thanks to Peter Mui and Doug Ling, the cofounders of the $10K Business Plan Competition in 1989 (now named the $100K Entrepreneurship Competition), for their memories of the early days of the competition and for private archival material, as well as to Joe Hadzima, David Verrill, Andrea Ippolito, Freddy Nguyen, Romi Kadri, Mitch Kapor, and Che-Chih Tsao.

I also want to express my thanks to the founders of the start-ups profiled throughout the book, who kindly fact-checked the stories about themselves and their firms. Numerous students have shared their enthusiasm about this project, which has been a motivating factor along the way. During each of my visits at MIT during my fieldwork, the MIT Industrial Performance Center and its director, Elisabeth Reynolds, kindly hosted me in the center's facilities. Professor Mary Rowe was particularly encouraging in pursuing this project, as she has always been with my endeavors since I met her many years ago, and she provided useful comments during this book project.

I am grateful to the reviewers of various versions of this book. Reading more than 200 pages, checking facts, and commenting on the text are no small feat for such busy people. My consulting editor, Michelle Choate, was an inspiring and invaluable writing partner who helped me turn my manuscript into a compelling story. Along the way, I benefited from the precious help of research assistants: Ankur Bansal, Pilar Carvajo Lucena ('17), Jean Choi ('07), and Attia Qureshi ('18). The interactions with them and with Michelle also made this journey less lonely. I wish to acknowledge my editor at MIT Press, Emily Taber, for having faith in my ideas and providing valuable guidance. Any errors that remain are my own.

NOTES

INTRODUCTION

1. Edward B. Roberts, Fiona Murray, and J. Daniel Kim, *Entrepreneurship and Innovation at MIT: Continuing Global Growth and Impact* (Cambridge, MA: MIT Sloan School of Management, 2015), http://web.mit.edu/innovate/entrepreneurship2015.pdf (accessed February 3, 2017).

2. *2019 Annual Report—Martin Trust Center for MIT Entrepreneurship* (Cambridge, MA: MIT, 2019), https://entrepreneurship.mit.edu/annual-report/ (accessed November 15, 2019).

3. MIT Innovation Initiative, *Innovation & Entrepreneurship Resources,* https://innovation.mit.edu/resources/ (accessed December 3, 2020).

4. J. Daniel Kim, "Early Employees of Venture-Backed Startups: Selection and Wage Differentials" (master's thesis, MIT, 2016), https://dspace.mit.edu/handle/1721.1/103 206; Roberts, Murray, and Kim, *Entrepreneurship and Innovation at MIT.*

CHAPTER 1

1. M. Roe Smith, "'God Speed the Institute': The Foundational Years, 1861–1894," in *Becoming MIT: Moments of Decision,* edited by David Kaiser (Cambridge, MA: MIT Press, 2012), 15–16.

2. See Professor David Mindell's comment in *The Ecosystem: Nurturing Entrepreneurship— MIT 150 Documentary (2011),* MIT Infinite History, Cambridge, MA, 2011, https://infinitehistory.mit.edu/video/ecosystem-nurturing-entrepreneurship"-mit150 -documentary-2011 (accessed August 27, 2019).

3. MIT Charter, 1861, the MIT Corporation, http://corporation.mit.edu/about-corp oration/charter (accessed December 3, 2020).

4. S. Rosegrant and D. Lampe, *Route 128: Lessons from Boston's High-Tech Community* (New York: Basic Books, 1992), 47. Also see Professor David Mindel in *MIT's Entrepreneurship Ecosystem*, YouTube, Cambridge, MA, 2016, https://www.youtube.com/watch?v=WSkDqpBctfA&t=17s (accessed August 30, 2019).

5. Rosegrant and Lampe, *Route 128: Lessons from Boston's High-Tech Community*, 61.

6. C. Lécuyer, "Patrons and a Plan," in *Becoming MIT: Moments of Decision* (Cambridge, MA: MIT Press, 2012), 69.

7. E. Roberts, *Entrepreneurs in High Technology: Lessons from MIT and Beyond* (New York: Oxford University Press, 1991), 34.

8. Henry Etzkowitz, *MIT and the Rise of Entrepreneurial Science* (New York: Routledge, 2002), 60.

9. David C. Mowery and Bhaven N. Sampat, "Patenting and Licensing University Inventions: Lessons from the History of the Research Corporation," *Industrial and Corporate Change* 10, no. 2 (June 1, 2001): 317–355, https://doi.org/10.1093/icc/10.2.317.

10. Lécuyer, "Patrons and a Plan," 70.

11. Lécuyer, "Patrons and a Plan," 75.

12. S. Ante, *Creative Capital: Georges Doriot and the Birth of Venture Capital* (Boston: Harvard Business Publishing, 2008), 75.

13. Etzkowitz, *MIT and the Rise of Entrepreneurial Science*, 78.

14. Etzkowitz, *MIT and the Rise of Entrepreneurial Science*, 87.

15. Etzkowitz, *MIT and the Rise of Entrepreneurial Science*, 88.

16. D. Douglas, "MIT and War," in *Becoming MIT: Moments of Decision* (Cambridge, MA: MIT Press, 2012), 95.

17. Robert Buderi, *The Invention That Changed the World. How a Small Group of Radar Pioneers Won the Second World War and Launched a Technological Revolution* (New York: Touchstone, 1996), 246.

18. Buderi, *The Invention That Changed the World*, 252–257.

19. Douglas, "MIT and War," 97.

20. Edward B. Roberts, *Celebrating Entrepreneurship: A Half-Century of MIT's Growth and Impact* (self-pub., 2018), 8.

21. Sachi Hatakenaka, "Flux and Flexibility: A Comparative Institution Analysis of Evolving University-Industry Relationships in MIT, Cambridge, and Tokyo" (PhD diss., MIT, 2002), 112, https://dspace.mit.edu/handle/1721.1/8434. See also Fred Hapgood, *Up the Infinite Corridor: MIT and the Technical Imagination* (Reading, MA: Addison Wesley, 1993), 75.

22. Buderi, *The Invention That Changed the World*, 257.

23. Ante, *Creative Capital*, 110.

24. "Leo L. Beranek," MIT Infinite History, https://infinitehistory.mit.edu/video/leo -l-beranek (accessed August 2, 2018).

25. Jeffrey Cruikshank, *Shaping the Waves: A History of Entrepreneurship at Harvard Business School* (Boston: Harvard Business Publishing, 2005), 104–105.

26. Scott Kirsner, "Venture Capital's Grandfather," *Boston Globe*, April 6, 2008.

27. Ante, *Creative Capital*, 145, Etzkowitz, *MIT and the Rise of Entrepreneurial Science*, 98, Rosegrant and Lampe, *Route 128: Lessons from Boston's High-Tech Community*, 134–135. Also see Annalee Saxenian, *Regional Advantage: Culture and Competition in Silicon Valley and Route 128* (Cambridge, MA: Harvard University Press, 1994), 15.

28. Everett Rogers and Judith Larsen, *Silicon Valley Fever: Growth of High-Technology Culture* (New York: Basic Books, 1984), 237.

29. Nithin Nohria, "Information and Search in the Creation of New Business Ventures," in *Networks and Organizations* (Cambridge, MA: Harvard Business Publishing, 1992), 255.

30. Sarah H. Wright, "Entrepreneurs Join in Celebrating MIT," *MIT Tech Talk*, March 12, 1997, http://news.mit.edu/1997/entrepreneurs-0312 (accessed April 15, 2018). See also interview with George N. Hatsopoulos '49, SM '50, ScD '56, October 28, 2009, https://infinitehistory.mit.edu/video/george-n-hatsopoulos-'49-sm-'50-scd- (accessed April 15, 2018).

31. Edward Roberts, "Entrepreneurship and Technology," *Research Management* (July 1968): 249–266.

32. Ante, *Creative Capital*, 170.

33. See *Teradyne's Early Days—the Chip History*, 2006, https://www.chiphistory.org/6 -alex-d-arbeloff-on-teradyne-s-early-days (accessed July 2, 2018).

34. "Edward B. Roberts '58, SM '58, SM '60, PhD '62," MIT Infinite History, March 8, 2016, https://infinitehistory.mit.edu/video/edward-b-roberts-58-sm-58-sm-60-phd-62 (accessed July 2, 2018). Also see *MIT Sloan School of Management: A Work in Progress* (Cambridge, MA: MIT Sloan School of Management, 2002); *Looking Back, Moving Forward* (Cambridge, MA: MIT Sloan School of Management, 2002).

35. This research was later compiled in Edward Roberts, *Entrepreneurs in High Technology: Lessons from MIT and Beyond* (New York: Oxford University Press, 1991).

36. Roberts writes, "Enrollment in those earlier years seldom was more than 20 students, but the subject persisted over time." Roberts, *Celebrating Entrepreneurship*, 12.

37. Interview with Ray Stata, Center for Ethics and Entrepreneurship, http://www .ethicsandentrepreneurship.org/20100208/interview-with-ray-stata/ (accessed July 2, 2018).

38. Interview with Ray Stata.

39. Interview with Ray Stata.

40. Wright, "Entrepreneurs Join in Celebrating MIT."

CHAPTER 2

1. David R. Lampe, ed., *The Massachusetts Miracle: High Technology and Economic Revitalization* (Cambridge, MA: MIT Press, 1988).

2. William Putt, *How to Start Your Own Business* (Cambridge, MA: MIT Press and the MIT Alumni Association, 1974), xv.

3. Edward B. Roberts, *Celebrating Entrepreneurship. A Half-Century of MIT's Growth and Impact* (self-pub., 2018), 19–20.

4. They were Charles Hieken, Frederick Lehman, Steven Lipner, Edward Roberts, Susan Schur, Robert Scott, Panos Spiliokos, Christopher Spraue, Martin Schrage, Carol Van Aken, and Edward Roberts. Source: Roberts, *Celebrating Entrepreneurship,* 20.

5. Putt, *How to Start Your Own Business*, xv.

6. Putt, *How to Start Your Own Business*, xv.

7. Edward B. Roberts and Charles E. Eesley, "Entrepreneurial Impact: The Role of MIT," *Foundations and Trends in Entrepreneurship* 7, no. 1–2 (2011): 1–149, 44, http://dx.doi.org/10.1561/0300000030.

8. The editorial board included George M. Berman ('45), Kenneth J. Germeshausen ('31), Donald R. Miller ('50), Richard S. Morse ('33), Denis M. Robinson ('31), Arthur F. F. Snyder, Fred G. Lehmann ('52), Panos D. Spiliakos ('66), and William D. Putt ('59). Source: Putt, *How to Start Your Own Business*.

9. Putt, *How to Start Your Own Business*.

10. Putt, *How to Start Your Own Business*.

11. Toshihiro Kanai, "Entrepreneurial Networking: A Comparative Analysis of Networking Organizations and Their Participants in an Entrepreneurial Community" (PhD diss., MIT, 1989), 91.

12. S. Rich and D. Gumpert, *Business Plans That Win $$: Lessons from the MIT Enterprise Forum* (New York: First Perennial Library, 1985), xv.

13. Kanai, *Entrepreneurial Networking*, 94.

14. Kanai, *Entrepreneurial Networking*, 89.

15. Roberts and Eesley, "Entrepreneurial Impact."

16. "The Independent Activities Period (IAP) is a special four-week term at MIT that runs from the first week of January until the end of the month during which members of the MIT community have the opportunity to organize, sponsor, and

participate in a wide variety of activities, including forums, lecture series, and contests." Source: Independent Activities Period, http://web.mit.edu/iap/ (accessed December 9, 2020).

17. Rich and Gumpert, *Business Plans That Win $$;* interview of Joe Hadzima on October 27, 2014.

18. S. Rosegrant and D. Lampe, *Route 128. Lessons from Boston's High-Tech Community* (New York: Basic Books, 1992), 153–157. Part of this growth can be attributed to the fact that, in 1978, the venture capital industry was boosted by the government allowing pension funds to invest a portion of their assets in higher-risk ventures.

19. Roberts and Eesley, "Entrepreneurial Impact," 89–90.

20. Michael Dukakis and Rosabeth Kanter, *Creating the Future* (New York: Summit Books, 1988); Nithin Nohria, "Information and Search in the Creation of New Business Ventures," in *Networks and Organizations* (Cambridge, MA: Harvard Business Publishing, 1992), 254–255.

21. Kanai, *Entrepreneurial Networking,* 91.

22. Annalee Saxenian, *Regional Advantage: Culture and Competition in Silicon Valley and Route 128* (Cambridge, MA: Harvard University Press, 1994), 67.

23. Saxenian, *Regional Advantage,* 66.

24. Michael L. Dertouzos, Robert M. Solow, and Richard K. Lester, *Made in America: Regaining the Productive Hedge* (Cambridge, MA: MIT Press, 1989).

25. Suzanne Berger and MIT Task Force on Production in the Innovation Economy, *Making in America: From Innovation to Market* (Cambridge, MA: MIT Press, 2013).

26. Jeff Engel, "Exit Interview: Lita Nelsen on MIT Tech Transfer, Startups & Culture," *Xconomy,* May 31, 2016, https://www.xconomy.com/boston/2016/05/31/exit-interview-lita-nelsen-on-mit-tech-transfer-startups-culture/ (accessed April 17, 2020). See also Edward Roberts and Denis Malone, "Policies and Structures for Spinning off New Companies from Research and Development Organizations," *R&D Management* 26, no. 1 (1996): 17–48.

27. Engel, "Exit Interview: Lita Nelsen."

28. Until then, entrepreneurship had raised only limited interest from students that materialized in tangible activities. For instance, Professor Edward Roberts writes about the "New Enterprises" class, the only pure graduate entrepreneurship class offered at MIT since 1961: "Enrollment in those earlier years seldom was more than 20 students, but the subject persisted over time." Roberts, *Celebrating Entrepreneurship,* 12.

29. E-Club home page, http://web.mit.edu/e-club/www/index.html (accessed December 9, 2020).

30. Interview of Peter Mui on November 17, 2019.

31. David Chandler, "Cementing Success," *MIT News,* May 14, 2010, https://news
.mit.edu/2010/100k-competition-0514 (accessed April 17, 2020).

32. Interview of Peter Mui.

33. Sloan New Ventures Association, http://web.mit.edu/50k/old-www/Attic/10kkit
.html#RXII (accessed December 9, 2020).

34. SNVA was discontinued in 1996–1997.

35. Chandler, "Cementing Success"; interview of Peter Mui; 1993 brochure about
the $10K Business Plan Competition provided by Doug Ling.

36. Email exchange with Doug Ling on September 3, 2020. This skepticism about
entrepreneurship is also echoed in "Edward B. Roberts," MIT Infinite History, Cambridge, MA, 2016, https://infinitehistory.mit.edu/video/edward-b-roberts-58-sm-58
-sm-60-phd-62 (accessed February 26, 2020).

37. Brochure about the $10K Business Plan Competition; Joost Paul Bonsen, "The
Innovation Institute: From Creative Inquiry through Real-World Impact at MIT"
(master's thesis, MIT, 2006), 66, https://dspace.mit.edu/bitstream/handle/1721.1
/37141/85813074-MIT.pdf?sequence=2 (accessed May 11, 2016); interview of Peter
Mui; email exchange with Doug Ling.

38. There is a little confusion about the exact number of contestants at the first
edition of the $10K, which varies between fifty-four and sixty-four, probably in part
because Joost Bonsen ('90) defended nine projects that year. Sources mentioning
sixty-four include the email exchange with Doug Ling and Bonsen, "The Innovation
Institute," 66. Sources mentioning fifty-four include Roberts and Eesley, "Entrepreneurial Impact," 101, and *MIT Entrepreneurship Center Annual Report 1997–1998*
(Cambridge, MA: MIT, 1998).

39. Roberts and Eesley, "Entrepreneurial Impact," 101.

40. Interview of Joe Hadzima on October 27, 2014.

41. Joseph G. Hadzima bio page, https://mitsloan.mit.edu/faculty/directory/joseph
-g-hadzima (accessed December 9, 2020).

42. Email exchange with Doug Ling; brochure about the $10K Business Plan
Competition.

43. "MIT Students Win 10K Prize," *Mass High Tech.,* May 17, 1993.

44. Interview of David Morgenthaler by Michelle Choate, May 16, 2016; Joe
Hadzima, "David Morgenthaler—a Man Who Knew Where to Place the Lever," *Huff-
post,* June 21, 2016, https://www.huffpost.com/entry/david-morgenthaler-a-ma_b
_10600412 (accessed December 9, 2020).

45. Hadzima, "David Morgenthaler."

46. "Edward B. Roberts," MIT Infinite History.

47. Bonsen, "The Innovation Institute," 33.

48. David Chandler, "Outside the Classroom, Students Create Future Businesses," *MIT News*, September 28, 2011, http://news.mit.edu/2011/entrepreneurship-extracurricular -0928 (accessed January 5, 2018).

49. Joe Hadzima, "Open Matters: MIT OpenCourseWare News and Information," *Daring to Show up, Year after Year* (blog), June 18, 2016, https://mitopencourseware .wordpress.com/category/entrepreneurship/ (accessed June 4, 2018); interview of Joe Hadzima.

50. Bonsen, "The Innovation Institute," 56.

51. "The Best Entrepreneurship Courses in America," Inc.com, February 19, 2009, https://www.inc.com/ss/best-entrepreneurship-courses-america (accessed October 10, 2018).

52. Since then, the seminar has been retitled "The Startup Experience at MIT."

53. Per Lita Nelsen, for accuracy, these are US patents; many universities also had foreign counterparts issued, but these are not included in the statistics and they vary widely.

54. Scott Shane, *Academic Entrepreneurship. University Spin-offs and Wealth Creation* (Northampton, MA: Edward Elgar, 2004), 59.

55. Sachi Hatakenaka, "Flux and Flexibility: A Comparative Institution Analysis of Evolving University-Industry Relationships in MIT, Cambridge and Tokyo" (PhD diss., MIT, 2002), 157, https://dspace.mit.edu/handle/1721.1/8434; Sachi Hatak-enaka, *University-Industry Partnerships in MIT, Cambridge, and Tokyo: Storytelling across Boundaries* (New York: Routledge, 2003); Engel, "Exit Interview: Lita Nelsen."

56. Engel, "Exit Interview: Lita Nelsen"; Shane, *Academic Entrepreneurship*, 103–138.

57. Engle, "Exit Interview of Lita Nelsen."

58. Roberts, *Entrepreneurs in High Technology*, 43; Bonsen, "The Innovation Institute"; Engel, "Exit Interview: Lita Nelsen."

59. "Roberts to Chair Entrepreneurship Center, Head Expansion," *MIT Tech Talk* 43, no. 23 (1999), https://news.mit.edu/1999/roberts-0317. See also "Celebrating a Half Century of MIT Entrepreneurship Conference. Building the MIT Entrepreneurship," Program Session, Cambridge, MA, 2016, https://www.youtube.com/watch?v=bWTjf -je5vg&t=1499s&pbjreload=10 (accessed April 4, 2020); Roberts, *Celebrating Entrepreneurship*, 26.

60. The *Entrepreneurship Center Annual Report 1997–1998* mentions, "The Massachu-setts Institute of Technology established the MIT Entrepreneurship Center with seed funding from the Kauffman Foundation, the Coleman Foundation, and the Lemel-son Foundation," 3.

61. "Edward B. Roberts," MIT Infinite History.

62. J. Engel, "MIT Boosts Resources for Entrepreneurs as Startup 'Fever' Rages," *Xconomy*, May 19, 2016, https://www.xconomy.com/boston/2016/05/19/mit-boosts -resources-for-entrepreneurs-as-startup-fever-rages/ (accessed August 16, 2018).

63. Roberts, *Entrepreneurs in High Technology*, 35; Roberts, *Celebrating Entrepreneurship*, 25; Bonsen, "The Innovation Institute."

CHAPTER 3

1. Pattie Maes, "Meet the Sixth Sense Interaction," TED Talk, https://www.ted.com /speakers/pattie_maes (accessed September 16, 2020).

2. Examples include Webline Communications (a winner of the $50K Entrepreneurship Competition) cofounded by Pasha Roberts ('04) and Firdaus Bhathena ('92); Stylus Innovation, cofounded by Mike Cassidy ('85), Kriztina Holly ('89), and John Barrus ('87); Direct Hit, cofounded by Gary Culiss, Steven Yang ('98), and the same Mike Cassidy; Silicon Spice (a winner of the 1995 $50K Entrepreneurship Competition), cofounded by Ian Eslick ('96), Rob French ('90), and Ethan Mirsky ('96); Flash Communications, cofounded by Rajeev Surati ('93); and Sohu, started by Charles Zhang ('94).

3. SenSAble Technologies was founded in 1995 by Thomas Massie ('93), and Z Corporation was founded by Marina Hatsopoulos ('93), Walter Bornhorst ('64), Jim Bredt MIT ('82), and Tim Anderson.

4. Software Arts was cofounded by Dan Bricklin ('73) and Bob Frankston ('70), and Lotus Development Corporation was cofounded by Mitch Kapor and Jonathan Sachs ('70) in 1982. Kenan Systems was founded by Dr. Kenan Sahin ('63), iRobot was founded by Colin Angle ('89) and Helen Greiner ('89), along with their MIT professor (and former director of the MIT Computer Science and Artificial Intelligence Laboratory) Rodney Brooks. Lexicus was founded by Rojon Nag ('91).

5. Interview with Mitch Kapor on November 5, 2019; interview with Bill Aulet ('94) on December 16, 2019; interview with Tim Rowe ('99) on November 4, 2016; also see https://en.wikipedia.org/wiki/Mitch_Kapor and https://en.wikipedia.org/wiki /Lotus_Software (accessed February 9, 2018); and Dan Power, "A Brief History of Spreadsheets" (n.d.), http://dssresources.com/history/sshistory.html (accessed September 5, 2020).

6. Bank of Boston, "MIT: The Impact of Innovation," 1997. "MIT Graduates Have Started 4,000 Companies with 1,100,000 Jobs, $232 Billion in Sales in '94," *MIT News*, March 5, 1997, http://news.mit.edu/1997/jobs (accessed February 9, 2018).

7. David Stone, "Interview with Alex Rigopulos—Part 1—GameCritics.Com," *Game Critics*, March 30, 2004, https://gamecritics.com/david-stone/interview-with-alex-rigopulos -part-1/ (accessed November 16, 2018).

8. Kris Graft, "Interview: Reinventing Harmonix," *Gamasutra,* August 11, 2011, https://www.gamasutra.com/view/news/126513/Interview_Reinventing_Harmonix .php (accessed December 9, 2020).

9. Charlie Hall, "With the Release of Rock Band 4, Harmonix Reveals Source of Investment," Polygon, October 5, 2015, https://www.polygon.com/2015/10/5/9454919/with -the-release-of-rock-band-4-harmonix-reveals-source-of-investment (accessed November 14, 2018).

10. Interview of Edward Roberts on October 14, 2014.

11. *MIT Entrepreneurship Center Annual Report 1997–1998* (Cambridge, MA: MIT, 1998).

12. Among those professionals were Howard Anderson and Noubar Afeyan ('87), two successful entrepreneurs turned venture capitalists; Alex d'Arbeloff ('49) (as Professor of the Practice); Tim Rowe, cofounder of an early internet company and the cofounder of the Cambridge Innovation Center; and Shari Loesberg, a former investment banker.

13. Edward B. Roberts and Charles E. Eesley, "Entrepreneurial Impact: The Role of MIT," *Foundations and Trends in Entrepreneurship* 7, no. 1–2 (2011): 1–149, 95, http://dx.doi.org/10.1561/0300000030.

14. Roberts and Eesley, "Entrepreneurial Impact," 90–91.

15. *MIT Entrepreneurship Center Annual Report 1997–1998.*

16. Interview of Kenneth Morse on January 11, 2020 and MIT's Endowment Report FY2019, "Richard S. Morse (1933) Fund."

17. Exchange with Kenneth Morse on October 21, 2019.

18. Interviews of professors Richard Locke on January 24, 2013, and Simon Johnson on May 11, 2016, by Michelle Choate. Also see my interview of Simon Johnson on May 9, 2018, https://mitsloan.mit.edu/action-learning/g-lab (accessed February 9, 2018).

19. MIT Management Executive Federation, "Entrepreneurship Development Program," https://executive.mit.edu/openenrollment/program/entrepreneurship_develop ment_program/ (accessed April 7, 2020).

20. This is from an interview of David Morgenthaler by Michelle Choate on May 16, 2016.

21. "Roberts to Chair Entrepreneurship Center, Head Expansion," *MIT Tech Talk* 43, no. 23 (1999), https://news.mit.edu/1999/roberts-0317 (accessed May 3, 2020).

22. VMS History, https://vms.mit.edu/mit-venture-mentoring-service/vms-history (accessed December 9, 2020). Professor Roberts provides a detailed narrative of the early days of VMS in Edward B. Roberts, *Celebrating Entrepreneurship: A Half-Century of MIT's Growth and Impact* (self-pub., 2018), 66–67.

23. Liz Karagianis, "Good Company," *MIT Spectrum,* Spring 2001, https://spectrum.mit.edu/spring-2001/good-company/ (accessed February 9, 2018).

24. Source: email of VMS from January 3, 2019.

25. Jerry Ackerman, "Alexander Dingee, Co-Founder of MIT Venture Mentoring Service, Dies at 88," *MIT News,* April 5, 2019, http://news.mit.edu/2019/alexander-dingee-co-founder-mit-venture-mentoring-service-dies-88-0405 (accessed February 9, 2018).

26. Alice Waught, "Venture Mentoring Service Backs Budding Businesses," *Slice of MIT,* April 24, 2018, https://alum.mit.edu/slice/venture-mentoring-service-backs-budding-businesses (accessed September 27, 2018).

27. Auto-ID Labs, http://autoid.mit.edu.

28. Bernd Schoner, *The Tech Entrepreneur's Survival Guide: How to Bootstrap Your Startup, Lead through Tough Times, and Cash in for Success* (New York: McGraw-Hill, 2014), 4.

29. Interview with Professor Charlie Cooney on March 2, 2020; David Chandler, "Bringing Innovation to the World," *MIT News,* October 18, 2010, http://news.mit.edu/2010/deshpande-1018 (accessed February 26, 2020). Professor Roberts also refers to conversations between Desh Deshpande and Alex d'Arbeloff leading to the creation of the Deshpande Center for Technology Innovation in "Edward B. Roberts '58, SM '58, SM '60, PhD '62," MIT Infinite History, March 8, 2016, https://infinitehistory.mit.edu/video/edward-b-roberts-58-sm-58-sm-60-phd-62 (accessed September 27, 2018).

30. "A Tribute to MIT Entrepreneurs Who Build Significant Companies and Pioneer New Industries—Session. Life Sciences and Biotechnology," Celebrating a Half Century of MIT Entrepreneurship Conference, Cambridge, MA, 2016, https://www.youtube.com/watch?v=KBXT1ulLSOg&t=3418s (accessed January 22, 2021).

31. Written exchange with Professor Charlie Cooney on November 12, 2020.

32. A list of the recipients of those prizes is available at https://entrepreneurship.mit.edu/awards/ (accessed October 8, 2020).

33. MIT VCPE, http://www.mitvcpe.com (accessed November 12, 2017).

34. Doug Ling ('87) reports that the alumnus Robert Goldberg ('65) funded the competition anonymously in the early 1990s.

35. *MIT Entrepreneurship Center Annual Report 1997–1998.*

36. Maw-Der Foo, "Team Design and Performance: A Study of Short-Term Entrepreneurial Teams" (PhD diss., MIT, 1999), 37, https://dspace.mit.edu/handle/1721.1/50526 (accessed January 16, 2020). Such figures, however, need to be taken with a grain of salt and should be considered indicative because it is not clear how rigorously they were collected.

37. MIT Global Startup Workshop, http://gsw.mit.edu/2020/ (accessed January 26, 2021).

38. MIT Entrepreneurs Club, http://web.mit.edu/e-club/ (accessed January 26, 2021).

39. Rob Matheson, "Biotech to the Rescue," *MIT News,* April 26, 2014, http://news .mit.edu/2014/ram-sasisekharan-startups-fight-disease-make-better-drugs-0428 (accessed September 27, 2018).

40. Matheson, "Biotech to the Rescue."

41. Interview with Professor Charlie Cooney on March 2, 2020.

42. VentureShips, http://web.mit.edu/sebc/vships/ (accessed December 9, 2020).

43. Denise Brehm, "Grad Student Sets up Program to Teach Java Course in Nairobi," *MIT News,* October 25, 2000, http://news.mit.edu/2000/kenya-1025 (accessed September 27, 2018). This article appeared in *MIT Tech Talk* on October 25, 2000.

44. Interview with Sally Susnowitz on October 27, 2014; interview with Alison Hynd on October 29, 2014; Amy Marcott, "Building a Better World: The Public Service Center Celebrates 25 Years," *MIT Technology Review*, April 23, 2013.

45. MIT—Division of Student Life, https://studentlife.mit.edu/pkgcenter/who-we -are/history (accessed December 14, 2017).

46. Joost Paul Bonsen, "The Innovation Institute: From Creative Inquiry through Real-World Impact at MIT" (master's thesis, MIT, 2006), 67–68, https://dspace.mit .edu/bitstream/handle/1721.1/37141/85813074-MIT.pdf?sequence=2 (accessed May 11, 2016).

47. *MIT D-Lab* (blog), http://d-lab.mit.edu.

48. *The D-Lab at MIT: The People's Engineering Team,* https://vimeo.com/67642337 (accessed December 21, 2017).

49. MLAsia was discontinued in 2003.

50. Sandy Pentland and Joost Paul Bonsen, "Media Ventures: Media Lab Entrepreneurship & Digital Innovations Seminar," https://www.media.mit.edu/posts/sample -venture-classes/ (accessed December 21, 2017).

51. Joe Hadzima, "Entrepreneurial Ecosystems: Cultivating Successful Businesses at MIT," MIT Alumni Association, *What Matters?,* June 2005.

52. Roberts and Eesley, "Entrepreneurial Impact," 113.

CHAPTER 4

1. Christine Ortiz, "Committee on Student Entrepreneurship (CSE) Letters to Community—Christine Ortiz, Dean for Graduate Education—Massachusetts Institute

of Technology," http://odge.mit.edu/dean/letters/letter20120217-2CSE.php (accessed March 4, 2018).

2. Fiona E. Murray and Vladimir Bulović, *The MIT Innovation Initiative: Sustaining and Extending a Legacy of Innovation December 3, 2014 PRELIMINARY REPORT* (Cambridge, MA: MIT, December 3, 2014); Vladimir Bulović and Fiona Murray, *MIT Innovation Initiative. Final Report of Community Feedback and Recommendations* (Cambridge, MA: MIT, January 2016), https://innovation.mit.edu/assets/MIT-Innovation-Initiative-Final -Report-Jan-2016.pdf (accessed February 3, 2017), 4.

3. Edward B. Roberts, Fiona Murray, and J. Daniel Kim, *Entrepreneurship and Innovation at MIT: Continuing Global Growth and Impact* (Cambridge, MA, MIT Sloan School of Management, 2015), http://web.mit.edu/innovate/entrepreneurship2015.pdf (accessed February 3, 2017), 15; Melissa Korn, "How to Make Entrepreneurs: MIT Lecturer Offers Steps for Potential Business Owners," *Wall Street Journal,* September 5, 2013.

4. See Professor Fiona Murray's talk at the European Central Bank on March 15, 2017, *Panel 3—Fostering Innovation and Entrepreneurial Ecosystems in the European Union,* Frankfurt, March 15, 2017, https://www.youtube.com/watch?v=DlqY--FHKPg &list=PLnVAEZuF9FZlg3wLNrClEdJUvjNgZuBCO&index=7 (at minute 26) (accessed February 3, 2018); Jeff Engel, "Xconomy: MIT Boosts Resources for Entrepreneurs as Startup 'Fever' Rages," *Xconomy,* May 19, 2016, https://www.xconomy.com/boston /2016/05/19/mit-boosts-resources-for-entrepreneurs-as-startup-fever-rages/ (accessed May 3, 2017); "A Cambrian Moment," *The Economist,* January 17, 2014, https://www .economist.com/special-report/2014/01/17/a-cambrian-moment (accessed February 3, 2017); Jeff Engel, "Exit Interview: Lita Nelsen on MIT Tech Transfer, Startups & Culture," *Xconomy,* May 31, 2016, https://www.xconomy.com/boston/2016/05/31/exit -interview-lita-nelsen-on-mit-tech-transfer-startups-culture/ (accessed June 3, 2016).

5. Murray, *Panel 3—Fostering Innovation and Entrepreneurial Ecosystems in the European Union.*

6. Engel, "Xconomy: MIT Boosts Resources for Entrepreneurs as Startup 'Fever' Rages."

7. Roberts, Murray, and Kim, *Entrepreneurship and Innovation at MIT.*

8. Murray and Bulović, *The MIT Innovation Initiative.*

9. Roberts, Murray, and Kim, *Entrepreneurship and Innovation at MIT.*

10. Roberts, Murray, and Kim, *Entrepreneurship and Innovation at MIT.*

11. Jinane Abounadi, "Sandbox," Microsoft PowerPoint presentation shared during interview, March 3, 2016.

12. Steve Lohr, "G.E. Makes a Sharp 'Pivot' on Digital," *The New York Times,* April 20, 2018, Business Day sec., https://www.nytimes.com/2018/04/19/business/ge-digital -ambitions.html (accessed December 3, 2018).

13. Thomas Friedman, *Thank You for Being Late: An Optimist's Guide to Thriving in the Age of Accelerations* (New York: Farrar, Straus and Giroux, 2016), 20–22.

14. "A Cambrian Moment."

15. Interview of Professor Alex (Sandy) Pentland on September 30, 2015; Joost Paul Bonsen, "The Innovation Institute: From Creative Inquiry through Real-World Impact at MIT" (master's thesis, MIT, 2006), 46, https://dspace.mit.edu/bitstream/handle/1721 .1/37141/85813074-MIT.pdf?sequence=2 (accessed May 11, 2016).

16. MIT D-Lab, "Scale-ups Fellowship," https://d-lab.mit.edu/scale-ups/about (accessed August 6, 2018); *D-Lab Annual Report 2014–2015* (Cambridge, MA: MIT D-Lab, 2015), https://drive.google.com/file/d/0B36nNXj12OvSRmEySkhSVlN3aUU/view (accessed August 6, 2018).

17. Sanergy, Home, http://www.sanergy.com (accessed December 10, 2020).

18. Anna Waldman-Brown and Georgina Campbell Flatter, *Scaling Sanergy: Growing a Promising Sanitation Startup (May 2018)*, case study (Cambridge, MA: MIT Legatum Center, 2018), http://legatum.mit.edu/wp-content/uploads/2018/07/Sanergy-Case-Study _6.29.2018.docx.pdf (accessed January 4, 2019), 2–3.

19. Sanergy, "Sanitation," http://www.sanergy.com/impact/ (accessed February 21, 2020).

20. These statistics are according to my estimates based on the MIT Course Catalogs (MIT Bulletin) 1990–2016.

21. "MBA E+I Track—Martin Trust Center for MIT Entrepreneurship," Martin Trust Center for MIT Entrepreneurship, 2018, http://entrepreneurship.mit.edu/mba-entre preneurship-innovation/ (accessed April 1, 2019).

22. Rob Matheson, "Engineering Course 'Demystifies' Entrepreneurship," *MIT News,* May 28, 2013, http://news.mit.edu/2013/engineering-course-demystifies-entrepre neurship-0528 (accessed August 9, 2018).

23. Dean, School of Engineering, "Reports to the President For the Year Ended June 30, 2013," 2013, http://web.mit.edu/annualreports/pres13/2013.04.00.pdf (accessed April 9, 2020).

24. President Reif wrote in his letter that "MIT will always be defined by its central focus on education and research. Yet more and more, innovation belongs to our mission as well." Rafael Reif, "Launching the MIT Innovation Initiative," Office of the President, MIT, October 17, 2013, http://president.mit.edu/speeches-writing /launching-mit-innovation-initiative (accessed November 8, 2018).

25. "Until quite recently, MIT had followed a 'hands off' approach toward entrepre-neurial engagement and the provision of more resources and infrastructure, in con-trast with many other universities in the United States and abroad: MIT has neither created an internal physical incubator space for ventures nor a venture capital fund to

enable prospective start-ups. That approach has permitted MIT to avoid the internal conflicts and occasional embarrassments that have plagued other academic institutions." Edward B. Roberts, Fiona Murray, and J. Daniel Kim, *Entrepreneurship and Innovation at MIT: Continuing Global Growth and Impact* (Cambridge, MA, MIT Sloan School of Management, 2015), http://web.mit.edu/innovate/entrepreneurship2015 .pdf (accessed February 3, 2017), 29. Also, Bill Aulet comments in a 2016 interview that since 2009, when he started his tenure as director of the Entrepreneurship Center, he has watched administrators' attitudes toward entrepreneurship change dramatically: "It's been a progression, but it really picked up, I would say, over the past six or seven years." J. Engel, "MIT Boosts Resources for Entrepreneurs as Startup 'Fever' Rages," *Xconomy,* 2016, https://www.xconomy.com/boston/2016/05/19/mit -boosts-resources-for-entrepreneurs-as-startup-fever-rages/ (accessed April 12, 2017).

26. Michael Patrick Rutter, "MIT Sandbox Invites 11,000 Students to Innovate," *MIT News,* January 25, 2016, http://news.mit.edu/2016/mit-sandbox-invites-students-to -innovate-0125 (accessed October 8, 2018).

27. Meg Murphy, "Helping Innovators to 'Keep Going.' How Does the Sandbox Funding Board Define Success? Everyone Learning," *MIT News,* June 8, 2016, http://news .mit.edu/2016/helping-engineering-innovators-keep-going-0608 (accessed October 8, 2018).

28. MIT Innovation Initiative—Lab for Innovation Science and Policy, "Reshaping Research Universities for Impact in the Innovation Economy," Challenges of the Innovation Economy Series, June 9, 2016, https://www.youtube.com/watch ?v=4gfpnXwXYbY (accessed December 10, 2020).

29. Sharon Lacey, "Creative Arts Competition Rewards Arts Entrepreneurship at MIT," *Arts at MIT,* May 10, 2017, https://arts.mit.edu/creative-arts-competition-rewards -arts-entrepreneurship-at-mit/ (accessed August 7, 2018).

30. E14, "From 'Deploy' to 'Scale,'" https://www.e14fund.com (accessed December 10, 2020).

31. "About MITdesignX," MITdesignX, https://designx.mit.edu/ (accessed November 8, 2018).

32. School of Architecture and Planning, "MET Fund Launched to Support MIT-designX," MIT News, April 9, 2019, https://news.mit.edu/2019/met-fund-launched -to-support-mitdesignx-0409 (accessed February 7, 2021).

33. Rafael Reif, "A Better Way to Deliver Innovation to the World," *Washington Post,* May 22, 2015, https://www.washingtonpost.com/opinions/a-better-way-to-deliver -innovation-to-the-world/2015/05/22/35023680-fe28-11e4-8b6c-0dcce21e223d_ story.html (accessed June 4, 2015).

34. Rafael Reif, "Letter to the MIT Community Regarding the Launch of The Engine," October 27, 2016, http://news.mit.edu/2016/letter-mit-community-regarding-launch -engine-1026 (accessed December 10, 2020).

35. Jeff Engel, "Transition in Tech Transfer: Will MIT Ever Start a Venture Fund?," *Xconomy*, March 11, 2016, https://www.xconomy.com/boston/2016/03/11/transition -in-tech-transfer-will-mit-ever-start-a-venture-fund/ (accessed January 18, 2018); MIT Innovation Initiative—Lab for Innovation Science and Policy, "Reshaping Research Universities for Impact in the Innovation Economy."

36. *Enhancing Collaboration between MIT and The Engine: Joint Findings of The Engine Working Groups. Final Report to the MIT Community* (Cambridge, MA: MIT, April 2018), http://web.mit.edu/ewgreport/introduction.html (accessed November 21, 2018).

37. The students were Robert Bruch ('04) and John Hebert ('03) from the Sloan School of Management and Martin Curiel and Tsafrir Vanounou from the Harvard Business School.

38. Rob Matheson, "The Half-Billion-Dollar Idea," *MIT News*, April 8, 2013, http:// news.mit.edu/2013/todd-zion-smartcells-0408 (accessed September 30, 2018).

39. Rafael Reif, "An Exciting Step Forward for Our Innovation Ecosystem," Office of the President, MIT, October 26, 2016, https://president.mit.edu/speeches-writing /exciting-step-forward-our-innovation-ecosystem (accessed August 25, 2020).

40. "From Lab to Market: The Path of a New Diabetes Treatment," *MIT Spectrum*, November 18, 2014, https://spectrum.mit.edu/continuum/from-lab-to-market-the -path-of-a-new-diabetes-treatment/ (accessed November 21, 2018).

41. Michael B. Farrell, "MIT Reboots Approach to Innovation—the Boston Globe," *BostonGlobe.com*, January 26, 2014, https://www.bostonglobe.com/business/2014/01 /26/mit-reboots-approach-innovation/TExxXWxI02WOR4NZKIHAFP/story.html (accessed October 8, 2018).

42. Liz Karagianis, "Why an Innovation Initiative Now?," *MIT Spectrum*, Spring 2015, https://spectrum.mit.edu/spring-2015/why-an-innovation-initiative-now/ (accessed August 11, 2018).

43. Jordan Graham, "Report Says MIT 'Bursting at Seams,'" *Boston Herald*, December 5, 2014, http://www.bostonherald.com/business/technology/2014/12/report_says_mit _bursting_at_seams (accessed August 11, 2018).

44. Murray and Bulović, *The MIT Innovation Initiative*, 4.

45. Ian Waitz, "Introducing Sandbox," *MIT Faculty Newsletter*, February 2016, http:// web.mit.edu/fnl/volume/283/waitz.html (accessed December 10, 2020).

46. "The idea is that, by offering time and credit for students working on entrepreneurial projects, MIT might be able to better hold on to bright young engineers who might otherwise abandon their studies—and the region—to start a company (hello, Mark Zuckerberg)." Curt Woodward, "MIT Unveils New Startup Program with Google, Greylock, Matrix VCs," *Xconomy*, February 7, 2013, https://www.xconomy .com/boston/2013/02/07/mit-unveils-new-startup-program-with-big-vcs/ (accessed August 11, 2018).

47. Interview of Ian Waitz, dean of engineering, on October 23, 2015.

48. "The ecosystem in Boston has really improved. Even three years ago, students felt that in order to get funded, they had to go out West. They see that differently now." Quoted in Lucia Maffei, "Trish Cotter about MIT Delta v and Student Entrepreneurship," *AmericanInno* (blog), November 6, 2017, https://www.americaninno .com/boston/50-on-fire/how-mit-plans-to-grow-its-delta-v-accelerator-program (accessed August 11, 2018).

49. "Drew Houston's Commencement Address," *MIT News,* June 7, 2013, http://news .mit.edu/2013/commencement-address-houston-0607 (accessed August 11, 2018).

50. Farrell, "MIT Reboots Approach to Innovation."

51. These were Sanjit Biswas ('05), John Bicket ('05), and Hans Robertson ('99).

52. Woodward, "MIT Unveils New Startup Program."

53. Woodward, "MIT Unveils New Startup Program."

54. Farrell, "MIT Reboots Approach to Innovation."

55. Farrell, "MIT Reboots Approach to Innovation."

56. Farrell, "MIT Reboots Approach to Innovation."

57. Samuel Jay Keyser, *Mens et Mania: The MIT Nobody Knows* (Cambridge, MA: MIT Press, 2011), 176. "MIT's revenue stream, such as it is, does not depend on profit. To help feed its education and research habit, it depends on gifts from alumni and other angels." Keyser, *Mens et Mania,* 182.

58. Max Stendahl, "Who's Donating $140 Million to MIT? The University Won't Say," *Boston Business Journal*, June 7, 2017, https://www.bizjournals.com/boston /news/2017/06/07/whos-donating-140-million-to-mit-the-university.html (accessed August 13, 2019).

59. Rich Auletta, "Get Rich U," *The New Yorker*, April 30, 2012, https://www .newyorker.com/magazine/2012/04/30/get-rich-u (accessed August 11, 2018).

60. "Legatum and MIT Announce the Creation of Academic Center Dedicated to Development and Entrepreneurship," *MIT News,* http://news.mit.edu/2007/legatum -0917 (accessed August 6, 2018); Rebecca Knightin, "MIT to Tutor Emerging Leaders," *Financial Times*, September 17, 2007.

61. See the example provided by Bulović and Murray about MIT professor Buonassisi's research in *MIT Innovation Initiative,* 18.

62. Elisabeth B. Reynolds, Hiram M Samel, and Joyce Lawrence, "Learning by Building: Complementary Assets and the Migration of Capabilities in U.S. Innovation Firms," MIT Industrial Performance Center Working Paper Series, Cambridge, MA: MIT, March 2013, https://ipc.mit.edu/sites/default/files/2019-01/13-001.pdf (accessed April 28, 2020).

63. ReviveMD, Home page, http://www.reviveintmed.com (accessed December 10, 2020).

64. Meg Murphy, "At MIT, a Culture of Innovation 'Never Gets Old,'" *MIT Engineering* (blog), June 2, 2016, https://engineering.mit.edu/admissions/student-spotlight /at-mit-a-culture-of-innovation-never-gets-old-0/ (accessed September 30, 2018).

65. Murphy, "MIT School of Engineering."

66. Biobot, https://www.biobot.io (accessed January 16, 2021).

67. Roberts, Murray, and Kim, *Entrepreneurship and Innovation at MIT*, 14.

68. Murray and Bulović, *The MIT Innovation Initiative*, 4.

69. Jenny Fowler, "Making a Difference One Grain at a Time," *Harvard Gazette*, June 26, 2014, https://news.harvard.edu/gazette/story/newsplus/making-a-difference-one -grain-at-a-time/ (accessed December 10, 2020).

70. Rob Matheson, "3 Questions: Fiona Murray on Female Entrepreneurship," *MIT News*, June 12, 2013, http://news.mit.edu/2013/3q-fiona-murray-on-female-entrepre neurship-0612 (accessed August 4, 2019).

71. Hussain Hanum, "Here's What Happens When You Bring 12 MIT Female Founders Together for the Weekend," MIT Innovation Initiative, May 21, 2019, https:// innovation.mit.edu/blog-post/heres-what-happens-when-you-bring-12-mit-female -founders-together-for-the-weekend/ (accessed December 10, 2020).

72. Meredith Somers, "10 MIT Alumnae Named to Inc.'s Female Founders 100," MIT Sloan, October 12, 2018, https://mitsloan.mit.edu/ideas-made-to-matter/10-mit -alumnae-named-to-incs-female-founders-100 (accessed December 10, 2020).

73. Engel, "Exit Interview: Lita Nelsen."

74. Li Zhou, "How Are Universities Grooming the Next Great Innovators?," *Smithsonian Magazine*, July 14, 2015, https://www.smithsonianmag.com/innovation/how -are-universities-grooming-next-great-innovators-180955792/ (accessed February 4, 2020).

CHAPTER 5

1. Samuel Jay Keyser, *Mens et Mania. The MIT Nobody Knows* (Cambridge, MA: MIT Press, 2011), x.

2. Edgar Schein, *Organizational Culture and Leadership* (Hoboken, NJ: John Wiley & Sons, 2017).

3. John Van Maanen and Edgar Schein, "Toward a Theory of Organizational Socialization," in *Research in Organizational Behavior* (Greenwich, CT: JAI Press, 1979), 209–269, https://dspace.mit.edu/bitstream/handle/1721.1/1934/SWP-0960-03581864.pdf.

4. *The Ecosystem: Nurturing Entrepreneurship—MIT 150 Documentary (2011)*, MIT Infinite History, Cambridge, MA, 2011, https://infinitehistory.mit.edu/video/ecosystem-nurturing-entrepreneurship"-mit150-documentary-2011 (accessed August 27, 2019).

5. *2013–2014 Annual Report—Martin Trust Center for MIT Entrepreneurship* (Cambridge, MA: MIT, 2015), http://entrepreneurship.mit.edu/wp-content/uploads/MTC-Annual-Report-2013-2014.pdf (accessed December 10, 2020), 17.

6. The Energy Initiative, http://energy.mit.edu; the Innovation Initiative, https://innovation.mit.edu; Solve, https://solve.mit.edu (all accessed December 10, 2020).

7. MIT Innovation Initiative—Lab for Innovation Science and Policy, "Reshaping Research Universities for Impact in the Innovation Economy," Challenges of the Innovation Economy Series, June 9, 2016, https://www.youtube.com/watch?v=4gfpnXwXYbY (accessed July 3, 2020).

8. "Nicholas Negroponte," MIT Infinite History, Cambridge, MA, March 8, 2016, https://infinitehistory.mit.edu/video/nicholas-negroponte-'66-mar-'66 (accessed July 8, 2020).

9. Jeff Engel, "Exit Interview: Lita Nelsen on MIT Tech Transfer, Startups & Culture," *Xconomy*, May 31, 2016, https://www.xconomy.com/boston/2016/05/31/exit-interview-lita-nelsen-on-mit-tech-transfer-startups-culture/ (accessed June 4, 2018).

10. http://www.mit.edu/about/ (accessed August 26, 2019).

11. Keyser, *Mens et Mania,* 100.

12. Benson Snyder, *The Hidden Curriculum* (Cambridge, MA: MIT Press, 1973); quoted by Keyser, *Mens et Mania,* 100.

13. Keyser, *Mens et Mania,* 188.

14. Zach Winn, "Redesigning Pharmacies with the Consumer in Mind," *MIT News,* February 13, 2019, http://news.mit.edu/2019/alto-pharmacy-jaime-karraker-0213 (accessed February 17, 2019).

15. David Chandler, "Outside the Classroom, Students Create Future Businesses," *MIT News,* September 28, 2011, https://news.mit.edu/2011/entrepreneurship-extracurricular-0928 (accessed April 10, 2018).

16. Douglas Shand-Tucci, *MIT. A Historical and Architectural Tour* (New York: Princeton Architectural Press, 2016), 8.

17. Leda Zimmerman, "Sophisticated Medicine," *MIT News,* December 15, 2014, http://news.mit.edu/2014/sophisticated-medicine-sangeeta-bhatia-1215 (accessed December 23, 2018).

18. School of Engineering, "3 Questions: Martin Culpepper on Making the Future Makers," *MIT News,* December 22, 2015, http://news.mit.edu/2015/3-questions-martin-culpepper-making-future-makers-1222 (accessed February 22, 2020).

19. Edward B. Roberts and Charles E. Eesley, "Entrepreneurial Impact: The Role of MIT," *Foundations and Trends in Entrepreneurship* 7, no. 1–2 (2011): 1–149, 77, http://dx.doi.org/10.1561/0300000030.

20. Chris Vogel, "How MIT Became the Most Important University in the World," *Boston Magazine* (blog), October 30, 2012, https://www.bostonmagazine.com/2012/10/30/mit-important-university-world-harvard/ (accessed December 10, 2020).

21. Rob Matheson, "High Probability of Success," *MIT News,* May 1, 2013, http://news.mit.edu/2013/ben-vigoda-lyric-0501 (accessed February 22, 2020).

22. MIT Sloan School, "Active Learning: Explore Our Labs," https://mitsloan.mit.edu/action-learning/all-labs (accessed April 4, 2020).

23. MIT Department of Mechanical Engineering, "MIT 2.007 Design and Manufacturing I," https://me-2007.mit.edu (accessed April 4, 2020).

24. "A Mechanical Engineering Rite of Passage at MIT," *MIT News,* December 15, 2015, https://news.mit.edu/2015/mechanical-engineering-rite-of-passage-1215 (accessed February 21, 2018).

25. MIT Undergraduate Research Opportunities Program, https://urop.mit.edu (accessed August 24, 2020).

26. *The Ecosystem: Nurturing Entrepreneurship—MIT 150 Documentary (2011),* MIT Infinite History, Cambridge, MA, 2011, https://infinitehistory.mit.edu/video/ecosystem-nurturing-entrepreneurship"-mit150-documentary-2011 (accessed August 27, 2019).

27. MechE Undergrad, "Choosing a 2-A Concentration," https://meundergrad.mit.edu/2A-degree/choosing-2A-concentration (accessed December 10, 2020); interview with Romi Kadri on October 26, 2018.

28. Lita Nelsen, "The Activities and Roles of M.I.T. in Forming Clusters and Strengthening Entrepreneurship," in *Intellectual Property Management in Health and Agricultural Innovation: A Handbook of Best Practices* (Oxford, UK: MIHR, 2007), http://www.iphandbook.org (accessed March 5, 2018), 309–316.

29. Deborah Chen, "Startups: A Hidden Lifestyle at MIT," *The Tech,* March 23, 2012, https://thetech.com/2012/03/23/startups-v132-n14 (accessed October 7, 2019).

30. Chandler, "Outside the Classroom."

31. Fred Hapgood, *Up the Infinite Corridor: MIT and the Technical Imagination* (Reading, MA: Addison Wesley, 1993), 89–107.

32. Steven Levy, *Hackers: Heroes of the Computer Revolution* (New York: Anchor Press, 1984).

33. Martin Trust Center for MIT Entrepreneurship, "Guiding Concepts and Initiatives," http://entrepreneurship.mit.edu/ecosystem/ (accessed October 7, 2019).

34. "Entrepreneurs Are Like Pirates Crossed with Navy SEALs," *MIT Spectrum*, August 13, 2013, https://spectrum.mit.edu/continuum/entrepreneurs-are-like-pirates-crossed-with-navy-seals/ (accessed February 7, 2019).

35. Jay London, "How Do You Hack Health Care?," *Institute for Medical Engineering & Science* (blog), July 20, 2015, http://imes.mit.edu/how-do-you-hack-health-care/ (accessed February 21, 2019).

36. Steven Leckart, "The Hackathon Is On: Pitching and Programming the Next Killer App," Wired, February 17, 2012, https://www.wired.com/2012/02/ff_hackathons/all/1/ (accessed July 21, 2018).

37. Kara Baskin, "Evolution of the Hack," *MIT Sloan* (alumni magazine) 12, no. 1 (Winter 2018): 20–27, https://mitsloan.mit.edu/sites/default/files/inline-files/MITSloan_Winter18_HR.pdf (accessed April 8, 2018).

38. Transcript of Morrill Act (1862), https://www.ourdocuments.gov/doc.php?flash=false&doc=33&page=transcript (accessed April 14, 2020).

39. Philip Alexander, *A Widening Sphere: Evolving Cultures at MIT* (Cambridge, MA: MIT Press, 2011), 165.

40. Keyser, *Mens et Mania,* 8.

41. "MIT's Building 20: 'The Magical Incubator,'" MIT Infinite History, Cambridge, MA, 1998, https://infinitehistory.mit.edu/video/mits-building-20-magical-incubator (accessed March 20, 2020).

42. "Building 20 Denizens Say Farewell to Former Home," *MIT News,* April 1, 1998, http://news.mit.edu/1998/b20main-0401 (accessed February 29, 2020).

43. Robert Buderi, *The Invention That Changed the World: How a Small Group of Radar Pioneers Won the Second World War and Launched a Technological Revolution* (New York: Touchstone, 1996), 14.

44. Sophia Roosth, *Synthetic: How Life Got Made* (Chicago: University of Chicago Press, 2017), 22.

45. Hapgood, *Up the Infinite Corridor*, 2.

46. "A Tribute to MIT Entrepreneurs Who Build Significant Companies and Pioneer New Industries," Celebrating a Half Century of MIT Entrepreneurship Conference, Cambridge, MA, 2016, https://www.youtube.com/watch?v=KBXT1ulLSOg&t=3418s (accessed December 10, 2020).

47. Melissa Korn, "How to Make Entrepreneurs: MIT Lecturer Offers Steps for Potential Business Owners," *Wall Street Journal,* September 5, 2013.

48. http://incubomber.com/the-incubomber/ (accessed July 9, 2018); Peter Reinhardt, "Incumbomber—Where Bomb Ideas Come to Life," *Slightly Delusional* (blog), January 17, 2011, http://reinpk.blogspot.com/2011/01/incubomber-where-bomb-ideas-come-to.html (accessed July 9, 2018).

49. Fred Turner, *From Counterculture to Cyberculture: Stewart Brand, the Whole Earth Network, and the Rise of Digital Utopianism* (Chicago: University of Chicago Press, 2008). See also David Mindell's comment in *The Ecosystem: Nurturing Entrepreneurship—MIT 150 Documentary (2011),* MIT Infinite History, Cambridge, MA, 2011, https://infinitehistory.mit.edu/video/ecosystem-nurturing-entrepreneurship"-mit150-documentary-2011 (accessed August 27, 2019).

50. Stewart Brand, *The Media Lab: Inventing the Future at MIT* (Harmondsworth, UK: Penguin Books, 1987).

51. Edward Roberts, *Entrepreneurs in High Technology: Lessons from MIT and Beyond* (New York: Oxford University Press, 1991), 339.

52. Susan Hockfield, *The Age of Living Machines: How Biology Will Build the Next Technology Revolution* (New York: W. W. Norton, 2019), 10 and 148.

53. Robert Buderi, *Engines of Tomorrow* (New York: Simon & Schuster, 2000), 120–130.

54. Turner, *From Counterculture to Cyberculture,* 19.

55. Peter Galison, "Trading Zone: Coordinating Action and Belief," in Mario Biagioli, *The Science Studies Reader* (New York: Routledge, 1999), 137–160; quoted in Turner, *From Counterculture to Cyberculture,* 19.

56. Buderi, *The Invention That Changed the World,* 251.

57. Buderi, *The Invention That Changed the World,* 255.

58. Hockfield, *The Age of Living Machines,* 21.

59. Hockfield, *The Age of Living Machines,* 21.

60. Hockfield, *The Age of Living Machines,* 167.

61. Hockfield, *The Age of Living Machines,* 158.

62. Alissa Mallinson, "Innovation and Entrepreneurship: The MechE Way," *MIT MECHE in the News,* June 26, 2013, http://meche.mit.edu/news-media/innovation-and-entrepreneurship-meche-way (accessed February 22, 2020).

63. David Chandler, "3 Questions: Neil Gershenfeld and the Spread of Fab Labs," *MIT News,* January 4, 2016, http://news.mit.edu/2016/3-questions-neil-gershenfeld-fab-labs-0104 (accessed January 5, 2016).

64. MIT News Office, "New Undergraduate Majors and Minors to Debut in Fall 2016," *MIT News,* April 8, 2016, http://news.mit.edu/2016/new-undergraduate-majors-and-minors-0408 (accessed February 22, 2020).

65. Hockfield, *The Age of Living Machines,* 165.

66. Alexander, *A Widening Sphere,* 243.

67. Juan Enriquez and Kathryn Taylor, "Battles of Tomorrow Being Waged in Kendall Square," *Boston Globe,* May 6, 2016, https://www.bostonglobe.com/specials/2016

/05/05/mit-and-kendall-square-center-universe/e6VuG1dAwCi1LF8zojZlsJ/story
.html (accessed June 19, 2019).

68. Biobot, home page, https://www.biobot.io (accessed December 10, 2020).

69. Alissa Mallinson, "Alumni Spotlight: Davide Marini, PhD '03," *MIT MECHE in
the News,* December 10, 2012, http://meche.mit.edu/news-media/alumni-spotlight
-davide-marini-phd-%E2%80%9803 (accessed December 10, 2020).

70. EECS Alumni/Ae: Taking EECS to the Limits, "News from the MIT Department
of Electrical Engineering and Computer Science," Fall 2010, https://eecs-newsletter
.mit.edu/articles/2010-fall/eecs-alumniae-creating-new-paths-everywhere/ (accessed
March 2, 2019).

71. Edward B. Roberts, *Celebrating Entrepreneurship: A Half-Century of MIT's Growth
and Impact* (self-pub., 2018), 147.

72. David Chandler, "Classes and Academic Research Help Launch Companies,"
MIT News, October 3, 2011, http://news.mit.edu/2011/entrepreneurship-academic
-1003 (accessed December 10, 2020).

CHAPTER 6

1. Joost Paul Bonsen, "The Innovation Institute: From Creative Inquiry through
Real-World Impact at MIT" (master's thesis, MIT, 2006), 40–41, https://dspace.mit
.edu/bitstream/handle/1721.1/37141/85813074-MIT.pdf?sequence=2 (accessed May
11, 2016).

2. Muddy Charles Pub, home page, http://muddy.mit.edu (accessed December 11,
2020).

3. Teresa Esser, *The Venture Café: Secrets, Strategies, and Stories from America's High-
Tech Entrepreneurs* (New York: Warner Business Books, 2002), 4–5.

4. Walter Frick, "How the MIT Energy Club Is Taking over the World One Beer at a
Time," *AmericanInno* (blog), March 13, 2012, https://www.americaninno.com/boston
/how-the-mit-energy-club-is-taking-over-the-world-one-beer-at-a-time/ (accessed September 27, 2018).

5. Bonsen, "The Innovation Institute," 56–57.

6. Climate Tech & Energy Prize@MIT, https://cep.mit.edu (accessed December 11,
2020).

7. Ubiquitous Energy, http://ubiquitous.energy; Ayar Labs, https://ayarlabs.com; Polar-
Panel, https://www.polarpanel.co (all accessed July 6, 2019).

8. Esser, *The Venture Café,* 5.

9. Fred Hapgood, *Up the Infinite Corridor: MIT and the Technical Imagination* (Reading,
MA: Addison Wesley, 1993), 91.

10. Jay London, "Inspired by MIT $100K Contest, MIT Alum Connects Entrepreneurs with Resources—No Strings Attached," *Slice of MIT,* April 4, 2016, https://alum.mit.edu/slice/inspired-mit-100k-contest-mit-alum-connects-entrepreneurs-resources-no-strings-attached (accessed December 11, 2020); Edmund Ingham, "What Inspired the Founder of the MassChallenge Accelerator to Try to Solve the 'World's Biggest Problems,'" *Forbes,* https://www.forbes.com/sites/edmundingham/2015/06/05/what-inspired-the-founder-of-the-masschallenge-accelerator-to-try-solve-worlds-biggest-problems/ (accessed July 6, 2019).

11. MassChallenge home page, https://masschallenge.org (accessed October 7, 2019).

12. Jessica Alpert, "Staying in the Neighborhood," *MIT Technology Review,* August 18, 2015, https://www.technologyreview.com/2015/08/18/166687/staying-in-the-neighborhood/ (accessed February 20, 2020).

13. "A Tribute to MIT Entrepreneurs Who Build Significant Companies and Pioneer New Industries," Celebrating a Half Century of MIT Entrepreneurship Conference, Cambridge, MA, 2016, https://www.youtube.com/watch?v=XEwp7OgIWrI&list=PLNAuCPSa5IAMLadx3E64Diw1pmtmnTeqq&index=6 (accessed December 10, 2020).

14. Olivia Vanni, "Perch: Weightlifting Form Tracker from an MIT Startup," *AmericanInno* (blog), January 18, 2017, https://www.americaninno.com/boston/first-look-boston/perch-weightlifting-form-tracker-from-an-mit-startup/ (accessed April 3, 2019).

15. Jay Cheshes, "When a Robot Makes You Dinner," *The New Yorker,* April 9, 2018, https://www.newyorker.com/magazine/2018/04/16/when-a-robot-makes-you-dinner (accessed April 4, 2020); https://www.spyce.com (accessed April 4, 2020).

16. According to LinkedIn, Peter Reinhardt has not yet completed his MIT degree and is on leave while he is launching Segment, a start-up based in San Francisco.

17. http://incubomber.com/the-incubomber/ (accessed July 9, 2018).

18. Peter Reinhardt, "Incubomber—Where Bomb Ideas Come to Life," *Slightly Delusional* (blog), January 17, 2011, http://reinpk.blogspot.in/2011/01/incubomber-where-bomb-ideas-come-to.html (accessed July 9, 2018).

19. Email exchange with Che-Chih Tsao on September 25, 2020.

20. Deborah Chen, "Startups: A Hidden Lifestyle at MIT," *The Tech,* March 23, 2012, https://thetech.com/2012/03/23/startups-v132-n14 (accessed October 7, 2019).

21. Chen, "Startups: A Hidden Lifestyle at MIT."

22. Delian Asparouhov, "How to Support a Student Entrepreneur," http://delian.io/how-to-support-a-student-entrepreneur (accessed July 13, 2018).

23. Robert McQueen, "Eric Grimson to Serve as Chancellor: 'I Need to Understand the Pulse of the Students,' Says EECS Prof," *The Tech,* February 11, 2011, http://tech.mit.edu/V131/PDF/V131-N4.pdf (accessed April 25, 2017).

24. This story is adapted from Teresa Esser, "Progressive Engineer: Profile—Tim Anderson," 2004, http://www.progressiveengineer.com/PEWebBackissues2002/PEWeb%20 33%20Dec%2002-2/Anders.htm (accessed May 29 2019).

25. SAP Concur, "Concur Hipmunk FAQs," www.hipmunk.com (accessed April 23, 2017).

26. Wade Roush, "Hipmunk, Conceived by David Pogue's Teenage Co-Author, Embarks on Mission to Make Travel Search Easier," *Xconomy*, August 18, 2010, https:// xconomy.com/san-francisco/2010/08/18/hipmunk-conceived-by-david-pogues -teenage-co-author-embarks-on-mission-to-make-travel-search-easier/ (accessed April 23, 2017).

27. The Lab for Computer Science is now known as CSAIL—Computer Science and Artificial Intelligence Lab.

28. Rob Matheson, "'Moneyball for Business,'" *MIT News*, November 4, 2014, http://news.mit.edu/2014/behavioral-analytics-moneyball-for-business-1114 (accessed August 12, 2018).

29. "Thomas Massie," Lemelson-MIT Program, http://lemelson.mit.edu/resources /thomas-massie (accessed February 21, 2018); Oleg Drozhinin, "'Phantom' Interface Takes Annual $10K," *The Tech* 115, no. 26 (May 16, 1995), http://tech.mit.edu/V115 /N26/phantom.26n.html (accessed February 21, 2018).

30. "2.75: Precision Machine Design. MIT Department of Mechanical Engineering," MIT MechE, February 16, 2015, http://meche.mit.edu/news-media/275-precision-ma chine-design (accessed February 21, 2018).

31. "Robopsy: A Low-Cost, CT-Guided, Tele-Robotic Percutaneous Lung Biopsy Assistant," https://ocw.mit.edu/courses/mechanical-engineering/2-996-biomedical -devices-design-laboratory-fall-2007/lecture-notes/robopsy_slide.pdf (accessed February 21, 2018).

32. Sasha Brown, "New Device Offers Assist in Needle Biopsies," *MIT News*, July 19, 2006, https://news.mit.edu/2006/robopsy (accessed February 15, 2018); Bonsen, "The Innovation Institute," 50–51.

33. "Nuts and Bolts of New Ventures, http://nutsandbolts.mit.edu/staff.php (accessed February 16, 2018); Bonsen, "The Innovation Institute," 50.

34. Sarah Foote, "Photo Finish: Sloanies Team up to Create Bounce Imaging," *MIT News*, November 21, 2012, http://news.mit.edu/2012/sloanies-team-up-to-create -bounce-imaging-startup (accessed July 3, 2018); Kelsey Atherton, "Police Will Throw This Camera Ball into Rooms," *Popular Science*, June 26, 2015, https://www.popsci .com/police-will-throw-camera-ball-rooms/ (accessed May 29, 2019).

35. Zach Winn, "With New Proto Ventures Program, MIT Innovation Initiative Turns Ideas into Impact," *MIT News*, April 2, 2019, http://news.mit.edu/2019/proto -ventures-program-innovation-initiative-0403 (accessed April 25, 2020).

36. Bonsen's web page is http://www.maximizingprogress.org, and a bio of this innovator can be found at http://nutsandbolts.mit.edu/staff.php (accessed October 6, 2018); also see Bonsen, "The Innovation Institute."

37. Jay London, "Google Glass: Inspired by Terminator," *Slice of MIT*, May 30, 2013, https://alum.mit.edu/slice/google-glass-inspired-terminator (accessed December 30, 2020); Bonsen, "The Innovation Institute," 53–54.

38. Bonsen, "The Innovation Institute."

CHAPTER 7

1. See http://entrepreneurship.mit.edu.

2. Bill Aulet, "Teaching Entrepreneurship Cultivating Antifragility: Why There's More to Entrepreneurship Education than Creating Startups," *BizEd Magazine*, November 18, 2019, https://bized.aacsb.edu/articles/2019/november/teaching%20entrepreneur-ship%20cultivating%20antifragility (accessed March 23, 2020); *2019 Annual Report—Martin Trust Center for MIT Entrepreneurship,* (Cambridge, MA: MIT, 2019), http://www.calameo.com/read/005056720756b3954a54d (accessed February 4, 2019), 4.

3. *2016 Annual Report—Martin Trust Center for MIT Entrepreneurship* (Cambridge, MA: MIT, 2016), http://entrepreneurship.mit.edu/wp-content/uploads/2016-Annual-Report-FINAL.pdf (accessed July 27, 2019), 9.

4. *2016 Annual Report—Martin Trust Center for MIT Entrepreneurship,* 8.

5. Trish Cotter, "Female Entrepreneurs: Gaining Ground," *MIT Sloan Experts* (blog), June 29, 2017, http://mitsloanexperts.mit.edu/female-entrepreneurs-gaining-ground-trish-cotter/ (accessed May 22, 2019).

6. *2018 Annual Report—Martin Trust Center for MIT Entrepreneurship* (Cambridge, MA: MIT, 2018), http://entrepreneurship.mit.edu/annual-report/ (accessed July 20, 2018), 3.

7. See http://entrepreneurship.mit.edu/t0/ (accessed July 27, 2018). Gregory Huang, "Kendall Square Innovation Festival, t=0, to Feature Brad Feld, Mitch Kapor, and (Probably) Entrepreneurial Walk of Fame, September 16–18," *Xconomy*, August 2, 2011, https://www.xconomy.com/boston/2011/08/02/kendall-square-innovation-festival-t0-to-feature-brad-feld-mitch-kapor-and-probably-entrepreneurial-walk-of-fame-september-16-18/ (accessed July 26, 2018).

8. Lauren Landry, "t=0, Where Every Place Has an Idea: MIT's Hackathon," *AmericanInno* (blog), September 15, 2011, https://www.americaninno.com/boston/t0-where-every-place-has-an-idea-mits-hackathon/ (accessed July 26, 2018).

9. http://entrepreneurship.mit.edu/accelerator/program/.

10. Initially, delta v was launched under the names "Founders Skills Accelerator," and then "Global Founders Skills Accelerator." In typical MIT "geek speak," it was

renamed "MIT delta v" in 2016, after the mathematical symbol for a change in velocity, caused by acceleration. The message, according to Aulet, is that "delta takes startups through the final stretch to 'escape velocity,' where they're ready to enter the market." See Rob Matheson, "Startups Show Promise, Progress at Demo Day," *MIT News,* September 12, 2016, http://news.mit.edu/2016/startups-show-promise -progress-demo-day-0912 (accessed March 4, 2019).

11. Bill Aulet, *Disciplined Entrepreneurship: 24 Steps to a Successful Startup* (Hoboken, NJ: John Wiley & Sons, 2013); Bill Aulet, *Disciplined Entrepreneurship Workbook* (Hoboken, NJ: Wiley & Sons, 2017).

12. Tom McGivan, "How Boston's Universities Are Producing Our Next Generation of Entrepreneurs," *Virgin,* September 23, 2016, https://www.virgin.com/entrepreneur /how-bostons-universities-are-producing-our-next-generation-entrepreneurs (accessed July 26, 2018).

13. Matheson, "Startups Show Promise, Progress at Demo Day."

14. LiquiGlide, https://liquiglide.com; Emerald, https://www.emeraldinno.com; Leuko, https://leuko.io (all accessed July 26, 2018).

15. *2018 Annual Report—Martin Trust Center for MIT Entrepreneurship,* 20.

16. Rob Matheson, "Is Your Meal Really Gluten Free?," *MIT News,* July 6, 2016, http://news.mit.edu/2016/portable-sensor-gluten-free-0706 (accessed July 14, 2019).

17. Agatha Kereere, "New Portable Sensor Tests for Gluten in Minutes," *Oakland North,* February 10, 2016, https://oaklandnorth.net/2016/02/10/new-portable-sensor -tests-for-gluten-in-minutes/ (accessed July 14, 2019).

18. *2018 Annual Report—Martin Trust Center for MIT Entrepreneurship,* 29.

19. *2017 Annual Report—Martin Trust Center for MIT Entrepreneurship,* 41, 50–52; *2018 Annual Report—Martin Trust Center for MIT Entrepreneurship,* 57.

20. Accion Systems, https://www.accion-systems.com; OKTA, https://www.okta.com; Ayar Labs, https://ayarlabs.com (all accessed January 26, 2021).

21. MIT Venture Mentoring Service (VMS), http://vms.mit.edu (accessed August 20, 2018).

22. "VMS Entrepreneurs," https://vms.mit.edu/entrepreneurs/vms-entrepreneurs (accessed August 20, 2018).

23. Roman Lubynsky and Karen Golz, "MIT Venture Mentoring Service Demo Day," April 26, 2018.

24. Accion Systems, www.accion-systems.com; Akselos, www.akselos.com; Cogito, www.cogitocorp.com; CoolChip Technologies, www.coolchiptechnologies.com; Leuko, www.leuko.io; PlenOptika, www.plenoptika.com (all accessed May 29, 2019). Ajua, https://ajua.com/media_blogs/msurvey-is-now-ajua-repositioning-for -growth-evolution-and-ambition/; SmartCells, https://www.merck.com/news/merck -to-acquire-smartcells-inc/ (both accessed February 4, 2021).

25. Rob Matheson, "Alumnus's Throwable Tactical Camera Gets Commercial Release," *MIT News,* June 26, 2015, http://news.mit.edu/2015/throwable-tactical-camera-bounce -imaging-0626 (accessed July 3, 2019).

26. Matheson, "Alumnus's Throwable Tactical Camera Gets Commercial Release."

27. Email exchange with Francisco Aguilar on May 27, 2020.

28. Jeff Engel, "After Escher Exit, MIT Sandbox Aims to Mold More Student Startups," *Xconomy,* March 8, 2018, https://www.xconomy.com/boston/2018/03/08/after-escher -exit-mit-sandbox-aims-to-mold-more-student-startups/ (accessed August 16, 2018).

29. Jinane Abounadi, "Sandbox," Microsoft PowerPoint presentation shared during interview, March 3, 2016.

30. Interview of Jinane Abounadi on April 23, 2019.

31. Kytopen, https://kytopen.com; Multiply Labs, https://multiplylabs.com; Escher Reality, https://nianticlabs.com/blog/escherreality/; ReviveMed, http://www.revivemed .io; FarmWise, https://farmwise.io; Yellowstone Energy, https://innovationcrossroads .ornl.gov/profile/yellowstone-energy (all accessed January 26, 2021).

32. MIT $100K Entrepreneurship Competition, https://www.mit100k.org (accessed December 12, 2020); David Chandler, "Cementing Success," *MIT News,* May 14, 2010, https://news.mit.edu/2010/100k-competition-0514 (accessed April 16, 2018).

33. Email exchange on May 30, 2019, with Cyrus David Schroeder, member of the organizing team of the 2019 $100K Entrepreneurship Competition.

34. Ash Bharatkumar, "Where Are They Now? A Reunion with MIT Business Plan Competition Alumni," *MIT Entrepreneurship Review,* October 3, 2013, https://miter .mit.edu/where-are-they-now-a-reunion-with-mit-business-plan-competition -alumni-2/ (accessed May 24, 2019).

35. Clean Energy Prize (CEP), http://cep.mit.edu (accessed May 24, 2019).

36. Sunhub, https://www.gvec.org/electric/sunhub-community-solar/; United Solar, https://unitedsolar.com; Heila Technologies, https://www.heilaiq.com; Infinite Cool-ing, https://www.infinite-cooling.com (all accessed May 24, 2019).

37. MIT Division of Student Life, http://studentlife.mit.edu/ideas (accessed June 8, 2018).

38. Hey, Charlie, https://heycharlie.org (accessed June 8, 2018).

39. Wecyclers, www.wecyclers.com (accessed September 30, 2018).

40. Kevin Sieff, "The World Is Drowning in Ever-Growing Mounds of Garbage," *Washington Post,* November 21, 2017, https://www.washingtonpost.com/world/africa/the -world-is-drowning-in-ever-growing-mounds-of-garbage/2017/11/21/cf22e4bd-17a4 -473c-89f8-873d48f968cd_story.html (accessed May 4, 2021).

41. D. D., "Why China Is Sick of Foreign Garbage," *The Economist,* August 21, 2017, https://www.economist.com/the-economist-explains/2017/08/21/why-china-is-sick -of-foreign-garbage (accessed December 20, 2020).

42. The Media Lab's website claimed that, as of 2019, more than 100 ventures had been spun off; see https://www.media.mit.edu/posts/spinoff-companies/ (accessed September 16, 2020).

43. ThruWave, https://www.thruwave.com; Wise Systems, https://www.wisesystems .com; Tulip, https://tulip.co/platform/ (all accessed September 19, 2020).

44. Steven Leckart, "The Hackathon Is On: Pitching and Programming the Next Killer App," *Wired*, February 17, 2012, https://www.wired.com/2012/02/ff_hack athons/all/1/ (accessed July 21, 2018). Hackathons are a variation of the "marathon bursts" of the 1960s at MIT, when students worked in twenty-four-hour stretches, as reported by Steven Levy in his book *Hackers: Heroes of the Computer Revolution* (New York: Anchor Press, 1984). Given this antecedent, it is not surprising that hackathons have been enthusiastically adopted at MIT in recent years.

45. MIT Hacking Medicine, http://hackingmedicine.mit.edu (accessed June 8, 2018).

46. Jay London, "How Do You Hack Health Care?," *Institute for Medical Engineering & Science* (blog), July 20, 2015, http://imes.mit.edu/how-do-you-hack-health-care/ (accessed February 21, 2018).

47. "Healthcare Hackathons: Model for Success," *ScienceDaily*, August 26, 2017, https://www.sciencedaily.com/releases/2017/07/170726132118.htm (accessed September 13, 2018).

48. "Doctor, Meet Entrepreneur," *MIT Sloan School of Management Newsroom*, September 10, 2013, http://mitsloan.mit.edu/newsroom/articles/doctor-meet-entrepreneur/.

49. Michael B. Farrell, "Data-Driven Scheduling Predicts Patient No-Shows," *Boston-Globe.com*, July 14, 2014, https://www.bostonglobe.com/business/2014/07/13/high -tech-cure-for-doctors-scheduling-pains/ylLD4Fwar8EElFJ32frI9I/story.html (accessed May 25, 2019).

50. PillPack, https://www.pillpack.com; Cake, https://www.joincake.com; Podimetrics, www.podimetrics.com; Augmented Infant Resuscitator, http://augmentedinfantresusci tator.com/wp (all accessed May 25, 2019).

51. *MIT Boston Grand Hack 2019*, Boston, 2019, https://www.youtube.com/watch ?v=5oIJFY-MoH0&feature=youtu.be (accessed February 17, 2020).

52. Interview of Andrea Ippolito on January 20, 2020.

53. Interview of Freddy Nguyen, coorganizer of Hacking Medicine, on February 17, 2020.

54. Interview with Nguyen.

55. Hacking Arts, www.hackingarts.com (accessed July 8, 2020).

56. MIT Creative Arts Competition, https://arts.mit.edu/start/entrepreneurship/crea tive-arts-competition/ (accessed July 8, 2020).

57. Roots Studio, https://rootsstudio.co (accessed July 8, 2020).

58. Rob Matheson, "Virtual-Reality System for the Elderly Wins Health Care Prize," *MIT News*, February 24, 2017, http://news.mit.edu/2017/virtual-reality-elderly-sloan-health-care-innovations-prize-0224 (accessed July 21, 2018).

59. Rob Matheson, "Sepsis-Curing Device Wins New Health Care Prize," *MIT News*, February 26, 2016, http://news.mit.edu/2016/sepsis-curing-device-wins-mit-sloan-healthcare-innovations-prize-0226 (accessed July 11, 2018).

60. Email exchange with Che-Chih Tsao on October 8, 2020.

61. MIT Venture Capital and Private Equity Club (VCPE), www.mitvcpe.com (accessed July 11, 2018).

62. Joost Paul Bonsen, "The Innovation Institute. From Creative Inquiry through Real-World Impact at MIT" (master's thesis, MIT, 2006), 69, https://dspace.mit.edu/bitstream/handle/1721.1/37141/85813074-MIT.pdf?sequence=2 (accessed May 11, 2016).

63. MIT StartLabs, http://startup.mit.edu (accessed December 11, 2020).

64. Lauren Landry, "MIT's Startlabs: Bringing Students through Entrepreneurship from Start to Finish," *AmericanInno* (blog), March 28, 2012, https://www.americaninno.com/boston/mits-Startlabss-bringing-students-through-entrepreneurship-from-start-to-finish/ (accessed July 25, 2018).

65. MIT Innovation Institute, https://innovation.mit.edu/opportunity/innovateedu-boston-venture-creation-program/.

66. www.mitgsw.org/ (accessed July 26, 2018).

67. This was initially called Africa Internet Initiative Africa, then Information Technology Initiative, and then Accelerating Information Technology Innovation—AITI.

68. See https://www.edx.org/course/entrepreneurship-101-who-is-your-customer.

69. Office of Digital Learning, "From MOOC to Bootcamp to MIT," *MIT News*, May 19, 2016, http://news.mit.edu/2016/mooc-bootcamp-mit-0519 (accessed May 13, 2019).

70. MIT Entrepreneurship and Maker Skills Integrator (MEMSI), https://memsi.mit.edu (accessed June 20, 2019).

71. Meg Murphy, "At Home in Hong Kong," *MIT News*, December 13, 2016, http://news.mit.edu/2016/students-faculty-alumni-hong-kong-1213 (accessed August 20, 2019).

72. *2018 Annual Report—Martin Trust Center for MIT Entrepreneurship*, 67 and 11.

73. MIT Innovation Initiative, "Entrepreneurship & Innovation Minor," https://innovation.mit.edu/education-practice/eiminor/ (accessed May 13, 2019).

74. MIT Media Lab, "Sample Venture Classes," https://www.media.mit.edu/posts/sample-venture-classes/ (accessed May 13, 2019).

75. MITdesignX, https://designx.mit.edu (accessed May 13, 2019).

76. Rob Matheson, "'IDEAS' to Change the World," *MIT News,* May 2, 2017, http://news.mit.edu/2017/ideas-global-challenge-awards-0502 (accessed July 20, 2018).

CHAPTER 8

1. "MIT Technology Licensing Office," https://tlo.mit.edu/ (accessed March 11, 2019).

2. Scott Shane, *Academic Entrepreneurship: University Spin-Offs and Wealth Creation* (Northampton, MA: Edward Elgar, 2004), 204.

3. Shane, *Academic Entrepreneurship,* 190.

4. "We are in the entrepreneurship by default, because large companies don't license university technologies." Interview of Leon Sandler, November 17, 2016.

5. Interview with Lita Nelsen on November 7, 2016.

6. Alison Takemura, "3Q: Lesley Millar-Nicholson on MIT's Technology Licensing Office," *MIT News,* October 5, 2017, http://news.mit.edu/2017/3q-lesley-millar-nich olson-mit-technology-licensing-office-1005 (accessed March 11, 2019).

7. Shane, *Academic Entrepreneurship.*

8. Eugene Fitzgerald, Carl Schramm, and Andreas Wankert, *Inside Real Innovation: How the Right Approach Can Move Ideas from R&D to Market—and Get the Economy Moving* (Hackensack, NJ: World Scientific, 2011), 18–19.

9. MIT Technology Licensing Office, http://tlo.mit.edu (accessed January 26, 2021).

10. Takemura, "3Q: Lesley Millar-Nicholson on MIT's Technology Licensing Office."

11. Takemura, "3Q: Lesley Millar-Nicholson on MIT's Technology Licensing Office."

12. Ross DeVol, Joe Lee, and Minoli Ratnatunga, *Concept to Commercialization: The Best Universities for Technology Transfer* (Santa Monica, CA: Milken Institute, April 2017), https://assets1c.milkeninstitute.org/assets/Publication/ResearchReport/PDF/Con cept2Commercialization-MR19-WEB.pdf (accessed March 11, 2019).

13. David Ewalt, "Reuters Top 100: The World's Most Innovative Universities—2017," Reuters, September 27, 2017, https://www.reuters.com/article/us-amers-reuters-ran king-innovative-univ-idUSKCN1C209R (accessed May 28, 2019).

14. Lincoln Laboratory conducts R&D related to national security for US government agencies. For more information, see its website, https://www.ll.mit.edu.

15. Many of these licenses were executed five to ten years previously.

16. *MIT Technology Licensing Office FY 2018 Fact Sheet* (Cambridge, MA: MIT TLO, 2018), https://www.dropbox.com/s/d125eq2341967l9/FY%202018%20fact%20sheet%20TLO .pdf?dl=0 (accessed January 26, 2021).

17. Edward B. Roberts, Fiona Murray, and J. Daniel Kim, *Entrepreneurship and Innovation at MIT: Continuing Global Growth and Impact* (Cambridge, MA: MIT Sloan School of Management, 2015), 18, http://web.mit.edu/innovate/entrepreneurship2015.pdf (accessed August 22, 2016).

18. See Financial Conflict of Interest in Research, https://coi.mit.edu/policy/application -guiding-principles (accessed September 5, 2020).

19. Thomas Allen and Rory O'Shea, "The Roadblock to Commercialisation," *Financial Times*, September 28, 2014, https://www.ft.com/content/a1ea7c72-18cc-11e4 -933e-00144feabdc0 (accessed November 3, 2019).

20. Jeff Engel, "Exit Interview: Lita Nelsen on MIT Tech Transfer, Startups & Culture," *Xconomy*, May 31, 2016, https://www.xconomy.com/boston/2016/05/31/exit -interview-lita-nelsen-on-mit-tech-transfer-startups-culture/ (accessed April 6, 2018).

21. David Chandler, "3 Questions: Lita Nelsen and the Technology Licensing Office," *MIT News*, November 7, 2014, http://news.mit.edu/2014/3-questions-lita-nelsen-tech nology-licensing-office-1107 (accessed June 3, 2019).

22. Shane, *Academic Entrepreneurship,* 171.

23. Adapted from *An MIT Inventor's Guide to Startups for Faculty and Students* (Cambridge, MA: MIT TLO, 2010), http://web.mit.edu/tlo/documents/MIT-TLO-startup -guide.pdf (accessed November 3, 2019).

24. Siluria, http://www.siluria.com/ (accessed May 28, 2019).

25. GVD Corporation, http://www.gvdcorp.com (accessed May 28, 2019).

26. MIT Deshpande Center for Technological Innovation, https://deshpande.mit .edu (accessed May 28, 2019).

27. Bowman Fishback, Christine A. Gulbranson, Robert E. Litan, Lesa Mitchell, and Marisa A. Porzig, *A New Model to Accelerate Start-ups,* SSRN Scholarly Paper (Rochester, NY: Social Science Research Network, July 1, 2007), https://papers.ssrn.com /abstract=1001926 (accessed March 21, 2019).

28. Interview with Leon Sandler, November 17, 2016.

29. David Chandler, "Bringing Innovation to the World," *MIT News*, October 18, 2010, http://news.mit.edu/2010/deshpande-1018 (accessed March 20, 2019).

30. Dealbook, "The Idea Incubator Goes to Campus," June 28, 2010, https://dealbook .nytimes.com/2010/06/28/the-idea-incubator-goes-to-campus/ (accessed March 20, 2019).

31. Nancy Stauffer, "A Battery Made of Molten Metals," *MIT News*, January 12, 2016, http://news.mit.edu/2016/battery-molten-metals-0112 (accessed July 11, 2020).

32. Paul Hunter, "In the Quest to Build a Better Battery, a Canadian Is Energizing the Field," *CBC News*, December 14, 2018, https://www.cbc.ca/news/technology/don -sadoway-david-bradwell-battery-invention-1.4945615 (accessed July 11, 2020).

33. MIT Deshpande Center for Technological Innovation, "Power Play," Case Study Series, https://deshpande.mit.edu/portfolio/case-studies (accessed July 11, 2020).

34. Queen's University—Faculty of Engineering and Applied Science, "A Cleaner Way to Power Our World," January 2, 2020, https://engineering.queensu.ca/curiositycreates /sustainable-energy.html (accessed July 11, 2020).

35. Hunter, "In the Quest to Build a Better Battery."

36. Source: Leon Sandler, director of the Despande Center.

37. MIT Deshpande Center for Technological Innovation, "Firefly BioWorks (Abcam)," https://deshpande.mit.edu/portfolio/project/firefly-bioworks-abcam (accessed March 20, 2019).

38. MIT Deshpande Center for Technological Innovation, "Case Studies," https:// deshpande.mit.edu/portfolio/case-studies (accessed March 21, 2019).

39. Rob Matheson, "Dental Scanner Allows Researcher to Sink His Teeth into Entrepreneurship," *MIT News,* August 21, 2013, http://news.mit.edu/2013/brontes -technologies-0821 (accessed March 21, 2019).

40. Jennifer K. Stine, *MIT Deshpande Center: Grantee (PI) Interviews. Summary and Analysis* (Cambridge, MA: MIT, August 6, 2014), https://deshpande.mit.edu/files /assets/MIT%20Deshpande%20Center%20Faculty%20Interview%20Report%20 2014.pdf (accessed March 22, 2019).

41. Chandler, "Bringing Innovation to the World."

42. Interview with Roman Lubinsky, program director, I-Corps at VMS, June 4, 2019.

43. Grants from the SBIR program or the STTR. The SBIR program aims at strengthening the role of innovative small businesses through federally funded R&D. Modeled after the SBIR program, it applies to government agencies with R&D budgets of $1 billion or more. See "The SBIR and STTR Programs," www.sbir.gov/about/about -sttr (accessed March 20, 2019).

44. National Science Foundation (NSF), About, https://www.nsf.gov/news/special_ reports/i-corps/about.jsp (accessed February 18, 2020); MIT News Office, "MIT Selected as Ninth NSF Innovation Corps Node; Set to Serve the New England Region," *MIT News,* September 4, 2018, http://news.mit.edu/2018/mit-selected-ninth-nsf-innovation -corps-node-new-england-0904 (accessed April 19, 2019).

45. Sandymount Technology, https://sandymount.com (accessed August 19, 2018).

46. Interview with Lubinsky.

47. S. Chapin, "Tiny Particles, Big Ideas: Interview with Firefly BioWorks' Dan Pregibon," *MIT Entrepreneurship Review,* March 22, 2011, http://miter.mit.edu/articletiny -particles-big-ideas-interview-firefly-bioworks-dan-pregibon/ (accessed April 18, 2019).

48. *Firefly BioWorks (Abcam) Video,* MIT Deshpande Center, Devices + Materials, Healthcare, 2010, https://deshpande.mit.edu/portfolio/project/firefly-bioworks-abcam (accessed April 18, 2019).

49. Rafael Reif, "A Better Way to Deliver Innovation to the World," *Washington Post,* May 22, 2015, https://www.washingtonpost.com/opinions/a-better-way-to-deliver -innovation-to-the-world/2015/05/22/35023680-fe28-11e4-8b6c-0dcce21e223d_ story.html (accessed August 23, 2018).

50. Rafael Reif, "An Exciting Step Forward for Our Innovation Ecosystem," Office of the President, MIT, October 26, 2016, http://president.mit.edu/speeches-writing /exciting-step-forward-our-innovation-ecosystem (accessed April 13, 2019).

51. Asma Khalid, "With $200 Million, MIT's The Engine Makes Its First Investments in 'Tough Tech,'" *Bostinno,* September 19, 2017, http://www.wbur.org/bostonomix /2017/09/19/with-200-million-mits-the-engine-makes-its-first-investments-in-tough -tech (accessed August 23, 2018).

52. Rafael Reif, "New MIT Innovation Hub Takes on World's Biggest Challenges—the Boston Globe," *BostonGlobe.com,* October 26, 2016, https://www.bostonglobe.com /opinion/2016/10/26/reif/oOI3OhgX8B1HYjYi04PzJL/story.html (accessed August 24, 2019).

53. Andy Rosen, "MIT's New Investing Engine Raises $200 Million—the Boston Globe," *BostonGlobe.com,* September 19, 2017, https://www.bostonglobe.com/business/2017 /09/19/mit-new-investing-engine-raises-million/meJc2KZhEjeQis1e7pnlhO/story .html (accessed March 18, 2019).

54. Adele Peters, "This New System Helps Bioengineering Happen 10,000 Times Faster," *Fast Company,* September 19, 2017, https://www.fastcompany.com/40468622 /this-new-system-helps-bioengineering-happen-10000-times-faster (accessed June 1, 2019).

55. *Enhancing Collaboration between MIT and The Engine: Joint Findings of The Engine Working Groups. Final Report to the MIT Community* (Cambridge, MA: MIT, April 2018), http://web.mit.edu/ewgreport/introduction.html (accessed November 21, 2018).

56. Rob Matheson, "MIT Launches New Venture for World-Changing Entrepreneurs," *MIT News,* October 26, 2016, https://news.mit.edu/2016/mit-announces -the-engine-for-entrepreneurs-1026 (accessed March 18, 2019); Alex Konrad, "MIT's $200M Venture Fund Invests in 7 Startups in Energy, Space and Smell," *Forbes,* September 19, 2017, https://www.forbes.com/sites/alexkonrad/2017/09/19/mit-venture -fund-the-engine-backs-7-startups/#576899d3226d (accessed April 13, 2019).

57. "One goal of The Engine is to help keep top talent around the Boston area research universities," said Kathy Rae, CEO and managing partner of The Engine. Source: Konrad, "MIT's $200M Venture Fund." See also Matheson, "MIT Launches New

Venture for World-Changing Entrepreneurs"; Rob Matheson, "Community Forum Gives Insight into How The Engine Will Run," *MIT News,* December 2, 2016, http://news.mit.edu/2016/the-engine-community-forum-1202 (accessed March 18, 2019).

58. MIT Startup Exchange, https://startupexchange.mit.edu (accessed April 13, 2019).

59. In 2017, Aptiv, previously known as Delphi Automotive, acquired nuTonomy. See "Delphi to Buy NuTonomy for $400M+ as Driverless Car Tie-Ups Continue," *Xconomy,* October 24, 2017, https://xconomy.com/boston/2017/10/24/delphi-to-buy-nutonomy-for-400m-as-driverless-car-tie-ups-continue/ (accessed April 21, 2019).

60. Industrial Liaison Program (ILP), *STEX Expands Startup Network in Year One: 2015 Startup Report* (Cambridge, MA: MIT, 2015), https://ilp.mit.edu/media/webpublications/pub/literature/STEX-Online-Brochure.pdf (accessed April 13, 2019).

61. Proto Ventures, https://innovation.mit.edu/ideas-to-impact/mit-proto-ventures -program/ (accessed January 25, 2021).

CHAPTER 9

1. Edward B. Roberts, Fiona Murray, and J. Daniel Kim, *Entrepreneurship and Innovation at MIT: Continuing Global Growth and Impact* (Cambridge, MA: MIT Sloan School of Management, 2015), http://web.mit.edu/innovate/entrepreneurship2015.pdf (accessed February 3, 2017).

2. Ryan Decker, John Haltiwanger, Ron Jarmin, and Javier Miranda, "The Role of Entrepreneurship in U.S. Job Creation and Economic Dynamism," *Journal of Economic Perspectives* 28, no. 3 (2014): 3–24.

3. Roberts, Murray, and Kim, *Entrepreneurship and Innovation at MIT*, 13.

4. The authors specify that these figures reflect gross firm creation (i.e., they do not take into account firms' survival).

5. This figure is probably an underestimation because younger alumni had had little time after graduation to patent invention.

6. MIT Industrial Liaison Program, http://ilp.mit.edu (accessed January 26, 2021).

7. Department of Material Science and Engineering (MIT DMSE), "MIT Startup Exchange: Connecting Industry to Startups," February 26, 2016, https://dmse.mit.edu /news/2016/mit-startup-exchange-connecting-industry-startups (accessed December 30, 2020).

8. Michael Blanding, "The Past and Future of Kendall Square: A Transformation in Five Acts," *Technology Review,* October 2015, https://www.technologyreview.com/s /540206/the-past-and-future-of-kendall-square/ (accessed June 8, 2019).

9. Patrick Sisson, "As Top Innovation Hub Expands, Can Straining Local Infrastructure Keep Pace?," *Curbed,* November 6, 2018, https://archive.curbed.com/2018/11/6

/18067326/boston-real-estate-cambridge-mit-biotech-kendall-square (accessed January 25, 2021).

10. John Kifner, "Creation of Life's Experiment at Harvard Stirs Heated Dispute," *The New York Times,* June 17, 1976.

11. John Durant, "'Refrain from Using the Alphabet': How Community Outreach Catalyzed the Life Sciences at MIT," in *Becoming MIT: Moments of Decision,* ed. David Kaiser (Cambridge, MA: MIT Press, 2012), 154.

12. Rob Matheson, "Birthplace of Biotech," *MIT News,* March 19, 2013, https://news.mit.edu/2013/kendall-square-birthplace-of-biotech-0319 (accessed June 19, 2019).

13. Scott Kirsner, "How Cambridge Became the Life Sciences Capital," *Beta Boston,* March 17, 2016, http://www.betaboston.com/news/2016/03/17/how-cambridge -became-the-life-sciences-capital/ (accessed June 19, 2019); Jim Miara, "The Reinvention of Kendall Square," *Urban Land Magazine,* February 17, 2012, https://urbanland.uli.org /development-business/the-reinvention-of-kendall-square/ (accessed June 21, 2019).

14. Interview with Mitch Kapor on November 5, 2019.

15. According to Tim Rowe, founder and CEO of Cambridge Innovation Center, and Bill Aulet. Sources: interview with Tim Rowe on November 4, 2016 and interview with Bill Aulet on December 16, 2019.

16. Susan Hockfield, *The Age of Living Machines: How Biology Will Build the Next Technology Revolution* (New York: W. W. Norton, 2019), 2.

17. MIT, "Kendall Square Initiative," https://kendallsquare.mit.edu (accessed June 21, 2019).

18. Globe Staff, "A Century of Innovation 1916–2016," *Boston Globe,* May 6, 2016, https://www.bostonglobe.com/specials/2016/05/05/century-innovation/263QTyw lVlr6Y5sVD8dYIO/story.html (accessed June 21, 2019).

19. Editas Medicine, https://editasmedicine.com (accessed June 19, 2019).

20. Damian Garde, "Her Next Project: Curing a Rare, Inherited Blindness Disorder," *Boston Globe,* May 6, 2016, https://www.bostonglobe.com/specials/2016/05/05/katrine -bosley-next-big-problem-solve-blindness-disorder/yMFUCb9dm3sT1OX87vEOpO /story.html (accessed June 20, 2019).

21. Heidi Ledford, "Start-ups Fight for a Place in Boston's Biotech Hub," *Nature News,* June 11, 2015.

22. Rob Matheson, "High Probability of Success," *MIT News,* May 1, 2013, http://news.mit.edu/2013/ben-vigoda-lyric-0501 (accessed July 9, 2019).

23. Samuel Jay Keyser, *Mens et Mania. The MIT Nobody Knows* (Cambridge, MA: MIT Press, 2011), 185.

24. Robert M. Krim, "'Bumping and Connecting': The Secret to Greater Boston's Four Centuries of Innovation," paper submitted to the Academy of Management, Framingham State University, Department of Business, Framingham, MA, January 2015.

25. Alfred Marshall, *Principles of Economics* (London: MacMillan, 1920).

26. *CONNECT 2018: CIC + Partners Global Impact Report,* CIC, April 8, 2019, https://cic.com/blogpost/connect2018 (accessed June 20, 2019).

27. MassChallenge, "About," https://masschallenge.org (accessed August 25, 2020).

28. MassChallenge, "Startups," https://masschallenge.org/startups (accessed August 25, 2020).

29. Dany Crichton, "12 Years in, Techstars Doubles Down on Corporate Relationships," *TechCrunch,* September 18, 2019, http://social.techcrunch.com/2018/09/18/12-years-in-techstars-doubles-down-on-corporate-relationships/ (accessed July 10, 2019).

30. Techstars, https://www.techstars.com/startups (accessed August 25, 2020).

31. Greentown Labs, https://www.greentownlabs.com (accessed June 20, 2019).

32. Learnlaunch, https://learnlaunch.com (accessed June 20, 2019).

33. Educational Testing Service, "New Edtech Accelerator from ETS and LearnLaunch Accelerator," *PR Newswire,* June 27, 2019, https://www.prnewswire.com/news-releases/new-edtech-accelerator-from-ets-and-learnlaunch-accelerator-300876338.html (accessed July 10, 2019).

34. Hub Angels, http://www.hubangels.com, MIT Alumni Angels of Bosotn, https://www.mitalumniangels.com, Castor Ventures, https://www.avgfunds.com/castor-ventures/ (all accessed December 12, 2020).

35. Hub Angels.

36. Henry Etzkowitz, *MIT and the Rise of Entrepreneurial Science* (New York: Routledge, 2002), 102–112; Stewart Gilmore, *Fred Terman at Stanford: Building a Discipline, a University, and Silicon Valley* (Stanford, CA: Stanford University Press, 2004).

37. SMART (Singapore-MIT Alliance for Research and Technology), https://smart.mit.edu (accessed January 25, 2021).

38. Magnanti also served as president of the Singapore University of Technology and Design (SUTD) during its early years.

39. SMART, "US$6 Million Venture Capital Raised for Biotech Spinoff from MIT SMART Centre," SMART, July 1, 2010, https://smart.mit.edu/news-events/us6-million-venture-capital-raised-for-biotech-spinoff-from-mit-smart-centre (accessed October 29, 2020).

40. Elizabeth Thompson, "Detecting Leaks with Robots, Wireless Sensors," *MIT Spectrum,* Summer 2015, https://spectrum.mit.edu/summer-2015/detecting-leaks-with-robots-wireless-sensors/ (accessed January 25, 2021).

41. Rob Matheson, "Startup Bringing Driverless Taxi Service to Singapore," *MIT News*, March 24, 2016, https://news.mit.edu/2016/startup-nutonomy-driverless-taxi-service-singapore-0324 (accessed January 25, 2021).

42. SMART, "SMART Develops a Way to Commercially Manufacture Integrated Silicon III-V Chips," *MIT News*, October 3, 2019, https://news.mit.edu/2019/mit-singapore-smart-way-to-manufacture-integrated-silicon-iii-v-chips-1003 (accessed October 12, 2020).

43. Written exchange with Professor Charlie Cooney on November 12, 2020.

44. Global MIT, http://global.mit.edu/map/browse-country/portugal (accessed June 20, 2019).

45. BGI Accelerator, https://www.bgi.pt/allprograms/BGI-Accelerator (accessed January 26, 2021); MIT Portugal Program, "MIT Portugal Collaboration Enters New Phase," *MIT News*, October 26, 2018, http://news.mit.edu/2018/mit-portugal-partnership-mpp-2030-launch-1026 (accessed June 23, 2019).

46. MIT Skoltech Program, https://skoltech.mit.edu (accessed June 22, 2019).

47. MIT Skoltech Program, "About," https://skoltech.mit.edu/about/history#E&I (accessed June 22, 2019); "Fostering U.S.-Russia Energy Innovation," *MIT News*, April 10, 2015, http://news.mit.edu/2015/fostering-us-russia-energy-innovation-0410 (accessed June 22, 2019).

48. Madrid-MIT M+Visión Consortium, http://mvisionconsortium.org (accessed June 22, 2019).

49. Institute for Medical Engineering and Science (IMES), http://imes.mit.edu (accessed June 22, 2019).

50. Leuko Labs, https://leuko.io (accessed June 22, 2019).

51. The impact-oriented biomedical translational research approach developed within M+Visión continues out of Cambridge as MIT LinQ, https://www.mitlinq.org (accessed June 22, 2019).

52. Rafael Reif, "Launching the MIT Innovation Initiative," Office of the President, MIT, October 17, 2013, http://president.mit.edu/speeches-writing/launching-mit-innovation-initiative (accessed November 8, 2018).

53. MIT Entrepreneurship and Maker Skills Integrator (MEMSI), https://memsi.mit.edu (accessed June 20, 2019).

54. Meg Murphy, "At Home in Hong Kong," *MIT News*, December 13, 2016, http://news.mit.edu/2016/students-faculty-alumni-hong-kong-1213 (accessed August 20, 2019).

55. Aavia, https://www.aavia.io (accessed December 12, 2020).

56. Email exchange on May 30, 2019, with Cyrus David Schroeder, member of the organizing team of the 2019 $100K Entrepreneurship Competition. The MIT Sloan

Office of Media Relations mentions similar numbers. MIT Sloan Office of Media Relations, "Acoustic Wells Wins 2019 MIT $100K Entrepreneurship Competition," *MIT Sloan,* May 16, 2019, https://mitsloan.mit.edu/press/acoustic-wells-wins-2019 -mit-100k-entrepreneurship-competition (accessed May 16, 2019).

57. Joost Paul Bonsen, "The Innovation Institute. From Creative Inquiry through Real-World Impact at MIT" (master's thesis, MIT, 2006), 52, https://dspace.mit.edu /bitstream/handle/1721.1/37141/85813074-MIT.pdf?sequence=2 (accessed July 16, 2018).

58. Email from Miguel Palacios on June 25, 2019.

59. MIT Global Startup Workshop (GSW), http://gsw.mit.edu/2018/ (accessed June 8, 2018).

60. Zach Winn, "Mentoring Model Developed at MIT Spreads to New Campuses," *MIT News,* May 31, 2019, http://news.mit.edu/2019/venture-mentoring-service-outreach -training-0531 (accessed June 1, 2019).

61. Rob Matheson, "A Model for Mentoring," *MIT News,* February 9, 2016, http://news .mit.edu/2016/vms-model-entrepreneur-mentoring-0209 (accessed May 29, 2019).

62. Matheson, "A Model for Mentoring."

63. Winn, "Mentoring Model.

64. MIT-CHIEF, https://www.mitchief.org (accessed December 12, 2020).

65. Rob Matheson offers a different perspective on CHIEF. He reports in an article in *MIT News* that the driving force behind the creation of CHIEF was the Chinese legislature's five-year plan to stimulate innovation and entrepreneurship in China in 2011, the same year that CHIEF was founded. Rob Matheson, "Inventing China's Future," *MIT News,* November 18, 2014, http://news.mit.edu/2014/mit-chief-us -china-entrepreneurship-1118 (accessed November 10, 2018).

66. Parking Network, "Smarking Signs Enterprise-wide Agreement with One Parking," https://www.parking-net.com/parking-news/smarking-signs-enterprise-wide-agreement -with-one-parking (accessed May 23, 2019).

67. "XtalPi: Cloud-Based Drug Development," https://www.mitchief.org/teams (accessed December 30, 2020).

68. MIT Initiative on the Digital Economy, http://ide.mit.edu (accessed August 2, 2018).

69. "MIT Sloan Announces Launch of Inclusive Innovation Competition," *MIT Management Sloan School Newsroom,* October 7, 2015, http://mitsloan.mit.edu/newsroom /press-releases/mit-sloan-announces-launch-of-inclusive-innovation-competition/ (accessed August 2, 2018).

70. Erik Brynjolfsson, "Technology Is Changing the Way We Live, Learn and Work. How Can Leaders Make Sure We All Prosper?," *World Economic Forum,* January 4, 2017,

https://www.weforum.org/agenda/2017/01/technology-is-changing-the-way-we-live
-learn-and-work-how-can-leaders-make-sure-we-all-prosper/ (accessed April 1, 2017).

71. Erik Brynjolfsson, Xiang Hui, and Meng Liu, "Artificial Intelligence Can Transform
the Economy," *Washington Post*, September 18, 2018, Opinions sec., https://www
.washingtonpost.com/opinions/artificial-intelligence-can-transform-the-economy
/2018/09/18/50c9c9c8-bab8-11e8-bdc0-90f81cc58c5d_story.html (accessed June 25,
2019).

72. Janelle Nanos, "Mobile App Marketplace Jana Pushes Deeper into the Developing World," *BetaBoston,* May 6, 2015, http://www.betaboston.com/news/2015/05/06
/with-a-new-loyalty-program-mobile-app-marketplace-jana-pushes-deeper-into-the
-developing-world/ (accessed April 23, 2020).

73. Rob Matheson, "Connecting the Masses," *MIT News,* May 5, 2015, http://news
.mit.edu/2015/startup-jana-free-mobile-data-0505 (accessed May 31, 2018).

74. Global Startup Lab (GSL), https://misti.mit.edu/global-startup-labs. GSL was
initially called Africa Internet Initiative Africa, then the Information Technology
Initiative, and then Accelerating Information Technology Innovation (AITI). Since
2013, GSL is no longer student run; it has been administered by MIT's International
Science and Technology Initiatives (MISTI).

75. Caroline Knox, "MISTI Global Startup Labs Celebrates 18 Years," *MIT News,* February 1, 2018, http://news.mit.edu/2018/mit-misti-global-startup-labs-celebrates-18
-years-0201 (accessed August 10, 2018).

76. Knox, "MISTI Global Startup Labs Celebrates 18 Years."

77. Julia Reynolds-Cuellar, "Successful MIT Global Startup Labs Alum Visits Campus,"
MIT News, August 29, 2014, http://news.mit.edu/2014/mit-global-startup-labs-invites
-back-alum (accessed August 10, 2018).

78. MIT D-Lab, https://d-lab.mit.edu/scale-ups/about (accessed July 28, 2018).

79. Melinda Beck, "The Challenge of Health-Care Innovation in Developing Nations,"
Wall Street Journal, September 25, 2016.

80. Alissa Mallinson, "Alumni Spotlight: 6dot Innovations," *MITMECHE in the News,*
June 26, 2013, http://meche.mit.edu/news-media/alumni-spotlight-6dot-innovations
(accessed August 9, 2018).

81. SurgiBox, https://www.surgibox.org (accessed July 28, 2018).

82. "SurgiBox: Mass General Trauma Surgeon Helps Bring Safer Surgery to the Field,"
Mass General Research Institute, December 13, 2018, https://d-lab.mit.edu/news
-blog/blog/surgibox-mass-general-trauma-surgeon-helps-bring-safer-surgery-field
(accessed June 6, 2018).

83. Nancy Adams, "D-Lab Scale-ups Awards Four Fellowships Totaling $80,000 to
Social Entrepreneurs," *MIT News,* July 25, 2016, http://news.mit.edu/2016/d-lab

-scale-ups-awards-four-fellowships-for-social-entrepreneurs-0725 (accessed August 8, 2018).

84. Legatum Center for Development and Entrepreneurship, http://legatum.mit.edu (accessed August 7, 2018).

85. *The Legatum Fellowship: 10 Years of Impact 2007–2017* (Cambridge, MA: MIT, 2017), http://legatum.mit.edu/resources/10-year-impact-report/ (accessed May 10, 2019).

86. Legatum Center for Development and Entrepreneurship, "The Zambezi Prize for Innovation and Financial Inclusion," http://zambezi.mit.edu (accessed May 10, 2019).

87. Wala, https://www.getwala.com (accessed December 12, 2020).

88. "SA Startup Wala Wins $100K Zambezi Prize for Innovation in Financial Inclusion," *Ventureburn* (blog), September 3, 2018, https://ventureburn.com/2018/09/wala-zambezi-prize/ (accessed July 28, 2019).

89. MSurvey, https://msurvey.co (accessed August 2, 2018).

90. Monty Munford, "MSurvey and Safaricom Continue Kenya's Mobile Money Revolution," *Forbes,* May 3, 2017, https://www.forbes.com/sites/montymunford/2017/05/03/msurvey-and-safaricom-continue-kenyas-mobile-money-revolution/ (accessed August 7, 2018).

91. ClimaCell, https://www.climacell.co (accessed January 26, 2021).

92. Dylan Martin, "High-Accuracy Weather Data Provider: ClimaCell Uses Wireless Networks," *AmericanInno* (blog), April 7, 2017, https://www.americaninno.com/boston/high-accuracy-weather-data-provider-climacell-uses-wireless-networks/ (accessed August 8, 2018).

93. Susan Adams, "Boston Startup ClimaCell Wants to Be the Bloomberg of Weather Forecasting," *Forbes,* June 29, 2017, https://www.forbes.com/sites/forbestreptalks/2017/06/29/boston-startup-climacell-wants-to-be-the-bloomberg-of-weather-forecasting/ (accessed August 8, 2018).

94. PKG, "IDEAS Social Innovation Challenge," https://pkgcenter.mit.edu/programs/ideas/ (accessed April 22, 2020).

95. Email exchange with Halley Kamerkar, communications and development manager of the Priscilla King Gray Public Service Center (PKG Center), on June 10, 2019.

96. Loop, https://loopcushion.org (accessed January 26, 2021).

97. Loop, https://ideasglobalchallenge.fluidreview.com/p/s/5220656/?&q=Loop&g=; Umbulizer, https://www.umbulizer.com (both accessed June 8, 2018).

98. MIT ODL Video Services, "CNN 'Innovators'—Susan Murcott," https://techtv.mit.edu/collections/h2o-1b/videos/469-cnn-innovators-susan-murcott (accessed August 8, 2018).

99. Rob Matheson, "IDEAS Winners Aim to Improve the World's 'Quality of Life,'" *MIT News*, May 6, 2014, http://news.mit.edu/2014/ideas-winners-aim-improve-worlds -quality-of-life-0506 (accessed July 20, 2018).

100. MIT Entrepreneurhip Development Program, https://executive.mit.edu/openenroll ment/program/entrepreneurship_development_program/ (accessed April 7, 2020).

101. MIT Management Executive Education, https://executive.mit.edu/blog/bringing -the-disciplined-entrepreneurship-process-to-ireland-a-q-a-with-edp-participant-dr -john-breslin (accessed September 30, 2020).

102. MIT Regional Entrepreneurship Acceleration Program (REAP), http://reap.mit .edu (accessed June 1, 2019).

103. Sarah Jane Maxted, "Farewell Letter from REAP Director, Sarah Jane Maxted," *MIT REAP*, https://reap.mit.edu/news-article/farewell-letter-from-reap-director-sarah -jane-maxted/ (accessed June 25, 2019).

104. MIT REAP, "Team Success Story: Scotland," http://reap.mit.edu/assets/Scotland2 -1.pdf (accessed June 1, 2019).

105. MIT Bootcamps, "MIT Bootcamps: Learn by Doing," https://bootcamp.mit.edu (accessed June 1, 2019).

106. edX, https://www.edx.org/course/entrepreneurship-101-who-is-your-customer (accessed January 26, 2021).

107. MIT Bootcamps, "MIT Bootcamps: Learn by Doing."

108. "Announcing the 2017 World's 50 Most Innovative Companies," *Fast Company*, February 13, 2017, https://www.fastcompany.com/3067756/announcing-the -2017-worlds-50-most-innovative-companies (accessed June 14, 2019).

109. Chi-Chu Tschang, Chi-Chi Zhang, and Yoni Dayan, "50 Startups, Five Days, One Bootcamp to Change the World," *MIT News*, August 29, 2014, http://news.mit .edu/2014/50-startups-five-days-one-bootcamp-change-world-0829 (accessed May 23, 2019).

CHAPTER 10

1. Michael Patrick Rutter, "MIT Sandbox Invites 11,000 Students to Innovate," *MIT News*, January 25, 2016, http://news.mit.edu/2016/mit-sandbox-invites-students-to -innovate-0125 (accessed July 12, 2018).

2. Bill Aulet, "What I've Learned about Teaching Entrepreneurship," in *2018 Annals of Entrepreneurship Education and Pedagogy*, vol. 3, ed. C. H. Matthews and E. W. Liguori (Northampton, MA: Edward Elgar Publishing, 2019), https://medium .com/@USASBE/bill-aulet-on-what-ive-learned-about-teaching-entrepreneurship -395117694e11 (accessed May 19, 2018).

3. Martin Trust Center for MIT Entrepreneurship, http://entrepreneurship.mit.edu /courses/ (accessed July 12, 2019); *2018 Annual Report—Martin Trust Center for MIT Entrepreneurship* (Cambridge, MA: MIT, 2018), http://entrepreneurship.mit.edu/annual -report/ (accessed July 12, 2018).

4. *2019 Annual Report—Martin Trust Center for MIT Entrepreneurship* (Cambridge, MA: MIT, 2019), http://entrepreneurship.mit.edu/annual-report/ (accessed July 12, 2019).

5. Martin Trust Center for MIT Entrepreneurship, "MIT E&I Track," http://entre preneurship.mit.edu/mba-entrepreneurship-innovation/ (accessed June 17, 2019).

6. Media Lab Entrepreneurship Program, https://www.media.mit.edu/posts/sample -venture-classes/; MITdesignX, https://designx.mit.edu; Sandbox, sandbox.mit.edu; StartMIT, https://entrepreneurship.mit.edu/startmit/ (all accessed April 24, 2020).

7. Martin Trust Center for MIT Entrepreneurship, "Entrepreneurship 101: Who Is Your Customer?," http://entrepreneurship.mit.edu/online-learning/ (accessed June 17, 2019).

8. Martin Trust Center for MIT Entrepreneurship, "Executive Education," https:// entrepreneurship.mit.edu/executive-education/ (accessed December 14, 2020).

9. Sloan School for Management, "Faculty Directory," https://mitsloan.mit.edu /faculty/faculty-directory#academic-groups:technological-innovation,-entrepreneur ship,-and-strategic-management (accessed July 12, 2020).

10. Bill Aulet, *Disciplined Entrepreneurship: 24 Steps to a Successful Startup* (Hoboken, NJ: John Wiley & Sons, 2013); Bill Aulet, *Disciplined Entrepreneurship Workbook* (Hoboken, NJ: Wiley & Sons, 2017).

11. Bill Aulet, "Entrepreneurship Is a Craft and Here's Why That's Important," *Sloan Management Review*, July 12, 2017, https://sloanreview.mit.edu/article/entrepreneurship -is-a-craft-heres-why-thats-important/ (accessed April 24, 2019).

12. Bill Aulet, "Teaching Entrepreneurship Is in the Startup Phase," *Wall Street Journal*, September 11, 2013, https://www.wsj.com/articles/SB100014241278873233249 04579042773539825050 (accessed July 12, 2018).

13. Sloan School of Management, "Action Learning," https://mitsloan.mit.edu /action-learning/ (accessed July 12-2018).

14. MIT I-Teams, http://iteams.mit.edu (accessed July 12, 2018).

15. Edward B. Roberts and Charles E. Eesley, "Entrepreneurial Impact: The Role of MIT," *Foundations and Trends in Entrepreneurship* 7, no. 1–2 (2011): 1–149, 77, http://dx.doi.org/10.1561/0300000030.

16. Luis Perez-Breva, "10.807/15.371 Innovation Teams Syllabus," February 2018, https://iteams.mit.edu (accessed January 26, 2021).

17. Interview of Luis Perez-Breva on May 1, 2019.

18. Interview of Professor Ed Roberts conducted by Michelle Choate on January 24, 2013.

19. The I-Teams class was first taught as a Special Studies course by "Ken Zolot ('95), in response to a request to help a student-initiated project." Source: Roberts and Eesley, "Entrepreneurial Impact." From 2008 on, Breva has been the lead faculty teaching the course.

20. Noam Wasserman, *The Founder's Dilemmas: Anticipating and Avoiding the Pitfalls That Can Sink a Startup* (Princeton, NJ: Princeton University Press, 2013); Edward Roberts, *Entrepreneurs in High Technology: Lessons from MIT and Beyond* (New York: Oxford University Press, 1991).

21. *2019 Annual Report—Martin Trust Center for MIT Entrepreneurship* (Cambridge, MA: MIT, 2019), 23, http://entrepreneurship.mit.edu/annual-report/ (accessed December 30, 2020).

22. MIT Course Catalog Bulletin 2020–2021, "Minor in Entrepreneurship and Innovation," http://catalog.mit.edu/interdisciplinary/undergraduate-programs/minors/entrepreneurship-innovation/ (accessed December 14, 2020).

23. Bill Aulet, "Teaching Entrepreneurship Cultivating Antifragility: Why There's More to Entrepreneurship Education than Creating Startups," *BizEd Magazine,* November 18, 2019, https://bized.aacsb.edu/articles/2019/november/teaching%20entrepreneurship%20cultivating%20antifragility (accessed March 23, 2020).

24. Stanford University, "David Danielson," https://energy.stanford.edu/people/david-danielson (accessed March 19, 2020).

25. "Doctor, Meet Entrepreneur," *MIT Sloan School of Management Newsroom,* September 10, 2013, http://mitsloan.mit.edu/newsroom/articles/doctor-meet-entrepreneur/ (accessed December 14, 2020); interview of Andrea Ippolito on January 30, 2020.

26. Congressman Thomas Massie, "About," https://massie.house.gov/about/ (accessed January 26, 2021).

27. Jeff Engel, "Exit Interview: Lita Nelsen on MIT Tech Transfer, Startups & Culture," *Xconomy,* May 31, 2016, https://www.xconomy.com/boston/2016/05/31/exit-interview-lita-nelsen-on-mit-tech-transfer-startups-culture/ (accessed June 4, 2018).

28. Anthony Wing Kosner, "Stanford vs. MIT: How Marketing Trumps Technology in Startups," *Forbes,* November 12, 2002, https://www.forbes.com/sites/anthonykosner/2013/11/12/stanford-vs-mit-how-marketing-trumps-technology-in-startups/#4b33ed9128a1 (accessed June 4, 2018); Michael B. Farrell, "MIT Retools to Aid Students with Startups," *Boston Globe,* January 26, 2014, https://www.bostonglobe.com/business/2014/01/26/mit-reboots-approach-innovation/TExxXWxI02WOR4NZKIHAFP/story.html (accessed May 21, 2019).

29. Bill Aulet, "Avoid Stagnation: Acceleration Trumps Incubation," *TechCrunch* (blog), 2014, http://social.techcrunch.com/2014/03/15/avoid-stagnation-why-acceleration -trumps-incubation/ (accessed December 14, 2020).

30. Luis Breva, *Innovating: A Doer's Manifesto for Starting from a Hunch, Prototyping Problems, Scaling Up, and Learning to Be Productively Wrong* (Cambridge, MA: MIT Press, 2018).

31. William Aulet and Fiona E. Murray, "A Tale of Two Entrepreneurs: Understanding Differences in the Types of Entrepreneurship in the Economy," *SSRN Electronic Journal*, 2013, https://doi.org/10.2139/ssrn.2259740 (accessed July 30, 2019), 3. See also Antoinette Schoar, "The Divide between Subsistence and Transformational Entrepreneurship," in *Innovation Policy and the Economy, Volume 10* (Chicago: University of Chicago Press, 2010), http://www.nber.org/chapters/c11765 (accessed July 30, 2019), 59–81.

32. Aulet and Murray, "A Tale of Two Entrepreneurs."

33. Catherine Fazio, Jorge Guzman, Fiona Murray, and Scott Stern, *A New View of the Skew: A Quantitative Assessment of the Quality of American Entrepreneurship* (Kansas City, MS: Kauffman Foundation, 2016), https://www.kauffman.org/neg/section-3 #anewviewoftheskew (accessed August 1, 2019).

34. Melissa Korn, "How to Make Entrepreneurs. MIT Lecturer Offers Steps for Potential Business Owners," *Wall Street Journal,* May 9, 2013.

35. Howard Stevenson and J. C. Jarillo, "A Paradigm of Entrepreneurship: Entrepreneurial Management," *Strategic Management Journal* 11 (1990): 17–27.

36. MIT Innovation Initiative, "Entrepreneurship & Innovation Minor," https:// innovation.mit.edu/education-practice/eiminor/ (accessed May 13, 2019).

37. MIT Innovation Initiative, "Innovation Ecosystems for Regional Entrepreneurship-Acceleration Leaders," https://innovation.mit.edu/education-practice/classes/real/ (accessed April 22, 2018).

38. Jorge Guzman and Scott Stern, "The State of American Entrepreneurship: New Estimates of the Quality and Quantity of Entrepreneurship for 32 US States, 1988–2014" (working paper, National Bureau of Economic Research, March 2016), https://doi.org /10.3386/w22095 (accessed August 1, 2018); Fazio et al., *A New View of the Skew*; Phil Budden, Fiona Murray, and Anna Turskaya, "A Systematic MIT Approach for Assessing 'Innovation-Driven Entrepreneurship' in Ecosystems" (working paper version 2.0, Cambridge, MA: MIT Lab for Innovation Science and Policy, February 2019).

39. Tom Gearty, "Entrepreneurship by Design," MIT School of Architecture and Planning, October 17, 2016, https://sap.mit.edu/news/entrepreneurship-design (accessed July 27, 2018).

40. MIT, "Better World," https://www.mit.edu/building-a-better-world/ (accessed July 27, 2018).

41. *2016 Annual Report—Martin Trust Center for MIT Entrepreneurship* (Cambridge, MA: MIT, 2006), 2, http://entrepreneurship.mit.edu/wp-content/uploads/2016-Annual -Report-FINAL.pdf (accessed July 27, 2018).

CHAPTER 11

1. Robert Buderi, *The Invention That Changed the World: How a Small Group of Radar Pioneers Won the Second World War and Launched a Technological Revolution* (New York: Touchstone, 1996), 14.

2. Jeff Engel, "Exit Interview: Lita Nelsen on MIT Tech Transfer, Startups & Culture," *Xconomy,* May 31, 2016, https://www.xconomy.com/boston/2016/05/31/exit -interview-lita-nelsen-on-mit-tech-transfer-startups-culture/ (accessed August 8, 2018).

3. Scott Kirsner, "Media Lab Director Joi Ito Planning New Fund That Would Put Money into Student Startups," *Boston.com,* March 7, 2013, http://www.boston .com/business/technology/innoeco/2013/03/media_lab_director_joi_ito_set.html (accessed January 26, 2020); *Enhancing Collaboration between MIT and The Engine: Joint Findings of The Engine Working Groups: Final Report to the MIT Community* (Cambridge, MA: MIT, April 2018), http://web.mit.edu/ewgreport/introduction.html (accessed August 27, 2018).

4. MIT News Office, "Letter Regarding the Creation of The Engine Working Groups and Idea Bank," *MIT News,* January 17, 2017, https://news.mit.edu/2017/letter -regarding-creation-engine-working-groups-and-idea-bank-0117 (accessed December 30, 2020).

5. Thomas Allen and Rory O'Shea, "The Roadblock to Commercialisation," *Financial Times,* September 28, 2014, https://www.ft.com/content/a1ea7c72-18cc-11e4-933e -00144feabdc0 (accessed April 1, 2020).

6. Bill Aulet, "What I've Learned About Teaching Entrepreneurship," in *2018 Annals of Entrepreneurship Education and Pedagogy,* vol. 3, ed. C. H. Matthews and E. W. Liguori (Northampton, MA: Edward Elgar Publishing, 2019), https://medium .com/@USASBE/bill-aulet-on-what-ive-learned-about-teaching-entrepreneurship -395117694e11 (accessed July 31, 2019).

7. Michael A. Cusumano, "The Puzzle of Japanese Innovation and Entrepreneurship," *Communications of the ACM,* October 2016, https://cacm.acm.org/magazines /2016/10/207761-the-puzzle-of-japanese-innovation-and-entrepreneurship/abstract (accessed August 11, 2018).

8. Richard K. Lester and Michael J. Piore, *Innovation—the Missing Dimension* (Cambridge, MA: Harvard University Press, 2004).

9. *2020 Annual Report—Martin Trust Center for MIT Entrepreneurship* (Cambridge, MA: MIT, 2020), 34, http://entrepreneurship.mit.edu/annual-report/ (accessed December 30, 2020).

INDEX

Moss, Frank, 60
Motivations related to
    entrepreneurship, 216–217, 233–234
Motorola, 157
mSurvey, 136
MTV Networks, 40
Muddy Charles Pub, 110
Mui, Peter, 26–27, 29, 107
Multidisciplinary approach to
    problem-solving, 103–107
Murcott, Susan, 202
Murray, Fiona, 42, 67, 70, 182, 203,
    221, 236
    on entrepreneurship as career path,
        58–59
    on female entrepreneurs, 79
    on innovation-driven
        entrepreneurship, 218
    on serendipity, 120

Nag, Rojon, 137
Nagle, Dennis, 199
NASA. *See* National Aeronautics and
    Space Administration (NASA)
National Aeronautics and Space
    Administration (NASA), 11, 16–17,
    23, 116, 157
National Institutes for Health (NIH), 12
National Science Foundation (NSF), 12,
    169
National Venture Capital Association
    (NVCA), 22
NBX Corporation, 111
Negroponte, Nicholas, 91, 95, 101
Nelsen, Lita, 26, 34, 91, 96, 155, 162,
    217
Networking and community- and
    career-building initiatives, 146–148,
    152–153
Newman, Bob, 13
New York MIT Venture Clinic, 21
New York Times, 166
Ngai, Tommy, 202

Nguyen, Freddy, 145
Nicholson, Lesley Millar, 218
Nigam, Akhil, 187
Nijhawan, Preetish, 112
Nima Sensor, 133
Njoroge, Paul, 52, 197
Noftsker, Russell, 22
Nondegree education programs,
    202–205
Notis-McConarty, Jean, 49
Novartis, 185
NuTonomy, 175, 190

Obama, Barack, 216
Obermayer, Arthur, 188
Office of Scientific Research and
    Development (OSRD), 10, 12
Ogunlana, Olumide, 197–198
OKTA, 134
Olguin Olguin, Daniel, 118
Olsen, Kenneth H., 14, 100, 107
OnChip Power, 148
$100K Entrepreneurship Competition,
    138–140, 193
OptiBit, 134
Orbitz, 116
Ortiz, Christine, 57
OSRD. *See* Office of Scientific Research
    and Development (OSRD)
Outreach, 148–149
Outsiders, embracing, 98–103

Packard, David, 107, 189
Palacios, Miguel, 193
Pappalardo, Neil, 20, 69
Parietti, Fred, 138
Parker, T. J., 144, 187
Patents, 8
    Bayh-Dole Act and, 31–34
PayPal, 60
Pentland, Alex (Sandy), 53–54, 60, 97,
    117–118, 196
Perch, 112–113